Demons are Closer than You Think

How Participating in New Age and Occult Practices Brought Demons Into My Life

Judy Hankel

PUBLISHING COMPANY
P.O. Box 220 • Goleta, CA 93116
(800) 647-9882 • (805) 692-0043 • Fax: (805) 967-5133
www.queenship.org

Library of Congress Number #2014959394

Published by:
Queenship Publishing
P.O. Box 220 • Goleta, CA 93116
(800) 647-9882 • (805) 692-0043 • Fax: (805) 967-5133
www.queenship.org

Printed in the United States of America.

ISBN 978-1 57918-437-7

Acknowledgments

This book is dedicated to Jesus Christ in gratitude for His Divine Mercy. I also want to thank Mary, the Mother of Jesus, for her powerful intercession on my behalf. It is through her intercessory prayers for me that this book has become a reality. I especially want to thank all of the saints who assisted me through their prayers and support, especially Padre Pio, St. Therese of Lisieux, St. Anthony of Padua, St. Joseph, St. Augustine, St. Maximillian Kolbe, St. Faustina, St. Jude the Apostle, St. Francis of Assisi, St. Paul, Pope St. John Paul II, St. Thomas Aquinas, and St. Mary Magdalen. God gave us the angels, and I owe a debt of gratitude to all of the angels who have assisted me with my daily problems, especially St. Michael the Archangel and my guardian angel, who watched over me during my most difficult times and during the course of this project. Last, but not least, I want to thank the Holy Souls in Purgatory for their intercessory prayers on my behalf.

Thanks to all those who assisted me among the living with this project! This includes those who reviewed my book and gave me concrete advice. I am grateful to Fr. John Hampsch, C.M.F., who spent many hours with me on the phone and via email assisting me and encouraging me to write this book. As demons attempted to stop the writing of this book, Fr. Hampsch prayed with me and encouraged me not to give up. I listened, and so this book is finally completed after ten years!

I also wish to thank Fr. Joseph Esper, who has been a friend and confidant for many years. He has given unselfishly of his time and talents to help me in my ongoing struggle with demons. He has provided a listening ear and advice many times during difficult moments.

I am also grateful for the advice of David Came, an editor who volunteered to assist me with this project. He provided valuable information, giving of his time very generously. God sent me the very best. Thank you, God for everything!

Table of Contents

Foreword

Even though the Catholic Church is on the front lines in the ongoing battle against the "prince of this world" (cf. Jn. 14:3), many Catholics—including, sadly, more than a few priests and religious—are unaware of this struggle and of its eternal significance. Some are quick to dismiss references to Satan and spiritual warfare as "medieval superstition"; others, while acknowledging these realities in theory, naively assume they personally are unthreatened and unaffected by them. Adopting an "out of sight, out of mind" mentality, many Catholics prefer not to think of such spiritual dangers; additionally, the fast pace of life in the early 21st century can be an attractive and compelling excuse to focus on more immediate and down-to-earth concerns.

The Catholic Church is very clear in her teaching on the reality of personalized evil in the form of Satan, or the devil (Catechism of the Catholic Church, n. 391), and of his unceasing attempts to deceive and ensnare humanity in sin (nn. 397, 414). Many Catholics have heard, read accounts, or seen cinematic portrayals (often sensationalized), of exorcisms—but wrongly conclude that, because they and their loved ones and personal acquaintances are not victimized by evil in this extreme way, the devil and his servants have no personal interest in them. Unfortunately, this assumption is unwarranted, for Satan and his evil spirits fiercely desire that all humanity be dragged down into Hell by and with them, there to share in "the eternal fire prepared for the devil and his angels." (Mt. 25:41).

Evil is an undeniable reality, and damnation is a genuine and frightening possibility. Yes, there definitely is a danger in ascribing too much power and influence to Satan, and in becoming obsessed over the possibility of losing one's soul; Jesus wants us to know and respond to our Heavenly Father out of love, not fear. "Fire and brimstone" sermons and threats of eternal damnation are usually not very helpful tools in forming and catechizing future citizens of the Kingdom—as previous generations of Church leaders and teachers have discovered. However, here in our own age the average Catholic is more likely to fall at the other end of the spectrum: not taking such dreadful realities seriously enough.

A proper balance in this regard is often difficult to achieve, but always of crucial importance. The Church has the duty of reminding her members that evil is real, but that God's love is more real; sin, and the resultant possibility of damnation, are a reality, but Divine Love and Mercy is an even greater reality.

For all of these reasons, Judy Hankel's book, is a valuable and timely resource for contemporary Catholics. The author humbly and honestly shares her own intense and important story, drawing from it many lessons and applications to modern life and the spiritual dangers often involved in it. Some may find parts of her testimony, or of the conclusions she draws and the advice she gives, hard to accept or upsetting—but, when we're dealing with matters even more important than "life and death," it can be a very good thing to have our assumptions and expectations challenged from time to time.

It is said that a smart person learns from his or her mistakes, while a wise person learns from other people's mistakes. Ms. Hankel frankly admits her own mistakes and failings, and in the process offers many useful lessons for the average reader—one who wants to grow closer to God, but who (quite possibly through no fault of his or her own) is only vaguely aware of how to recognize and overcome the obstacles presented by the world, the flesh, and the devil. By being innocent as doves but wise as serpents (cf. Mt. 10:16), may all of us come to be numbered among those who have conquered the evil one by the Blood of the Lamb. (cf. Rev. 12:11)

Rev. Joseph M. Esper

Author of

Spiritual Dangers of the 21st Century

Catholicism in Crisis

Defiance: The Antichrists of History and their Doomed War Against the Church

After the Darkness

On the Brink, America and the Coming Divine Judgment

Preface

This book was given to me by Jesus Christ. It is a grace and mercy of the Lord. I don't deserve it. I have committed sins that warrant eternal damnation, yet Jesus has helped me and is allowing me to use my sordid life as an opportunity to evangelize. I give thanks and praise to Jesus Christ for He has strengthened me and entrusted this book to me through the power of the Holy Spirit. On my own, I can do nothing, but ***with God all things are possible.*** (Matthew 19:26 NIV)

I was involved in new age and the occult for several years. Most new age spirituality and all occult practices are pagan. As a result of my participation in these deceptive practices, I have been tormented by demons of all kinds. I have to tell you, however, that I was very ignorant on the subject of the occult, new age spirituality and demons. When I went to school back in the 1950's and 1960's, we did not discuss the evils of new age spirituality or the occult in the Catholic schools I attended. Of course, they weren't an issue back then. People were not exposed to the preponderance of new age and occult practices that are permeating our society today. However, I learned that when we participate in new age or occult practices, it can have devastating consequences and lead to serious sin. Satan has a grip on us, whether we know it or not.

Serious offenses cause demons to enter our lives. If we persist in these sins, we may begin to suffer from the effects (the consequences) of our actions. These consequences may include attacks by demons, who manifest themselves in many ways, including, but not limited to: depression, oppression, obsession, possession, temptations, and infestation.

Demons of new age and the occult have been with me since 1994 due to my involvement in new age and occult sinful practices. I believe these are demons of oppression. Oppression is demonic harassment, but the demons do not use the person's body. The demons harass me and speak to me 24 hours a day. However, God does allow me to sleep most of the time without interference.

However, if I wake up, they start speaking right away. They try to tempt me and to interfere with any good that I try to do, whether it is prayer, a work of charity, reading a religious book, watching a religious TV program, or going to Mass, Confession or Adoration of the Blessed Sacrament. Writing this book has increased the spiritual battle, but God is in control.

I have tried to write this book several times during the past 10 years. However, every time I tried to write it, I was in such a spiritual battle that I either got off track or became discouraged and gave up on it. This time I intend to persevere no matter how much demonic interference there is. I do have more experience now, and I am determined to do the will of God. Satan did his best to stop this book from being written because it reveals his tactics and gives glory to God. Satan will try to squelch any attempt to reveal that he really exists and how he works. Satan does not want this book to be written, but Jesus Christ does. So I put my faith in Him as I write this now. Jesus, I Trust in You!

This is the true story of my life in the new age and the occult and how Jesus' Divine Mercy helped me through it. I am Catholic, but I am writing this book for everyone, particularly those who are most in need of God's mercy. Although I still have demons with me as I am writing my story, I have repented and confessed my sins. I am writing my story as I go through my trials to give you hope and to show you that no matter what you may be going through, that you, too, can go on if you trust in Jesus. Is my life difficult? Yes, it is. But Jesus gives us the graces we need to persevere even in the most extreme circumstances. Jesus is a forgiving, merciful Savior who understands our weaknesses. If we repent and surrender to His Will, we cannot fail. I have been wounded in the spiritual battle, but I am not defeated.

Many of you may be engaged right now in a new age or occult practice which you do not recognize as sinful. For example, perhaps you are participating in yoga or tai chi, consulting a psychic, using astrology, reading horoscopes in the newspaper, or reading a book on Wicca or some other new age or occult practice without recognizing the moral errors. All of these practices and more are spiritually dangerous. Like me, you may have embraced new age or occult philosophies innocently without realizing that it can bring demons into your life. These sins offend Almighty God. The fact is that participation in new age and occult practices is against the First Commandment: ***I am the Lord your God: You Shall Not Have Strange Gods Before Me.*** (Traditional Catechetical Formula, Catechism of the Catholic Church).

I have met people, some of them daily Catholic Mass attendees, who are having dreams and visions that, in my opinion, are demonic. Some of them are hearing audible voices pretending to be a saint or Jesus. They think their messages are from God, but communications from God will not contain moral errors. Other people are seeing angels, but are they properly discerning whether or not these encounters are from God? God certainly does permit supernatural experiences that come from Heavenly beings, but Satan and demons mimic things of God, who allows these deceptions due to our fallen nature. I have learned that demons are very clever, and it is easy to be duped.

One major problem is that new age and occult practices and teachings are within the Catholic Church. I approached several priests from the very beginning of my demonic manifestations who dismissed my experiences or did not have a clue as to how to help me. At one time, I spent the better part of a year trying to find a priest who could advise me. I did end up with many spiritual directors, but the majority of them did not know anything about new age or the occult, and I did not get adequate spiritual direction. Some priests (and in one case, a nun) were in a spiritual battle themselves. Some of them had new age or occult practices going on in their own retreat centers or colleges. It was like the blind leading the blind.

Despite my inability to get proper spiritual direction, I take responsibility for my own sins. I made some incorrect choices and didn't always pay attention to the Holy Spirit. We all have free will, and I have committed serious sins. I "own" them, a common expression today for admitting responsibility for one's guilt or problems. I have repented and Jesus helped me along the way. Jesus will not abandon us. Trust in the Lord Jesus, who is the Way, the Truth, and the Life. He is the Good Shepherd who keeps watch over His sheep. He does not want any of His flock to be lost. In the Bible, it says that Jesus Himself will shepherd us. (Ezekiel 34:11) Jesus did help me. In fact, He personally read the Bible to me every night for a few hours over a period of several months when I was having demonic attacks during the early years. He would always begin by saying: "I am Jesus, Son of the Living God..." As a result, I began to read and study Holy Scripture. I also started a Bible study group and had a good Catholic writer and apologist lead it. It bore good fruit.

Jesus has given me the grace to persevere and taught me how to deal with the demons in my life. He sent the Holy Spirit to give me the remedies, ways to make reparation (restitution) for my sins, which have given me the graces necessary to go on and actually become closer to God in the process. I want you all to know there is hope and Jesus' Divine Mercy is there for all of you. Jesus loves you. If you repent, He is there to forgive you and welcome you back to Him with open arms. Don't give up! Resist the devil. He is a loser, and we all know who is going to win the final spiritual battle. Set your heart and mind on Jesus Christ.

In the Diary of St. Faustina, Jesus tells her that *the greater the misery of a soul, the greater its right to My mercy: Urge all souls to trust in the unfathomable abyss of My mercy, because I want to save them all.*[1] There is hope if we trust in the Lord. This is my story—a story of pain and heartache—but also one full of extraordinary graces, forgiveness, mercy and the undying love of Jesus Christ. It is a story of Divine Mercy.

---

1 Kowalska, Saint Maria Faustina, *Divine Mercy in My Soul, Diary of Saint Maria Faustina Kowalska,* Marian Press; 3rd edition with revisions (29th printing), 2013.

Introduction

First of all, I would like to give you some general information on the New Age Movement and the occult. Some of you may be familiar with new age and the occult, but many of you may not be. Therefore, this is intended to be a very brief overview before I begin my own personal testimony.

What is the New Age Movement (NAM)?

"New age" is a broad term consisting of many different types of alternative therapies, pagan practices, and idolatrous beliefs. New agers have an increased interest in spirituality, mysticism, meditation, and holism (a philosophy whereby it is believed that parts of a methodology can only be understood in terms of the whole). One popular tenet of the New Age Movement is the belief that we can heal ourselves. New age practices are widely accepted by people and are found everywhere today in society. I would guess that most people have encountered many new age practices and beliefs, especially in recent years, because of their increased popularity.

The New Age Movement (NAM) is not a structured group nor is it an organization. It is a worldview. Perhaps this is partly why new age tenets are so readily embraced by many people in different cultures from all walks of life. Focus on the Family defines a personal worldview as: *...a combination of all you believe to be true, and what you believe becomes the driving force behind every emotion, decision and action. Therefore, it affects your response to every area of life: from philosophy to science, theology and anthropology to economics, law, politics, art and social order—everything.* In contrast, *a biblical worldview is based on the infallible Word of God. When you believe the Bible is entirely true, then you allow it to be the foundation of everything you say and do.*[2]

New age practices go back to before the time of Christ. We view them as new because they are new to us. Perhaps people are

2 Tackett, Del, *What's a Christian Worldview?* Focus on the Family, http://www.focusonthefamily.com/faith/christian_worldview/whats_a_christian_worldview.aspx, 1997-2014.

drawn to new age practices and beliefs who really do not know God, but still have an inward craving for the spiritual side of life. Although new age practices and beliefs may seem on the surface to satisfy this spiritual hunger, they are really a tactic of the devil to lead people into moral errors. The devil is a liar. St. Peter warns us: ***Be alert and of sober mind. Your enemy the devil prowls around like a roaring lion looking for someone to devour. Resist him, standing firm in the faith, because you know that the family of believers throughout the world is undergoing the same kind of sufferings.*** (1 Peter 5:8-9 NIV) We need to be fed with biblical truths.

Unfortunately, more and more people have been exposed to new age practices and beliefs and are actively participating in new age spirituality. The truth is that new age practices are not compatible with Christian beliefs even though parts of some practices may be acceptable. I say this with hesitation because any acceptable parts of any new age practices are rare. Many new age practices are a mixture of truth and lies, and it is difficult for most people to discern which is which. Therefore, I urge complete abstention.

Many new age practices come from pagan Eastern religions. Because many of us have never been exposed to religions such as Hinduism, Buddhism, and Taoism, new age practices intrigue us, and we gravitate towards them out of curiosity or because everyone is using them. When we even participate in one course or practice, it puts us in the middle of the battle between good and evil. From using or participating in even one practice, you are inviting the devil and demons into your life. That's how dangerous they are. These deceptive practices and beliefs are inundating Western civilization. The devil is propagating the errors of atheistic countries in the Western hemisphere, and we have embraced them through ignorance and lack of proper discernment. Belief and participation in spiritually dangerous new age practices is causing our Judeo-Christian society to revert to paganism.

In general, the term "New Age" consists of five primary tenets which summarize the scope of its beliefs. These tenets are inherent in pagan practices and many organizations connected with new age today throughout the world. The five tenets are: (1) All is one, and everything is a part of the whole. (2) Everything is God, everything is in God, and God is in everything. (3) Man is a part of God. (4) Man never dies, but is reincarnated until he reaches spiritual perfection. (5) Man can create his own reality through altered states of consciousness.

God and Energy

In new age spirituality, energy is believed to be a life force (God) that permeates everything in the world, including man. Man is thought to be different vibrations of this energy, which is believed must be kept in balance for the best results. This is called Monism (meaning "all is one"). According to the Vatican document, *Jesus Christ the Bearer of the Water of Life: A Christian Reflection on the New Age,* Monism is ***the metaphysical belief that differences between beings are illusory. There is only one universal being, of which everything and every person is a part.***[3] New agers believe that we can access this energy through altered states of consciousness. Some methods include practices such as hypnosis, guided imagery, and visualization. It is believed that by doing this, we can heal ourselves and get in touch with our own divinity. In this worldview, God is an impersonal life force or energy instead of a personal, loving God whom we should trust implicitly to provide for all of our spiritual and temporal needs. The truth is that we can do nothing without God, and, therefore, we are not divine and we cannot heal ourselves.

We are Gods

In new age, we are taught that we are gods. This is called Pantheism, which is the belief that ***everything is God or, sometimes, that everything is in God and God is in everything (Panentheism). Every element of the universe is divine, and the***

---

3 *Jesus Christ the Bearer of the Water of Life: A Christian Reflection on the New Age* www.vatican.va/.../pontifical_councils/interelg/documents/rc_pc_inter-lg_doc_20030203_new-age_en.html - 216k - 2003-02-20, Section 7.2.

divinity is equally present in everything.[4] Therefore, man is a god, too, and potentially has all of the powers and attributes of the Creator. Actress and new age promoter Shirley MacLaine once wrote: *Each soul is its own God. You must never worship anyone or anything other than self. For you are God. To love self is to love God.*[5] You will hear references to the "God Within," "Christ Consciousness," "Cosmic Christ," or "Higher Self." These are all different names for the god within us. We divinize ourselves, and leave the one, true God out of the picture. We see the sin of pride in these beliefs which place an emphasis on ourselves instead of God.

The first sin of pride was committed by our ancestors, Adam and Eve. Their sin affected all humanity, which includes us. The serpent (the devil) used pride as a temptation for them to disobey God's command not to eat of a certain tree in the center of the Garden of Eden. The devil enticed them to eat of it by telling them that if they ate the fruit of the forbidden tree, they would become like gods, knowing what is good and evil. New age thought today persuades us that we, too, can be gods. Pride is the root of all sin.

Since we are gods, new agers believe that we can determine for ourselves what is right and wrong. This is called "moral relativism." It puts us in control, setting our own standards for morality. This is not biblical because God gave us the Ten Commandments, and we are expected to obey them. When we stand before God after we die, is He going to determine whether our own moral judgments supersede one or more of His Commandments? Of course not. In the Bible we read: ***I am the Lord; that is My name! I will not yield My glory to another or My praise to idols.*** (Isaiah 42:8 NIV) We cannot compete with God. Therefore, moral relativism is against the First Commandment. You will be judged on whether or not you obeyed God's statues, not your own. If people's freedom is based on moral relativism, there can't help but be chaos. It makes any laws interpretive and is an obstacle to the common good. On World Peace Day in 2012,

4 *Ibid.*

5 Shirley MacLaine, *Dancing in the Light,* Toronto; Bantam Books, 1985, 343, as seen in Pacwa, Mitch, S.J., *Catholics and the New Age,* Servant Publications, Ann Arbor, Michigan, 1992.

Pope Benedict XVI said: *Authentic freedom can never be attained independently of God.*[6]

In new age, we try to control our own destiny. New agers do this by seeking psychics to divine their future, using astrology and horoscopes, balancing their chakras, relying on dreams for answers, worshipping gods and goddesses, meditation, holistic health, shamanism, and more. In the Bible, we read: ***See to it that no one takes you captive through hollow and deceptive philosophy, which depends on human tradition and the elemental spiritual forces of this world rather than on Christ.***(Col. 2:8) New age is a false philosophy designed by the devil to take our minds and hearts away from God. Our daily actions must conform to God's plan, not the devil's plan or our own plans.

People are mesmerized by new age ideas and latch onto this movement through ignorance and a desire for something better and new. However, it is old paganism revived with devastating consequences. If many people adhere to the new age doctrine, the world will become void of true Christians—those that still believe in Jesus Christ, Holy Scripture and truth. As Christians, we understand that we are in a battle between good and evil, and that Satan works very hard on us to fall into serious sin. We are a major target of the devil, who is filling our world with his version of the "truth." Be aware of this and be sure to place Jesus Christ first in your life. If any non-Christians are reading this book, I urge you to accept Jesus Christ into your lives and to read the Bible to learn truth. Jesus loves you and will welcome you with open arms. You are even more susceptible to demonic attacks because you don't know Jesus Christ, who is the Son of God and our Redeemer.

A survey by Pew Research in 2010 showed that Christians in the world were still slightly in the majority, comprising 31.5% of the world's entire population.[7] Muslims accounted for 23.2% of the world's population, and the third largest segment (16.3%) was categorized as "unaffiliated." I can't help but wonder how many of these "unaffiliated" people are new agers since new

6 Pope Benedict XVI, *Address for the Celebration of the World Day of Peace,* 1 January 2012.

7 *Global Religious Diversity,* Pew Research, Religion & Public Life Project, April 4, 2014, http://www.pewforum.org/2014/04/04/global-religious-diversity/

agers are a loose network of people not necessarily affiliated with a religion. I also wonder if any of them are fallen-away Catholics. It is no secret that the Catholic Church is losing more and more members. Could this be partly because of new age and occult practices within the Catholic Church which can lead to a watering down of the faith?

All people need to read and understand the Bible, especially Catholics. Other Christian denominations put us to shame because, to their credit, they rely heavily on Holy Scripture and many can quote the Bible. God bless them! Catholics need to know and understand their faith because it is the <u>one true faith</u> handed down to us by Jesus Christ Himself. All other denominations can be traced back to a person who founded the religion. The Catholic Church is the only denomination that can trace its roots back to Jesus Christ.

All people need to understand the dangers of participating in new age and the occult so that they don't end up with demons in their lives. In order to understand the dangers of new age and the occult, it is important to first know Jesus Christ.

Marilyn Ferguson's Influence on the New Age Movement

Marilyn Ferguson was very influential in promoting and spreading the New Age Movement through her book, *The Aquarian Conspiracy: Personal and Social Transformation in the 1980's,* which was first published in 1980.[8] The movement was a synthesis of pagan beliefs and Christianity, which seemed to appeal to all people, both non-Christians and Christians alike. Her ideological ideas conveyed personal fulfillment and limitless potential. It was a cultural movement dominated by increased interest in pagan practices in the Western Hemisphere that came from Eastern religions, such as Hinduism and Buddhism. Consequently, practices such as yoga, Transcendental Meditation, tai chi, and alternative therapies such as acupuncture became popular with people who had never been exposed to them before.

---

8 Ferguson, Marilyn, *The Aquarian Conspiracy: Personal and Social Transformation in the 1980's*, Houghton Mifflin; First Printing Edition. (February 1, 1980)

These practices were not really new. They had been propagated in the 1800's by Thoreau, Emerson, Wordsworth and through Theosophy, which was introduced by Madame Helena Blavatsky (1831-1891).[9] However, during that time, the practices had not taken root on a global scale. Marilyn's book changed that. After the publication of her book in the 1980's, the New Age Movement became popular with people in all walks of life. The book "sold over 500,000 copies in its first seven years in print."[10] This was without benefit of the internet. Today, many people all over the world have adopted some form of new age thought and participated in pagan or spiritually dangerous practices through the influence of Ferguson's book. Ferguson and other advocates who became mesmerized by *The Aquarian Conspiracy* made it widely acclaimed all over the world.

The word conspiracy implied a "breathing together," a merging of opposing forces to produce personal and social changes throughout the world. People in every discipline were drawn to it by a uniform desire to create a new level of consciousness. Today, we find new age practices and beliefs in every field, including medicine, psychology, spirituality, politics, education, government, science and more. The result is the watering down of Christianity and an increase in pagan new age and occult practices. I believe it was a demonically-inspired effort to slowly bring about the reign of the Anti-Christ. When the Anti-Christ reigns, most of the world will be under the control of Satan and believe in false, non-Biblical tenets.

In *The Aquarian Conspiracy,* Ferguson discusses the connection between the New Age Movement and its relationship to a certain sign of the zodiac. The zodiac is believed to be *a belt of the Heavens within about 8° either side of the ecliptic, including all apparent positions of the sun, moon, and most familiar planets. It is divided into twelve equal divisions or signs (Aries, Taurus, Gemini, Cancer, Leo, Virgo, Libra, Scorpio, Sagittarius, Capricorn, Aquarius, Pisces).*[11] The zodiac

9 Hoyt, Karen, *The New Age Rage,* Spiritual Counterfeits Project, Fleming H. Revell Company, Old Tappen, NJ 07675, 1987, p. 22-24.

10 ABC-CLIO, Laderman, Gary and Leon, Luis D., *Religion and American Cultures: An Encyclopedia of Traditions, Diversity and Popular Expressions,* Volume 1, 2003, p. 245.

11 *Google Definitions,* https://www.google.com/webhp?sourceid=chrome-instant&ion=1&espv=2&ie=UTF-8#q=definition+of+zodiac.

and its twelve signs are part of Astrology, which is *the study of the motions and relative positions of the planets, sun, and moon, interpreted in terms of human characteristics and activities.*[12] Astrology is a forbidden practice for Catholics and considered divination. (CC 2116).

The sign of the zodiac Ferguson focused on was Pisces. It was scheduled to begin on January 1, 2001. Pisces is symbolized by two fish swimming in opposite directions. For Ferguson, this symbol envisioned a different world that would begin at that time, one dominated by more metaphysical phenomena and planetary awareness. It would be a new world using esoteric and scientific knowledge and incorporating Eastern mysticism and modern psychology. People would begin to think on a global level. She envisioned a powerful network dominated by more metaphysical phenomena and planetary awareness. It would be a new world bringing about radical changes in the way we live; in short, a personal and social transformation. It would be a millennium of peace and harmony, understanding, and love.

It sounds great—a worldwide network of people conspiring with each other to create a millennium of love and light. New age presents itself as good. Who doesn't want to live in peace and harmony, respect the planet and protect the environment? However, the devil's distortions of truth often convey a seemingly good motive. Underneath the facade lies rebellion. New age beliefs are a rebellion against Christianity and against God Himself. I believe that the fascination with new age is a continuation of the war against evil. The spiritual battle will continue until the end of the world.

To me, the Pisces symbol has a religious connotation. I see one fish as being symbolic for Jesus because a fish is often used as a symbol for Jesus among Christians. I believe that the other fish is symbolic for Satan. The fish are going in opposite directions, therefore, they are diametrically opposed to one another. We see these opposing forces in our world today. We have staunch Christians who believe in Jesus Christ and follow His commandments and teachings. On the other hand, we see people in the New Age Movement following spiritually deceptive

12 *The Free Dictionary by Farlex,* http://www.thefreedictionary.com/astrology.

and immoral pagan practices that have become more acceptable since the publication of Marilyn Ferguson's book.

Ferguson maintained that the New Age Movement would change our worldview and create distinct changes in the way we live. It certainly has, but not for the better. We are becoming our own gods. We also base much of our beliefs on personal experiences, which we do not discern. Personal experiences can be good or evil. Evil experiences (which are sins against the Ten Commandments) are never from God. The book, *The Aquarian Conspiracy,* is often referred to as "The New Age Bible." We need to read the Bible handed down to us by the apostles of Jesus Christ, which tells us how to get to Heaven. Frank Sinatra recorded a song years ago called, *My Way.* Our way, if we continue to follow the *New Age Bible,* may lead to eternal damnation. In the Bible, Jesus states, ***I am the way and the truth and the life. No one comes to the Father except through Me.*** (John 14:6 NIV)

The Influence of Pierre Teilhard de Chardin on the New Age Movement

According to well-known Catholic writer Ted Flynn, in his book, *Hope of the Wicked: The Master Plan to Rule the World,* Fr. Pierre Teilhard de Chardin is *praised in progressive Catholic circles as a great religious thinker and a scientific genius. His influence goes far beyond Catholic circles as evidenced by the fact that he is the most widely read author in the New Age Movement...In The Aquarian Conspiracy by Marilyn Ferguson, arguably the most important and comprehensive modern work on the New Age Movement, there are at least sixteen different references to Pierre Teilhard de Chardin.*[13]

In 1957, de Chardin's new age writings, especially his writings dealing with evolution and his pantheistic views that include his view that both man and the universe are divine, were condemned by the Holy Office in the Catholic Church. However, in recent years his new age writings are once again growing in popularity. Due to his vast influence in the New Age Movement today, I am going to give a very brief biography of him.

---

13 Flynn, Ted, *Hope of the Wicked: The Master Plan to Rule the World,* MaxKol Communications, Inc., Sterling, VA 20166, 2000, p. 56.

Pierre Teilhard de Chardin was born in 1881 in Sarcenat, France. His mother was a pious Catholic. His father was an amateur scientist and collected geological specimens. His mother influenced him spiritually, and his father cultivated his interest in nature. Consequently, Pierre often explored the extinct volcanos in the Clermont-Ferrand area near his home from which he developed an interest in geology and paleoanthropology. Over time, he became obsessed with the universe and nature, which he attempted to analyze from a Christian perspective.

In 1892, Pierre entered a Jesuit college and in 1899, he entered the Jesuit Novitiate near Marseilles, France. Due to the influence of the anti-Catholic war minister, Catholic schools were closed, so Pierre finished his studies at a seminary in St. Helier, Jersey capital of the British Channel Islands. It was here that he studied geology, Scholastic theology and philosophy. It was while studying here that matter, life and energy became his focus and his ideas of "cosmic-consciousness" evolved. Nature and the universe became synonymous with God for him; in other words, he believed that both the universe and God were divine. This is Pantheism, and is against the First Commandment. He attempted to blend the physical and spiritual worlds under the banner of evolution.

Following his ordination as a priest in 1911, Pierre got into trouble with the Catholic Church on his theory of evolution. He did not regard the Darwinst theory of evolution as merely a scientific concept, *but one which could be spiritualized into a cosmic reality.*[14] His views were "Gnostic," meaning that they were based on hidden knowledge (occultism). He made a religion of the earth into a religion of Heaven and actually, a cult. A religion without a personal God is not Christian at all.

In his own time, Chardin was heavily denounced by many Jesuits and other orthodox clergy as "inventing his own language" around evolution and liberal causes. Chardin was key player as the Church began to lose its way in the latter half of the twentieth century.

What do other Christians think about Fr. Pierre Teilhard de Chardin? Alan Morrison, a Christian writer for the SCP

14 Terego, Alex, *Pierre Teilhard de Chardin and the Cosmic Christ*, Kindle Edition, http://www.amazon.com.

Journal, states in his article *From Old Gnosticism to New Age,* that *the real appeal of Teilhard de Chardin is that his teachings provide a philosophical groundplan for all those with Gnostic inclinations who are today seeking to develop a global religious, scientific and political climate which is conducive to the annihilation of the concept of the transcendent, judging, sovereign God portrayed in the Bible and the establishment of a satanically inspired reign of peace and justice on the earth.*[15]

Fr. Mitch Pacwa, a Jesuit priest who initially favored Fr. Pierre Teilhard de Chardin's doctrines, finally could no longer accept his teachings. Fr. Pacwa states: *I shifted away from his thought to a doctrinal position capable of including a fuller understanding of teachings on sacred revelation about God, Christ, the future of the world, sin and redemption."*[16]

Gary Kah, in his book, *The Demonic Roots of Globalism,* makes this comment: *Teilhard de Chardin saw every aspect of existence, from the earth itself to human beings as moving in a purposeful forward, upward motion to his concept of the Omega Point.*[17] *For him, Christogenesis, the movement by which the universe turns completely into Christ, is simply the last phase of evolution. He presented to the people of his day a religion which he still tried to call Christian. But the result was in every sense a vehicle for moving theologically into a new mindset which accepts a futuristic view of a supposed golden New Age to come. This age, would, of course, be ushered in by man's own efforts.*[18]

Some Catholic priests and religious promote the new age writings of Fr. Pierre Teilhard de Chardin today. I believe that the Vatican needs to address this growing problem. Should Catholics, especially priests, be speaking, writing, reading, or preaching on the new age writings of Fr. Pierre Teilhard de Chardin? These include his pantheistic ideas of the cosmos and also his other moral errors dealing with evolution.

---

15 Morrison, Alan, *From Old Gnosticism to New Age*, SCP Journal, Vol. 2 9:2 - 2 9:3, 2005.

16 Pacwa, Mitch, S.J., *Catholics and the New Age*, Servant Publications, Ann Arbor, MI, 1992.

17 Wikipedia, *Omega Point*, http://en.wikipedia.org/wiki/Omega_Point. The Omega Point is a term coined by Pierre himself. The Omega Point is the purported maximum level of complexity and consciousness towards which some believe the universe in evolving.

18 Kah, Gary, H., *The Demonic Roots of Globalism*, Huntington House Publishers, 1995, p. 93-94.

In the book, *Hostage to the Devil,* Fr. Malachi Martin (an exorcist) cites a case of possession of a man who was reading the writings of Pierre Teilhard de Chardin. The man became mesmerized with de Chardin's writings to the point where a demon entered his body.[19] When we give Satan an opening, he will take it. Demons came into my life from reading the work of a new age and occult author. Do you want to risk it? Pierre Teilhard de Chardin is one of the leading men responsible for the popularity and practice of new age today.

The New Age Movement and the Occult

The occult is part of new age spirituality. The occult is very dangerous for those who participate in its practices and beliefs, especially on a regular basis. The occult is seeking hidden knowledge or secrets (Gnosticism) to obtain power by using diabolical methods. Occult practices are intriguing and appealing to people because they provide quick answers and predict the future. They are especially attractive to young people, who unfortunately, have learned it from J.D. Rowling's Harry Potter book series and other occult books and movies geared to children. Harry's magic gives him power and the books subtly infuse in readers the quest for power and the seemingly good results that follow. However, many people of all ages get drawn into the occult without realizing the inherent spiritual dangers. I was one of them, and I can tell you from personal experience that delving into the occult can be deadly.

Technology promotes interest in the occult through the entertainment media i.e., movies, sitcoms, video games, websites devoted to mediums and psychics, spells, witchcraft, and even Satanism, which seems to be more prevalent today. The occult deals directly with spirit entities and spirit guides. These are demons who speak through a person or are conjured up through a magic spell or a psychic reading, crystal ball, Ouija Board, or other occult technique or device.

All occult practices are intrinsically evil. Beware! Demons are

19 Martin, Malachi, *Hostage to the Devil: The Possession and Exorcism of Five Living Americans, Father Boanes and Mr. Hatch,* Harper San Francisco, a Division of Harper Collins Publishers, 1992, p. 107.

easily let into your life, but they are not always easy to get rid of. Demons of the occult are some of the strongest demons.

Occultists believe that Jesus Christ is just a prophet, not the Son of God. He is referred to as a "Spiritual Master," but He is not the God depicted in Holy Scripture. Satan is clever, and Jesus was called "Master" by his disciples when He walked the earth. Satan is now using that term to deceive those who lump the concept of God and the occult "spiritual masters" all into one category. People who do not profess that Jesus is the Son of God are false prophets because it is contradictory to Holy Scripture. Christians believe that Jesus, the Son of God, was sent by His Father to redeem us after Adam and Eve's sins of disobedience and pride closed the gates of Heaven for all of us. By Jesus Christ's Suffering and Death on the Cross and His Resurrection, He repaired the damage done by Adam and Eve, re-opening the gates of Heaven for us. We received forgiveness for our sins. However, we were left with free will, which means that we can still choose to do what is good or evil. Our choices determine whether we will go to Heaven or Hell.

The real purpose of new age and occult practices is to bring about the One World Order in which the Anti-Christ will reign over the entire world. Read the Book of Revelation in the Bible. I believe this is not too far away unless people change their lives soon and stop participating in new age and occult practices. Satan is duping many people in the entire world right now. The One World Order network of people, especially Freemasons and the group called the Illuminati, believe in Gnosticism, which is "secret knowledge." They believe they are "chosen" people who are receiving "enlightenment" from spiritual beings who are sent from God. However, because Gnosticism is connected with the occult, they are really hearing from evil spirits. The group working to bring about a One World Order is delving into the occult to obtain knowledge and power. Consequently, they are actively working for Satan, whose real name is Lucifer. This is why those working for the One World Order are often referred to as Lucifernarians.

Synopsis

New age and all occult activities, practices and beliefs are against the First Commandment. It seems to me that people often think that this commandment is not applicable to today's world. After all, in the Old Testament, people worshipped golden calves and molten images and that's in the past. However, this commandment means that anything that takes the place of the one, true God is immoral. This means that new age and occult practices, which place an emphasis on ourselves or an impersonal energy or seek answers through attempts to contact the spirit world, are against the First Commandment. The Bible forbids all forms of idolatry, which includes divination, magic, sorcery, all attempts to unveil the future, seeking hidden powers or making our primary focus a creature. This can include obsessions with just about anything, which I believe are spiritual problems designed to take our focus off of God and place it on a "creature," an earthly desire.

The Catholic Catechism says: ***Idolatry not only refers to false pagan worship. It remains a constant temptation to faith. Idolatry consists in divinizing what is not God. Man commits idolatry whenever he honors and reveres a creature in place of God, whether this be gods or demons (for example, Satanism), power, pleasure, race, ancestors, the state, money, etc. Jesus says, 'You cannot serve God and mammon.'*** (CC2113)

Everywhere I go I see new age and occult practices being advertised. As I travel down streets, I see signs advertising "Acupuncture," "Yoga," and "Psychic Readings." I've seen it at my doctor's office in magazines, which have articles that incorporate new age. Doctors also use new age techniques. I've heard it at musical concerts, where new age lyrics have been incorporated into songs. I've seen it at craft fairs which sold aromatherapy and homeopathic products. I've seen it at school book fairs, which sold new age and occult books. I've seen it at the checkout in grocery stores, where books on horoscopes and magazines with new age articles in them are sold. I've seen it on restaurant place mats, which often have the signs of the zodiac. It's even in hospitals and medical facilities such as Boston's Children's Hospital which use guided imagery, Reiki, acupuncture, yoga, and therapeutic touch for children. You get the idea—new age and the occult is everywhere in every aspect of our lives.

What disturbs me the most is seeing it so prevalent in my beloved Catholic Church, the church founded by Jesus Christ. It is in most schools, seminaries, retreat houses, convents, Catholic hospitals and medical facilities and even in spiritual direction ministries. I hope that will change through sharing my own story and by the grace and mercy of Jesus Christ.

We all need to learn the truth, which is found in Holy Scripture. If we recognize truth, we do not need to contact the spirit world for further information. God sent us the Holy Spirit to help us discern His will for our lives and to guide us in the truth. Do not be duped by new age and occult distortions of it. If you are involved in new age or the occult now, I urge you to correct your behavior. You are in Satan's grasp and spiritually contaminated. Get out of it now while you still can. Don't let demons rule your life. Focus on the Bible and Jesus Christ. You need to do this to save your soul!

Today everyone needs to be educated on what constitutes new age and occult practices from a Christian perspective. Catholic and orthodox Christian articles and books on the subject are required reading for anyone who wants to protect themselves from demonic harassment and stay close to God. Education is essential today so you do not get duped by these moral errors which are prevalent in our culture at this time. If you do not want demons in your life, do your homework.

Chapter One

The Early Years

I was born in 1947 in Madison, Wisconsin, the oldest of four children. My dad was Protestant and had a good job working for the State of Wisconsin. My mother was a devout Catholic and did not work outside the home. Her life was centered on Jesus and her family. We lived in a typical middle class neighborhood.

My siblings (two sisters and a brother) and I were raised Catholic, and I attended Catholic schools for 12 years. From second grade on, I took piano lessons. Eventually I learned to play the organ, too, and got a job in our local Catholic Church when I was in eighth grade. I played for Masses, weddings, funerals, and devotions until I graduated from high school.

I do have fond memories of my early childhood. I particularly enjoyed my mother's parties. She had birthday parties for her friends, and, of course, birthday parties for us kids, too. We used to play Bunco, a dice game that I really enjoyed, at these parties. My siblings and I always enjoyed playing cards and board games, and we had hours of fun doing this. My dad took us on camping trips. We used to pitch a tent and then cook, hike and just enjoy life.

Our family always had dogs, which were friendly and playful, except for the poodle that bit the mailman. Luckily, he didn't press charges. However, I enjoyed our parakeets the most and birds became my favorite pets. I taught them to talk and had one who really could carry on quite a conversation! His name was Windy.

One of my sisters and I used to have a club. Another playmate from the neighborhood joined us. Although we were only a "club" of three, we made money by selling lemonade, which we used to buy candy. We enjoyed playing hopscotch, jump rope, jacks, hide-and-seek, and playing in the park that was just down the street. Our third club member had a lot of comic books, and I used to love to read the Superman comics.

I remember our first TV and watching Lawrence Welk with my mother. It was good family entertainment. I walked to school and church, which was only a couple of miles away. I loved the fresh air and sunshine. I also loved reading books and by the age of 11, I'd read most of Shakespeare's works and many novels.

However, I do remember some bad experiences. As a child, I would often stay overnight at my grandmother's house (on my dad's side of the family.) Since I was her first grandchild, my grandmother doted on me. My grandmother was a widow. (I never met my grandfather because he died before I was born. However, I discovered that my grandfather was adopted and a French Canadian Indian.)

My grandmother lived in a large home she and my grandfather had purchased. Since his death, my grandmother rented the upstairs rooms to men, usually transient individuals. Some would stay a week and others would stay for months. As early as the age of four or five, I remember finding a man hanging in my grandmother's garage. He was one of her boarders, who had committed suicide. I was too young to process this at the time because I did not understand it. I do remember telling my grandmother that a man was hanging in the garage. I also remember standing at a distance watching the police cut him down and taking his body away.

From the time I was about three years old, I would frequently walk in my sleep, carrying my pillow with me. Although I slept upstairs at home, I would usually end up in the downstairs kitchen, where my parents would be enjoying their nightly dessert together around midnight. They would wake me up and put me back in bed. This happened for a few years and I do not know for sure when it stopped, but I believe it was about the age of seven.

I was an incorrigible child from an early age. I had temper tantrums and was rebellious. When I started kindergarten at age five, I kept walking out of school and going home. Finally, my dad disciplined me enough so that I remained in school. My temperament did not improve, however, until I was in my late teens.

God was good to me. I received many graces from going

to daily Mass during my childhood. This was how we began each day at the Catholic grade school I attended. I also received graces from receiving the Sacraments of Baptism, Confession, the Eucharist, and Confirmation. By second grade I had made my first confession. Thereafter, my mother saw to it that I confessed once a week.

About the age of 11, I began to menstruate. From the very beginning, the blood flow was much more than normal. I began to suffer from severe anemia and enormous fatigue on a regular basis. My parents were puzzled by the fact that, during menstruation, I would wake up in the morning and I would be in a puddle of blood even though I had on two super pads and a tampon. I did not know how this happened either. I find it amazing that despite my enormous fatigue and monthly hemorrhaging, I was able to do well in my studies and to excel in subsequent jobs. At the time, I didn't realize that this was a great grace being given to me by God.

I was fortunate to be able to attend a Catholic high school. My parents made sacrifices to do this because the tuition was high. The ability to play organ and sing in church, which meant attendance at many Masses and devotions, also provided very necessary graces for me.

My dad was in a serious car accident in 1962. He was on a business trip and his car overturned and rolled into a deep ravine as he was making a turn on a highway near Mauston, Wisconsin. He was thrown from the car. He had a concussion, ten broken ribs, a punctured lung, a mangled hand, and he was paralyzed on his left side. As a result of the accident, he was in a coma.

I was 15 years old at the time and a sophomore in high school. I remember that the principal announced the accident over the public address system after she told me about it. The entire high school prayed for my dad, and he miraculously survived. The doctors had told my mother he would die. However, he spent a year and a half in the hospital because, when he came out of the coma, he had amnesia. He did not remember anything about his life, his background, his family, or his job. The time he spent in the hospital included one year in the psychiatric ward to help him regain his memory. During that time, my mother had many hardships. When my dad was released from the hospital, he was healed of his physical problems and he had remembered most of his life. However, he was traumatized and could not handle a family with a wife and four children. Consequently, he lived with his mother (my grandmother) until her death in the late 1960's. After that he returned home and lived with my mother until his death in 1994.

My mother was a real blessing in my life, although I didn't appreciate her until years later. She went to three Masses each morning and prayed each night for many people. When I quit my job as organist, she replaced me. She had taken organ lessons in her spare time, and she played in church for the next 25 years. She worked very hard to raise me and my siblings with a devout love for Jesus and Mary. She often gave me books to read on the saints, approved apparitions, or other religious topics. She performed many acts of charity. After her death from Alzheimer's, I inherited her religious library. I found prayers she had tucked into other prayer books. I was moved to tears by her devotion to Jesus and the Eucharist. Today, in spite of my sinfulness, I share this devotion.

Rejection of God

In my late teens, I became engaged to someone I met in church. After two and a half years, he asked me to marry him. Unfortunately, my fiancée got cold feet and told my mother to tell me that he couldn't marry me the day before I was scheduled to have a wedding shower. Later, I discovered that it was not the first time he had broken off an engagement. I began to attend daily Mass in order to deal with this problem. I forgave him and went on with my life.

Six months after the breakup, someone else asked me to marry him, and I consented. I married him on the rebound. On our wedding night I was unable to consummate the marriage because I became traumatized. I felt like I was going to have a nervous breakdown. Despite the rocky beginning, however, my husband and I had three children. I was leading a life close to God and performed all of my duties as a wife and mother as best I could.

Good Christians are always a target for Satan, and I began to have temptations. I had started to work outside the home with the public, and men began to take an interest in me. Some wanted liaisons. After awhile, I did see one or two of them once or twice. I began to feel guilty and that I wasn't a good wife. This time I did not turn to God in prayer, and left my family and filed for divorce at age 30. Looking back, I realize that I was really in a spiritual battle. I began to see another man quite steadily. My husband and I were divorced in 1980 and I remarried outside the Catholic Church in 1981.

When I remarried outside of the Catholic Church, I committed a serious sin because I did not have an annulment from my first marriage. In other words, I was not free to marry in the eyes of God. A legal divorce is only a civil dissolution of the marriage and is not grounds for remarriage within the Catholic Church.

My second marriage lasted seven years, and I was single once again by 1988. After I was divorced the second time, I began to date and lead a sinful life of fornication.

In 1994, I went to confession and made the decision to be celibate, and I have not faltered. Once I made the decision to be celibate, I received graces. The temptations of impurity did not cease, but the temptation to have sexual relations did stop. Eventually, purity and chastity became a way of life as I began to resist the temptations and make a firm purpose of amendment. The Bible says: ***Submit yourselves, then, to God. Resist the devil, and he will flee from you.*** (James 4:7 NIV)

Chapter Two

The Miracle

After I divorced my second husband in 1988, I purchased a condo. I began to date my next door neighbor, a friendly guy named Jerry. While Jerry and I were getting to know each other, I was dating other men. One night while one of my gentleman friends and I were conversing in the living room, we heard a loud squeal. Trying to find the source, my date discovered a bugging device underneath the sofa. Panic-stricken, I called the police. After ransacking my home, they found another device upstairs in my bedroom.

During the time the police spent with me, I found out the devices were short-range. I suspected they had been planted by Jerry, who lived in the other half of my townhouse condo. After a serious conversation with Jerry the following day, he denied planting the devices. However, a few weeks later he confessed. He was jealous of my other relationships because he liked me so much. While I did not condone his behavior and was taken aback by his insecurity, I did forgive him, and we continued to see each other.

The following year, 1989, Jerry asked me if he could move in with me. I had fallen in love with him by this time, and I felt sorry for him because he had recently declared bankruptcy and needed a place to stay. So I consented.

Two days after Jerry moved in, I awakened shortly after retiring one evening feeling quite strange. I had trouble staying conscious. I called to Jerry, who was sleeping in a bedroom across the hall, and feebly asked him to call 911. When the paramedics arrived, my blood pressure and heart rate were low, so I was taken to the hospital. After getting oxygen and an IV, I remained in the hospital for observation. However, I was sent home the next day without a diagnosis. I was troubled by the incident, but went on with my life.

I soon discovered Jerry's problems went much deeper than insecurity and bankruptcy. My new neighbor, who had purchased Jerry's condo, came over to introduce himself one day. During the conversation, he declared, *I really love the condo, but whoever lived here before me really had a problem! I found empty gin bottles all over the house in the strangest places.* Jerry was standing next to me at the time. I'll never forget the look on his face. That's how I found out Jerry was an alcoholic.

I was in shock. When Jerry and I had first met, he drank beer and gin frequently. When I became concerned and discussed it with him, he said he would stop drinking if it bothered me. I'd never seen Jerry take another drink since that conversation.

Now, I felt betrayed. I asked Jerry to look for other housing. After he moved out, however, I continued to see him for the next two and a half years. I still loved him and kept hoping he would change. I even went to alcoholism counseling with him. But he did not stop drinking. In January of 1992, I reluctantly told Jerry that I could no longer see him. Although I regretted losing the man I loved, I was able to deal with the breakup very well because I was emotionally prepared for it. Jerry, however, had become so dependent on me that he could not live without me. He seemed almost obsessed with me, and he began to stalk me.

For the next nine months, my life was a living nightmare. Jerry would sit across the street and watch my house at all hours of the day and night. He would call me repeatedly and hang up. He followed me. On one occasion, I was having dinner with a male friend at a restaurant, and he gave the waitress his business card to give me so I would know he was there. Then he followed us when we left the restaurant. A neighbor told me that he had seen Jerry following me when I took my daily outdoor exercise walks, being careful to stay far enough behind so I wouldn't see him. He was also seen taking my mail. I was getting answers to personal ads I had placed seeking male companionship, and he was intercepting them.

All of these things were quite naturally disturbing to me. I had no privacy. The stress was physically taking a toll. I had always had heavy periods, but during 1992, I bled for a total of 26 weeks straight. In August, I ended up in urgent care, hemorrhaging and very weak. I was given a prescription to stop the bleeding. When I went to a neighborhood drug store to fill the prescription, Jerry was there to greet me when I came out. He was the last person I wanted to see. I went home extremely agitated.

All of these things were bad enough, but when I began to suspect that Jerry was coming into my house, I was panic-stricken. How was he getting in? I had changed all of the locks on my doors when we broke up. But I was sure he was getting in. A friend and I had planned to take a trip so I could get away from it all, and I hadn't told anyone about it. Yet, only a day after I had gotten my itinerary, which I left lay on the couch in the living room, Jerry called me up and said, *Have a nice trip!* The words sent chills right through me. Frightened, I asked, *How did you know that I was going to take a trip? You've been in my house, haven't you?* Of course, he denied it.

I began to have insomnia, afraid I was not alone, unnerved by the whole situation. What was he capable of? This was not normal behavior. I had heard of stalking cases on television, but never thought it would happen to me. I became even more rundown and caught a virus.

On a Saturday night in late August 1992, although it was only 7 p.m., I retired for the night. Shortly afterwards, I was awakened with a start by the sound of my overhead garage door going up underneath my bedroom. My first thought was, *Oh, my God, someone's in the house!* I immediately suspected it was Jerry and prepared for a confrontation. (While my car was in the garage, it was not necessarily a sign that I was home since, when I went on a date, the man usually picked me up in his car). A few minutes later, I heard the garage door go back down, and I knew he had left. It was one of the only times that I had locked the access door leading into my house from the garage. God was really with me that night! Even in my sinful state, He was still looking out for me.

I called the police, but they said I needed a restraining order to arrest Jerry. I later discovered that he had programmed his garage door opener to mine before our breakup, which explained how he had been gaining access to my house. He merely entered the garage using the opener and then walked into the house through the access door in my garage, which I normally left unlocked.

Subsequently, I filed the necessary papers to get the restraining order and prepared to go on my trip. I took a blessed trip to Europe, touring England, France, Switzerland and Italy. For the next two weeks, I forgot about all of my problems. When I returned home from this trip, I was in a different frame of mind. I went to court to get the restraining order and settled back into a normal life. Jerry finally left me alone.

Jerry and I had no contact again until Spring of 1993, when he called and asked me to attend the play, *Jesus Christ Superstar,* with him. I was hesitant, but agreed to go. I think often emotions get in the way of common sense. On April 3, 1993 we went to the play, which was held in a large arena. I was very tired. I had started a new job a couple of months earlier and had been working long hours. During the applause at the end of the play, I suddenly blacked out with no warning. (I actually think that I fell asleep). When I woke up, I was screaming. Luckily, it was muffled by the applause. An ambulance took me to the hospital, where I had several tests. I was diagnosed with neurocardiogenic syncope, a fancy name for a condition of the nerves of the heart that cause it to slow down, lowering blood pressure, which causes fainting. However, as further evidence will show, this diagnosis was incorrect.

In September 1993, I was outdoors washing my car. After I finished, I lay down on the couch to rest. I fell sleep, but awoke within ten minutes, unable to breathe. The same thing happened again about a week later. Subsequently, I saw a pulmonary specialist who did tests. When I met with him to get the test results, he was puzzled. He confirmed that I had chronic bronchitis, which I had been diagnosed with in 1989. However, he said I didn't fit the profile of the average person who typically has this problem. Most people are male, smoke, have a family history of respiratory problems or have been exposed to pollution. None of these factors applied to me. He also told me that he detected a heart murmur, but could not determine the underlying cause. He went on to say that all the breathing tests were normal except when I hyperventilated. But when did I hyperventilate? He had no answers and suggested that I see an internist to pursue further testing.

Subsequently, I did see an internist, and had many tests, which were all negative. The internist who was going to manage my case finally suggested that I see a gynecologist. For the past three years I'd had an elevated temperature. In fact, I kept my thermostat at 58 degrees year round, which was comfortable to me. Since I also had frequent insomnia and night sweats, I began to believe I had symptoms of menopause. I was 46 years old at the time. The gynecologist did several tests to determine hormone levels in my body, but told me everything was normal. I was not in menopause yet.

By December 1993, I was having attacks continually after I went to sleep. I would be hit in the center of my forehead and would always feel like I was dying. My heart rate and pulse would be very low during and immediately after the attacks. I came close to death. Paramedics came several times and took me to the hospital. The attacks increased in frequency to the point where they began to happen every night every time I went to sleep. They were accompanied by various other symptoms, including tingling in my arms, paralysis from the waist down, sweating, and trouble breathing.

In January 1994, I had severe pain in my forehead as the number and force of the attacks increased. Also, during the attacks I experienced sheer terror. I was only able to get about ten minutes of sleep a night. I was not able to work at the office full-time anymore because I was exhausted from lack of sleep. My boss was kind enough to let me work out of my home. I couldn't drive because I was too weak and dizzy so people had to drive me around, and I could not stand for any length of time. My life was falling apart.

Because of my weakening condition, I decided to make my peace with God. I felt like I was dying a slow death, and I decided to prepare for it. Because I had been away from the Catholic Church for over ten years, I called a priest from a local parish who came over to my home to hear my confession. After making a general confession, I had peace.

A few days later, a friend of mine gave me a small prayer book called *The Pieta Prayer Book.*[20] It contained a novena given to St. Bridget by Our Lord in the year 1350, commemorating the Passion and Death of Jesus. I began to say this novena every night before bed. I also included a prayer of Consecration to Jesus

20 *Pieta Prayer Book,* Miraculous Lady of Roses, LLC, Hickory Corners, MI 49060-0111, 2006. It is available in small and large print. Also see www.mlor.com.

through Mary which followed the novena in the prayer book. From that time on, I prayed daily. I also had someone take me to Sunday Mass every week. I didn't know what was going to happen to me, but I put my trust in God, surrendering everything to Him. Then, every night, in my own words I prayed to Jesus for healing. I also asked Mary to intercede for me to her Son, Jesus, to help me get better.

I decided to consult a psychologist because both my internist and gynecologist had suggested it. I was able to make an appointment with an experienced, Catholic psychologist who had an opening in his schedule. After reviewing my case, he ordered a complete psychological profile and conducted a test on my nervous system. Electrodes were hooked up to the nerves in my upper back to register their sensitivity. The results of this test stunned him. He said that the dial was off the monitor. It was as if I was mummified! Indeed, my back was so tense that this did not surprise me.

The psychologist diagnosed me with Post-Traumatic Stress Disorder. I had never heard of it. He said I was a trauma survivor, meaning that something so terrible had happened to me in the past that the memories of it had been blocked out as a protective mechanism. Because the attacks happened shortly after I fell asleep (which is the deepest dream stage), he surmised that I was most likely dreaming about the traumatic incident(s), which caused the attacks and accompanying symptoms. He stated that my body was most likely duplicating symptoms of the traumatic event over and over as if it were happening today. The stress of the hidden memories was taking a toll on my body. Because the attacks were happening so frequently and violently, he warned me that I may need psychotherapy for the rest of my life. He explained that I would need to remember what had happened to me in order to deal with it, which could take years. I left his office in shock. I thought to myself, *A trauma survivor—how can I handle this?*

Coincidentally, the very next day I received a copy of a newsletter in the mail from a local psychiatric hospital that explained all about the disorder. The newsletter explained that traumatization is often associated with victims of physical, sexual and emotional abuse. Frequently, this abuse occurs during childhood. It is associated with an event that happens that is so terrible that the memories are blocked out for an extended period of time. The diagnosis is difficult, since repressed memories can remain dormant for many years, only to resurface later through one or more symptoms. It is natural to look for physical causes of those symptoms since no memory of the traumatic experience exists. Occasionally, the trauma surfaces as a result of a similar or other stressful event that may have recently occurred.

The first memories of the traumatic event in my life from the past came during a visit from a friend. My friend was a former Catholic psychologist who had dealt with memory repression cases during his career. During our conversation, he began to ask me leading questions designed to trigger my memory.

I immediately remembered a night during my childhood when I was living at my grandmother's house on my dad's side of the family. I had moved in, somewhat reluctantly, at my grandmother's request at age 11 because she was lonely. It was a large, older home. She had converted her large dining room into a bedroom for the two of us. We slept on opposite ends of this room. Adjacent to this room was the kitchen with a back door, which was used by family members. There was also another door on the opposite side of the kitchen which led either to the front door which went outside or upstairs to the boarders' rooms. The front door was used by my grandmother's four boarders because it went right upstairs to their rooms. On this particular night, I was asleep when I heard the sounds of someone come into the house through the back door. My first thought was, *Oh, my God, someone's in the house!*

At this point my friend discontinued his questions because he became uncomfortable. He had left psychology to go into another field because he could no longer deal with his patients' pain. We talked about other subjects before he left. However, the similarity between the recent incident when Jerry tried to enter my home while I was sleeping and the dreadful night from the past was apparent. It seemed as if Jerry had triggered the memory of the night of the trauma.

My friend remarked that many people thought that what I was experiencing was the struggle between good and evil. I pondered this comment. The psychologist that was treating me had observed that it was unusual that during the attacks I was hit in the **center** of my forehead. He said typically attacks of this nature affected the **side** of the head. I wondered about it also.

At the next session with the psychologist who was treating me, he talked about how he was going to proceed with my case. I told him what I had already remembered during the visit with my friend. He said he was going to use various techniques to trigger further memories beginning with my next appointment. I was afraid and very nervous.

The next Sunday, I prayed hard at Mass. One of the songs sung that day was "Be Not Afraid," and I prayed not to have any fear during my next appointment. The next day, when I arrived at my scheduled appointment with the psychologist, he was amazed by my calmness. So was I. I had not been that calm for many years. The Lord really did help me.

During my first appointment and subsequent ones, the psychologist used guided imagery and hypnosis. I later learned that both guided imagery and hypnosis can be considered new age techniques. Guided Imagery is visualization designed to place the patient into an altered state of consciousness. In my case, my psychologist asked me to visualize a peaceful scene by a lake or in a garden and to focus on it while he guided me into a progressive state of relaxation, blocking out any intrusive thoughts.

Hypnosis used in cases of memory repression places the patient in a trance-like state in order to help repressed memories return to the conscious mind. Although hypnosis was supported by Pope Pius XII in his address to an audience of obstetricians and gynecologists on January 8, 1956, he believed that the morality of hypnosis would be based on need in grave situations and with a licit end. I believe that its use today is abused and often unwarranted, causing more problems than good.

Bishop Donald Montrose, D.D. says: *Although hypnotism is now used sometimes by respectable doctors, dentists and therapists, it was linked in the past with the occult and with superstition. Even when it is legitimate, there are certain real dangers that must be very carefully considered. In hypnotism, one surrenders for a time his own capacity to reason; there is a dependence of the one hypnotized on the will of the hypnotist; also there can be unfortunate after effects that result from this technique. Except for a very serious reason, avoid submitting to a hypnotist; never do it for the purpose of entertainment.*[21]

Although the psychologist attempted to use guided imagery and hypnosis in my case, I did not willingly and actively participate in them, but focused on other thoughts, including Jesus, when he tried to use them. Although there may be legitimate circumstances when hypnosis benefits the patient, I personally was not comfortable with either hypnosis or with guided imagery. I believe that these cautions came from the Holy Spirit because I was not familiar with these methods at all at the time.

During the first session with my psychologist that I had after praying at Sunday Mass, I remembered more about the night that I had recalled with my Catholic friend. These memories came back naturally. I remembered that when my grandmother and I were asleep, I was awakened by the sounds of someone coming into the house. The person came in the back door, the one normally used by family members. As I looked towards the swinging door that led from the kitchen into our bedroom to see who would enter, the thought came to me that it must be my dad, since he frequently came over to check on us. But it was unusual for him to come over so late. Then I did not remember any more until my grandmother awakened because I was screaming. She turned on the lamp next to her bed and asked me what was wrong. I said there had been a man in the room.

The psychologist then delved into my memories of the men I knew during this time in my life. He was attempting to help me identify the perpetrator (the term for the person who abuses the victim). He asked me if I remembered any of my grandmother's boarders. I did. There were two that I recalled, but only one stood out in my mind. He was a handsome man that I'd had a schoolgirl crush on. I would always dress up and be sure to look my best when he came to pay the weekly rent. He was always friendly, and I flirted with him, although I did not remember his name.

The psychologist asked if I was afraid of this man. I said, "No."

21 Montrose, Bishop Donald W., *Spiritual Warfare* : The *Occult Has Demonic Influence*, www.ewtn.com/library/bishops/occult.htm.

Consequently, he probably eliminated him as a suspect. He then began to pursue my relationship with my dad. I knew where he was going with this line of questioning. He was pursuing the possibility that the abusive act had been committed by my dad. Because my dad and I had not been especially close, I began to believe that he had tried to molest me. This was naturally very disturbing to me.

Over the next six weeks, I met with the Catholic psychologist twice a week. The attacks continued. They were actually panic attacks that occurred after I went to sleep. The psychologist said he could do nothing to stop them. My internist prescribed some medications such as sleeping pills and anti-depressants, but they only increased the force of the attacks because I fell into a deeper sleep. Consequently, although specialists tried to do all they could for me, I grew progressively worse.

During the sessions with my psychologist, he began to focus exclusively on my relationship with my dad. This caused me to believe more and more that my dad had abused me. I decided that whoever did it, I would forgive him. At the time, both of my parents were still alive. I never told my parents what I was going through. I treated my dad with respect. I know I was given the grace to do this.

In the meantime, the attacks became so strong that sometimes I would wake up with my hands braced on the floor next to my bed for support. It felt like a sledge hammer hitting me. My head began to hurt continually from the force and frequency of the blows. I know that Satan can exacerbate the symptoms in a case like this. Was he? Or was he even causing the symptoms?

One night I had the sense of being suffocated with a pillow. I began to dread going to bed because I knew what I would be facing. I was only able to get a few minutes of sleep a night. Physically, I was growing weaker, but, ironically, my ability to reason and to think was not impaired. That was miraculous. My mind was clear, and this was demonstrated by the fact that I could still perform my job at home accurately. I worked as a print production coordinator and had to give detailed instructions to suppliers.

However, by February 25, 1994, I could not go on. My doctor

did not know what else he could do for me and he gave me two options. First, he could try to find a psychiatrist to take my case, but he said that would take some time. Second, he could admit me to the hospital. This was not a solution for me because I did not have adequate insurance, and I would have run out of money. I was supporting myself. Also on this day, I informed my boss that I could no longer work, even at home. Of course, that meant that the company could no longer pay me.

On that day, February 25, 1994, at 6 p.m., I experienced a miracle. I was trying my best to go on and I forced myself to walk on my treadmill. While I did this, I turned on the radio because music usually lifts my spirits. After only a few minutes, the song, "Let It Be," came on the radio. All of a sudden, I felt the presence of the Blessed Mother standing right in front of me. The words of the song seemed to speak to me: "Let It Be." In other words, let go of the past. I heard, "There will be an answer." I felt peace as though I was being healed. I got more energy, but by this I mean more strength, because I was physically weak. By the end of the song, I was completely healed!

That night I did not have an attack for the first time in months. It was a miracle! I slept through the entire night. However, when I put on a tape recorder the following night before I went to sleep out of curiosity, I did record me having an attack. I heard my voice saying, "No, get away from me!" The attacks had not stopped, but I had no memories of them, and they did not disrupt my sleep. I was able to drive to work at the office immediately and my boss, who had personally witnessed my decline because he had brought me work to do at my home, was amazed at my recovery. For a few weeks, he kept coming over to my desk and asking me if I really was okay.

I had such peace that I can't put it into words. I was more relaxed than I'd ever been in my entire life. My back was no longer tense after many years, and I no longer had night sweats. My body temperature became normal. I was not yet in menopause, which didn't occur for another few years. Also, the hemorrhaging I'd had during my periods since age 11 stopped after 35 years. A week later, my psychologist retested my nervous system, which was completely normal. He could not attribute it to anything other than a miracle. He told me that in 30 years of practice, he had never witnessed any transformation as dramatic as mine. During my next office visit with my internist, he also confirmed that I had a miracle. I no longer had chronic bronchitis or a heart murmur.

I believe that Jesus healed me through the intercession of the Blessed Mother. I believe that the attacks had demonic influence, but the Blessed Mother is the woman who will crush the head of Satan, and she is a powerful intercessor. One of the promises for saying the novena given to St. Bridget commemorating the Passion and Death of Jesus is that if you are to die, your life will be prolonged. I do think I may have died if the attacks had continued much longer because I virtually had only a few minutes of sleep for months, and it was taking a real toll on me. In addition, the novena given to St. Bridget is a meditation on the Passion and Death of Jesus, which I know is a powerful prayer of reparation.

I also know that other people were praying for me. In addition, it is too coincidental that *The Pieta Prayer Book*, with the prayers in it that I said, was given to me just in time. I had also surrendered my life to Jesus through Mary and had made a good confession. I was in the state of grace. I had started to attend daily Mass.

In reflecting on this part of my life today, I believe my healing was brought about by forgiveness of the perpetrator, Confession, the Mass, the Eucharist, prayer, completely surrendering my life to God, and intercessory prayer by the Blessed Mother to her Son, Jesus. I do not believe that PTSD victims should focus on past abuse nor should they covet money or wish for someone to pay the price for their pain. Jesus has already paid the price for all of our sins. All of us have some form of suffering. We need to offer it up for the salvation of souls. It may not be God's will that we all have a miracle of healing, but prayers can help us cope. It is also wonderful that we have Mary, the saints, angels, and the prayers of the souls in Purgatory to pray for us and with us to God for our needs.

I do not believe that the victim needs to remember what happened to be healed. I think the memories should be allowed to progress naturally. The spiritual prayers and devotions I mentioned can help victims in a way that psychology cannot. Also, today victims must be careful because the field of psychology is steeped in new age and occult practices, which will only add to the problem. I suggest that victims start or join a prayer group for support and pray the Rosary and the Chaplet of Divine Mercy. I also think forgiveness is crucial to healing.

It's been 20 years since the miracle, and I have been doing well. The miracle has stood the test of time. Over the past 20 years, I have become convinced the panic attacks I had at night were strictly demonic. I had some attacks again, but they were intermittent. They did not cause problems like those I have just described in this chapter. I would guess I had a total of 12 attacks during the last 20 years, and I was hit in the center of my forehead. I believe they were demonic, spiritual attacks by Satan. The fact that I was hit in the center of my forehead is a big clue. Also, I know that evil spirits of trauma can cause demons to come into people's lives. I still believe that I experienced a miracle. I will never forget that moment.

Life is a struggle between good and evil. I know some people commented to me that no miracle could happen during a song by the Beatles because of their sinful lifestyle. But don't you think this is judgmental? Don't we all have both good and evil in our lives?

In an article by Catholic writer Charlotte Allen, she writes about the song, *Let It Be,* saying: *Though dedicated to Paul McCartney's earthly mother, whose name was Mary, it can also be understood as a song to the Virgin Mother.*[22] The words are reminiscent of Mary's fiat to the angel Gabriel, who asked Mary if she would be the Mother of Jesus. Mary's answer was: ***Behold, the handmaid of the Lord: let it be done to me according to your word.*** (Luke 1:38)[23] It is a beautiful prayer of surrender to the will of God. I had just done that. The Bible says to take what is good and discard the rest.

On its own merits, the song, *Let It Be,* is inherently good. It talks about Mother Mary coming to us in times of darkness. It truly was my hour of darkness. But the song's message goes far beyond my own personal situation. Don't we live in evil times—

22 Allen, Charlotte, *Catholic Digest,* September 2001.

23 Scripture taken from *The New Testament*, St. Paul Catholic Edition, 2000, by the society of St. Paul.

times of darkness? Mary has come to us in her many approved apparitions requesting prayer, fasting and penance for world peace. The world is full of wars, violence, hatred, prejudice and terrorism. There is still a chance that we, the broken-hearted people, may see. We are all sinners in need of repentance. Let's pray for peace in our families, in our country, in our world. Let us pray and love one another.

Chapter Three

The Psychic

After the miracle in 1994, my life settled down during the next few months. However, then I began to have a lot of questions. What did happen to me during the evening of the trauma? Who tried to molest me? Was it my dad? I did not remember who attempted to molest me, only the circumstances surrounding the attack. I began to pray to the Blessed Mother for the answer, the answer that the song, "Let It Be," seemingly indicated would come. Unfortunately, sometimes we do not get immediate answers to prayer. Jesus has a perfect plan, and we are just to take one day at a time and trust in Him. I should have just "let it be," but I wanted instant answers. We must be patient and keep praying. Everything happens in God's time. I actually think these are spiritual tests to test our faith.

About two weeks after the miracle, a co-worker gave me the name of a psychic[24] woman, a Catholic, who she said had a gift. Her gift was giving people a sense of direction by telling them things that were supposedly from God about their lives and their future. My co-worker gave me the psychic's name and phone number and urged me to contact her. My friend confided to me that the woman had helped her, and she thought I would benefit from contacting her, too.

I took the information home and left it on my kitchen counter. I didn't understand these things. I'd never heard of a psychic. At first, I was not going to call this woman. I was afraid that she would tell me that I would have more attacks and problems. I couldn't face it. But, eventually, I thought to myself, *Well, what harm can it do?* I was about to find out.

The psychic lived in another city in my state. She knew nothing

24 Psychics are individuals who receive knowledge from evil spirits. In part, this happens through visions, mental telepathy and use of demonic tools, such as Tarot cards, astrology and other forms of divination. It is against the First Commandent to consult a psychic.

about me. For the first few minutes of our phone conversation, she explained to me that she'd had a gift of seeing the future since the age of four. It fact, the gift ran in her family. She assured me that she was Catholic, and that she was using this gift to help people.

Following this brief conversation, there was complete silence for about five minutes. (I think she may have been using Tarot cards[25] during this time lapse). Then the psychic asked me when my birthday was. This determined for her which sign of the Zodiac applied to me. She said, *Oh, you're a Taurus.* At the time, this went completely "over my head," so to speak. Now I recognize it as Astrology.[26]

The psychic began by telling me some things about myself that no one knew. They pertained to my personality, and she was correct. But what she said next took me aback. She said, *You've had a miracle happen to you recently.* She began to relate the entire incident of the night of the trauma from my childhood. She said that I was asleep and I heard someone come into the house through the back door. She said one of my grandmother's boarders came in that night and attempted to sexually molest me. I blacked out in sheer terror and when I came to, I was screaming. He then took a pillow and tried to suffocate me to shut me up because my grandmother was stirring. As my grandmother awakened further, he ran out of the room. The psychic described the boarder I had mentioned to my psychologist—the man I had been attracted to and flirted with at age 11. She told me his name, which I had not remembered, but it jogged my memory, and I realized that she was correct. She said that my grandmother suspected that he had tried to molest me that night and asked him to leave the premises. I did remember that my grandmother spoke to this boarder the following day, and he did leave the home. She was correct about this, too!

I thought to myself, *Who could know this except God?* No one

25 Tarot cards are a deck of 78 cards used to reveal hidden truths. They are often used by psychics and mediums. It is against the First Commandment to use Tarot cards.

26 Astrology is a divining practice that determines our destiny by the position of the stars. Astrologers use birthday-based predictions to determine a person's temperament and future. If any part of our free will is predetermined, we would not be able to choose good and evil for ourselves.

had been there except my grandmother, and she had been dead for 26 years. (What I did not know at the time is that psychics can give some accurate information, but the information always comes from Satan and demons.)

I was amazed and from that point on, I hung on every word that she said. Truthfully, I did not call this woman with the intent of trying to learn more about who abused me. I did not even mention anything about it to her, which made what she told me even more remarkable. I was also quite vulnerable. The fact that the song, "Let It Be," seemed to indicate I would get an answer was still fresh in my mind. Therefore, I believed that this was the answer.

The psychic said that I would write a book on miracles. I would travel to many places where I would meet people who had miracle stories. Thus, the book would consist of several different types of miracles gotten from people all over the country. She said that it was God's will that I do this, and that I would have protection from Heaven. She told me to read stories about angels, and that St. Therese the Little Flower was with me. Can you imagine? The devil uses religion when it suits his purposes. He is very clever. St. Therese the Little Flower happened to be the saint I had taken as my confirmation name. Doesn't this sound like something from God? At least I thought so. I was hooked. In fact, I decided the word, "prophet," would actually be a better description for her, and I decided to use that term in describing her. This was a grievous error.

Over the course of three years, the psychic and I talked often. When she requested that I pay $25.00 an hour for her time, I willingly did so. I believed that some monetary compensation was justified. It was only fair. I fell for the bait hook, line, and sinker. I discovered later that all psychics charge money for their time. So it was that beginning in 1994, I entered the heretofore unknown world to me of new age and the occult.

Looking back, I see Satan's strategy. I had just returned to the Catholic Church and was in the state of grace. Satan had me in his grasp for many years, and he wanted me back. He doesn't need to worry about the people in mortal sin. He wants those who are with the Lord. He wasn't about to let me go so easily.

He knew all of my sins and weaknesses. He also knew I wanted answers in my PTSD case, in which he definitely had influence. He used this very weakness against me.

Satan also detests the Blessed Mother, who was instrumental in my healing. He fears her the most because she is his exact opposite. While Satan is full of pride, Mary is meek and humble. Her plan in salvation history is to be a mother to us all. When we consecrate our lives to Jesus through Mary, which I did in my hour of darkness by reciting the prayer in *The Pieta Prayer Book,* she goes to battle for us and helps us as much as she can. I believe that if we ask Mary to intercede for us to Jesus with any of our problems, we will not be disappointed. How can Jesus deny her anything?

Psychics are considered part of the occult because they divine the future using various techniques which come from the devil. Divining the future is against the First Commandment: ***You shall worship the Lord your God and Him only shall you serve.*** (Matthew 4:10 NIV). ***The First Commandment summons man to believe in God, to hope in Him, and to love Him above all else.*** (CC 2134).

The Catechism also states: ***Consulting horoscopes, astrology, palm reading, interpretation of omens and lots, the phenomena of clairvoyance, and recourse to mediums all conceal a desire for power over time, history, and, in the last analysis, other human beings, as well as a wish to conciliate hidden powers. They contradict the honor, respect, and loving fear that we owe to God alone.*** (CC 2116)

The Book Begins

During the course of writing the book on miracles, I was led to many new age and occult practices and beliefs. I was continually running into people who promoted these practices or teachings, with which I was not familiar. I ran into them in my travels or through chance encounters with people in various places in the Milwaukee area. Some were mentioned to me by the psychic. At the time, I sincerely believed she had a gift from God.

During the course of three years, the psychic would suggest

places where I should travel and people whom I should interview to get miracle stories. In retrospect, I realize she was leading me, with help from Satan and evil spirits, to stories that had some element of new age or the occult in them. However, God in His mercy, allowed me to go to some places where I did receive genuine miracle stories. These were places where I decided to go or where friends suggested that I go, not places where the psychic directed me to go.

Satan presents good with evil. He does not mind throwing in truth along with lies to deceive us. What I learned is that much in a book can be morally sound, but it's the parts that are evil that Satan uses to deceive us. Thus, we should not read books that contain any moral errors. The parts that are scripturally and morally sound would have to be extracted and made into a separate book by someone qualified to discern.

At one point, the psychic decided to write and produce her own play. She was the star, and there was only a handful of other actors and actresses. Knowing what I do now, I recognize the play as filled with new age ideas. During the play there were auras around people. An aura is a light or energy field that supposedly surrounds a person or object. The color of the light is believed to determine the person's emotional and intellectual moods. I actually began to see auras around people, which I eventually learned was demonic. When I began to dismiss these lights I saw around people, I stopped seeing them.

During the play, the psychic spoke with a character who was a spirit guide. She communicated with her deceased grandmother, which is form of spiritualism. To show how the devil works, during the play there were large pictures of Jesus and Mary on the stage. However, they really had nothing to do with the play. Satan has no qualms about adding something religious to anything that is predominantly new age or occult because he is hoping that people will believe it all is from God. The psychic talked me into donating money towards this project. Of course, I regret it.

During the three years that I consulted the psychic, her temperament slowly changed. She became short-tempered and irritable at times. She was actually so rude to me at times that it brought me to tears. In hindsight, maybe I was getting too many good stories. One thing I did do was to try to become closer to God. I began to pray for souls in Purgatory after watching a show on EWTN with Mother Angelica, attended Sunday Mass regularly, went to confession, and attended Marian conferences. Despite the moral errors and poor judgment on my part, God, in His infinite mercy, was trying to lead me to truth.

Some of the new age and occult practices I ran into during the time I wrote the book were channeling, auras, spiritism, holistic health remedies, energy therapies, tea leaf reading, shamanism, dream therapy, and reincarnation. When I began to research these things from a Catholic or Christian perspective, I discovered they were not in line with Scripture. It didn't happen overnight, however. I learned slowly through finding Catholic or Christian articles on one or more of the subjects and had to read and digest them. Sometimes, I met good Catholics during my travels and learned from them, or I heard a good speaker at a Catholic conference. It was actually a mercy of the Lord that I was led to truth a number of times. I also had some help from Jesus Himself.

When I discovered the psychic was incorrect about a practice that she recommended to me, for example, Healing Touch (an energy therapy), I just chalked it up to human error and explained to her that I discovered it was against Catholic teaching. This was a fatal error on my part. I should have realized that God would not be speaking to me through someone who did not know right from wrong. I continued to call her for advice and readings, and it reached a point where I could not do anything without her. At this point, I believe that mortal sin occurred.

We cannot look to anyone or anything other than God for answers to our problems. We are not to worry about the future; God is already there. We are to trust in Him and pray to the Holy Spirit for guidance and discernment. I made excuses for the psychic because I still thought the book was from God, in part due to the seemingly miraculous way that I was getting stories. But I should have paid attention to the Holy Spirit, who was trying to warn me that I was not on track. But I didn't listen.

The warning signs from the Holy Spirit included realizing that the psychic was leading me to new age practices (which

I shrugged off), not leading a Catholic/Christian life herself at times, justifying her joining a psychic network (which was shortly before my book on miracles was scheduled to be printed), charging me money, and most of all, looking to her for answers instead of relying on God.

Not only did I not heed the warnings, I actually contacted another psychic or two out of curiosity to see if another psychic would tell me the same things as she did. This was in 1996 to the best of my recollection. I cannot excuse my poor behavior, but I can tell you that one sin leads to another and to another and to another....

One day at work, a co-worker suggested that members of our department do tea leaf reading, which I later learned is an occult technique to divine the future. I participated in this, which I eventually seriously regretted because it is a sin. Our department was small, about six people. I did not know anything about it at the time, and we did it "for fun," which was our goal. However, it is not a "fun" thing to do because it can bring evil spirits into your life.

Tea leaf reading, known as tasseography, is a form of divining the future using tea leaves, which is against the First Commandment. The practice originated in Asia, the Middle East and Greece. Loose tea is used, and there is a specific set of rules to follow. Symbols supposedly form in the leaves, which are then interpreted to divine the future.

All forms of divination are to be rejected; recourse to Satan or demons, conjuring up the dead or other practices falsely supposed to "unveil" the future. (CC 2116). The source of this teaching is from Deuteronomy 18:10 in which the Lord declares all "diviners" to be an abomination to Him. So it was that, during the course of writing the book on miracles, I actively lived the struggle between good and evil.

For three years, I travelled to many states and received miracle stories from perfect strangers. I wrote one story at a time and in 1996, had enough stories for a book. When I finished the book, I had a vision of a shower of roses coming down from Heaven when I was awake, accompanied by fireworks, cherubs and other spiritual phenomena. I thought it was from St. Therese the Little

Flower, but I know now it was demonic. The chain on my Rosary also turned from silver to gold. I was sure this was a sign that God was blessing me. However, I learned that Satan can change the color of a Rosary from silver to gold and visions can come from both sides, good and evil.

I tried to find a publisher. I had gone to the apparition at Medjugorje, and on the plane trip home, I had a vision of the Holy Spirit. After a conversation with a Catholic writer, who happened to be sitting next to me on the plane, she agreed to help me find an agent to try and place my book with a publisher. I was certain this was from God because of my vision and because of the coincidence of sitting next to her on the plane. However, I learned that Satan can give us a vision of the Holy Spirit and even set up coincidences. I want to stress that Satan mimics things of God, and there are coincidences that really come from God and those that are not from God. (A few years later, after I knew more about new age, I recognized new age beliefs in this woman's own "Catholic" books. Therefore, I understand why Satan put us together. We were both being tempted in a similar manner.) I learned we must discern and stay close to God through daily prayer, frequent reception of the Sacraments, frequent Adoration, reading the Bible and other religious devotions.

Subsequently, the writer I met on the plane followed through and sent my book to one of the largest publishers in the United States. However, after six months, the publisher rejected it and would not print it. I thank the Lord for that now, but at the time, I was disappointed. It was actually Divine Mercy.

Since I was not able to find a publisher for the book I wrote, I self-published it in December of 1997. The psychic had encouraged me to do this. I printed 10,000 copies and paid a company to store them. I attempted to market the book, but the book did not sell well. In the meantime, I racked up many debts.

Chapter Four

My Battle with Demons

I opened a door for evil spirits to enter when I allowed the psychic to come into my life despite the fact that I thought that she was sent to me from God. I consented to the situation. I accept responsibility for it. My life changed in ways I never anticipated. I learned that there are consequences for all of our actions.

I began to have experiences from both God and Satan immediately after I started to write the book on miracles in 1994. I had many encounters with Satan, demons, and people who went to Hell. (I am going to refer to people who went to Hell as "disembodied damned human souls.") On the other hand, I also had supernatural experiences with God the Father, Jesus, souls in Purgatory, angels and saints in Heaven.

My very first demonic experience was a vision I had of Satan in June, 1994. One night after I went to bed, Satan appeared to me. He had a black spirit body, and his red eyes were glowing in the dark. He looked just like the image of Satan in the cloud of smoke after the World Trade Center bombing although my experience happened years before this event. The room was ice cold, a frequent sign of a demonic presence. It was horrible, but I didn't consider it unusual because some saints had experiences with Satan. This was not because I thought that I was a saint, but I accepted it as God's will. I thought it was spiritual warfare because I was writing a book for the Lord, and I just accepted it. I continued to go to Mass on Sunday and pray.

Shortly after Satan's visit, Jesus had mercy on me. I was shown in a dream to hold up a wooden crucifix with the Corpus on it and say, *Satan, begone in the name of Jesus Christ,* when I was being attacked. I purchased a crucifix and kept it on my nightstand because the attacks happened at night. Satan left immediately *every time* I used it. St. Ignatius said, *When the devil wants to attack and harass a man with peculiar bitterness, he prefers to work at night.*[27] The spiritual assistance I received from Jesus helped me cope with the attacks by Satan and other evil spirits as they continued through the years.

A short time later, I saw St. Michael in a dream with his foot on the head of Satan. I was led to purchase a statue of St. Michael the Archangel and have it blessed. I began to pray to St. Michael when I was having demonic attacks. I learned that the St. Michael prayer, which was written by Pope Leo XIII, is a powerful exorcism prayer that fights evil. I saw St. Michael come and fight the demons for me several times. St. Michael's army of good angels in white battled the fallen angels in black in my bedroom. My bedroom was full of warring angels! I owe St. Michael a lot because he really protected me.

Later on, Jesus told me to say the St. Michael prayer over and over each night after retiring. I still say this prayer, and if I do not, the demons start tormenting me by speaking, demonic noises and other forms of harassment. I fall asleep today saying the St. Michael prayer. Sometimes the demons wake me up by harassing me in the middle of the night, but I begin reciting the St. Michael prayer over and over, and they leave me alone every time. I was also led to say the Chaplet of St. Michael.

One day I purchased a CD which listed ten religious songs, but when I played it, there were actually eleven songs on it. The last song was a sung version of the St. Michael Prayer followed by the words: *I won't be afraid, Lord, for You lead me. I know Your goodness and Your love will be with me.* It was a pleasant surprise and a personal message for me. It was a reminder to say the St. Michael Prayer and also to trust in Jesus.

Eventually, I was led to use Holy Water against the evil spirits when they attacked. When I used it I sometimes heard a long audible, "sssssssssss," like a fire being put out. I was also led to use Blessed Salt and Holy Oil. This assistance was given to me by Jesus; I did not get this knowledge from a priest or anyone in this world. Jesus would either show me what to do in a dream or vision or lead me to read about what to do somewhere along the

27 Taken from the book, *Thoughts of St. Ignatius Loyola,* translated from the *Scintillae Ignatianae* of Father Gabriel Hevenesi, S.J. by Alan G. McDougall, published by Benziger Brothers, 1928.

way. I did not know anything about spiritual warfare.

Between June 1994 until sometime in 2002, I literally had thousands of physical attacks by Satan, demons and disembodied damned human souls. By physical attacks I am referring to attacks where I actually felt a spirit body on me or with me, physically wrestled with demons, was paralyzed by a demon who immobilized me so I could not even move, or received blows to my body. These blows did not leave visible marks on my body, but I could feel the force of them. I was, however, actually paralyzed and unable to move during many attacks. I got very little sleep and suffered from exhaustion. However, God gave me the grace to endure it.

Satan, demons and disembodied damned human souls from Hell came every night between one and seven times. When Satan appeared, Jesus usually gave me the distinct knowledge that it was him. Demons would often come in the form of hideous beasts, animals or other grotesque images. Disembodied damned human souls would come as presumably the person they were on earth except they had a spirit, opaque body without flesh. There were men, women and even children among them. They were similar to an apparition or a ghost. They were all different ages, shapes and sizes, just like people on earth.

Some of these experiences would begin in the dream stage, but at some point I would be aware of what was happening on a conscious level and rebuke them in the name of Jesus Christ, using the crucifix I had purchased. They left every time. I believe these experiences were not "just dreams" but actual encounters with demonic entities and damned souls. I say this because I also saw these entities when I was awake with my eyes open. I always felt "negative energy," which is hard to describe. I would say it was a feeling of oppression, fear, an ominous feeling, in the room. In 2002, after I made a general confession with a Catholic priest, the experiences happened less often.

A Sampling of My Experiences

One night when I went into my bedroom, my room was filled with demons. I could feel their presence. I could also hear the sound of crackling fire. When I sprinkled holy water all over the room, they left immediately, and I felt peace. I never believed in sacramentals before, but I do now! Sacramentals are blessed sacred articles that help us spiritually to combat evil.

Late one night, I heard Satan's voice. He said, *A movie,* and proceeded to show me a movie. It started just like a motion picture, depicting a gold horse within a gold frame. Then the movie showed an ugly man dancing. I commanded Satan to leave in the name of Jesus Christ, and he did.

Satan came to me in the form of a serpent and slithered up my body more than once, often on the first of January, the feast of the Solemnity of Mary, Mother of Jesus. While I could not see Satan, I actually felt a snake slithering up my body. On January 1, 2003, I was sleeping. In the middle of the night, I was awakened by my right arm being lifted slightly up. I was lying on my back at the time. I realized a huge snake was crawling up my torso. It was Satan in the form of a serpent. He paralyzed me for awhile before I could call out to Jesus for help. I commanded him to leave in the name of Jesus, but before he did, I saw a vision of a huge brownish-colored snake with large beady eyes staring into mine. I was not afraid. God is more powerful than Satan. But this confirms the fact that Satan can take the form of a serpent and does even today. We should not worship creatures, but God alone.

I remember a time when a demon tried to choke me and another time a demon wanted to throw me out of bed against the wall, but Jesus would not let him. Jesus was and is always in control. Demonic entities can only do what God permits them to do.

One night a disembodied damned human soul came and stood next to me in a dream. I knew he was really with me in my bedroom, but I didn't want to open my eyes and look at him. Then he took the form of a skeleton, and I saw out of the corner of my eye his skeletal hand with white, thin flesh flapping from the bone. I cried out and then opened my eyes and prayed for him to *Begone in the name of Jesus Christ.* Then I saw a vision of a skeletal head with its jaws open. It fell a few inches in midair and disappeared. I called on the angels to come, and they came and gave me much peace. St. Michael the Archangel came.

Late one night I was attacked by a group of disembodied

damned human souls of men. I rebuked them in the usual manner and they left, but before they did, I saw a vision of the men and one turned into a skull. I think the message was that these men had died in mortal sin and now were going to be dead in every way, including being separated from God.

On another occasion, I was sleeping and dreamt that a man who had gone to Hell was attacking me from behind. However, this was a real encounter with a disembodied damned human soul. He had his arms around me and I was fighting him off. I felt his spirit body against me. I sensed that this damned soul didn't really want to do what he was doing. I fought him with my arms at first, but he grabbed me by the wrists to pin me down. No doubt people who end up in Hell are unhappy with their choices. I am sure they wish they could go back and redo their lives. I think this particular man was very unhappy that he had chosen by his actions to go to Hell, which was probably why he seemed reluctant to attack me. However, people who go to Hell cannot undo their eternal state. They have made their choice and it's final.

The Motorcycle Rider

One night I was awakened by a knock on my bedroom furniture. Then I saw a disembodied damned human soul of a man riding a motorcycle. He actually rode right through my bedroom wall and stopped on the right side of my bed. He was between 35 and 40 years old, had dark hair, and was quite heavy set. He wore a leather jacket. I remember hearing the loud roar of his motorcycle. I told him to "Begone in the name of Jesus Christ," and he left.

Satan came in the form of a handsome young man one night to visit me, but I was given the knowledge that it was Satan by the Holy Spirit. He had the shape and features of a good-looking young man, yet he was still a spirit. I think this experience was allowed by God to let us know that Satan can take the form of a person even though he is an angel of darkness.

Clairvoyance (Also called Extrasensory Perception (ESP), Precongnition and Mental Telepathy

Beginning shortly after I had contact with the psychic, I began to experience clairvoyance. This is also referred to as extrasensory perception (ESP), precognition or telepathy. It is an ability to acquire information without benefit of the senses, and it is typically connected with psychic ability or paranormal activity.

After speaking with the psychic the first time, I began to just "know" things that would later occur. The thoughts would just come into my mind. For example, one day, the thought of a person and a message just came to me. It was: *Phone call—Mary Alice Short* (not her real name). Within an hour or so, this person called me. This was remarkable because I did not know the person, had never spoken with her, and had never met her. She also lived in different state. I had, however, forwarded a letter to her office to resend to someone else. I had asked her to just re-address the envelope and forward the letter. I requested that she not read the letter. However, she had opened it and read it and called to discuss it with me. However, I do not think it was a coincidence that she called me right after I had a message that she would call. I certainly never expected this call. This type of knowledge had been given to me frequently in the months following my contact with the psychic. Thoughts of future events would come into my mind before they actually happened. I personally do not believe that Satan knows the future with absolute certainty, but he can guess at it. His goal is to get us to rely on these paranormal experiences instead of God for answers.

I believe that anyone who has participated in a new age or occult practice has opened themselves up to paranormal activity caused by demons. I also believe that demons can transmit thoughts or knowledge to individuals and also between two or more people due to the door they have opened for evil spirits to enter through their sins.

Native Americans, who practice paganism, sometimes have ESP. Bobby-Lake Thom, in his book, *Spirits of the Earth*, states: *For years I wondered how my grandfather knew a flood was coming. A lot of people were amazed at the so-called psychic premonitions and power he often demonstrated.*[28] My contention is that participation in pagan practices is a conduit for evil spirits, giving them permission to transit thoughts into people's minds.

A friend of mine who I'll call Ann (not her real name) told me about an incident that happened to her involving clairvoyance. Her husband had hired an attorney, but began to be suspicious of his credentials. Ann began to research the lawyer's background for any improprieties. Ann's sister, who used new age and occult practices such as Transcendental Meditation, Astral Projection, and a Ouija Board, called her one day. Her sister mentioned the fact that Ann was looking through public records to obtain information on the lawyer. Neither Ann nor her husband had told her sister this because it was a private matter. Ann suspected that her sister's knowledge came from demons.

The Woman in Washington, D.C.

Years ago a friend of mine had a very scary experience on two occasions. This man and I had sexual relations outside of marriage a few times, but then we began to have a platonic relationship. One day several months after our sexual dalliances had ended, he went on a business trip to Washington, D.C. After a day of meetings, he took a bus back to his hotel. A woman seemed to be following him to the bus stop. When he got on the bus, she got on, too, and sat right next to him. She turned to him, and said, "You entered the woman." Her statement shook him up, but he went back to his hotel room and dismissed the encounter.

A few months later, my friend had to return to Washington, D.C. again on business. This time he stayed in a hotel in a different part of the city. When he got on the bus to return to his hotel at the end of the day, the same woman he had met months earlier sat down next to him again. When he got off the bus, she followed him. Finally, he turned around to confront her. Before he could speak, she said to him: *You entered the woman, the woman who cried. And you need to do it again.* She then quite graphically described in

28 Thom, Bobby Lake, *Spirits of the Earth: A Guide to Native American Nature Symbols, Stories, and Ceremonies*, Penguin Books USA, Inc., New York, NY, 1997, p. 9.

detail how he should have sexual relations with me.

My friend was so unnerved by this encounter that he immediately ran to his hotel as fast as possible. The first thing he did was call me. He told me everything, and I was shocked. I was the "woman who cried," because every time I had sexual relations all of my life I cried during intercourse. This was probably due to being molested at my grandmother's house. My husband never knew I cried even though we were married for ten years because we were always in the dark, and I wiped my tears right away so he wouldn't know. But this man had seen me cry.

I believe this woman knew about our sexual relations and my friend's trips through clairvoyance. Demons communicate with those people who have allowed them to come into their lives. Satan and demons monitor our activities in order to tempt us. I think the woman who followed my friend in Washington, D.C. was a human being working for the devil. I believe that she was given detailed knowledge by demons through clairvoyance about his sexual relations with me and also his itinerary. As a willing instrument of Satan, she used the information to tempt him. Just as God has given us each a guardian angel to watch over us, I believe that Satan also has one or more members of his kingdom watch us. This is probably why we are all tempted daily.

Since all temptations begin as a thought, they can be placed into my minds by demons. Therefore, if demons can place temptations into our minds, they can certainly communicate information to those who are willing participants in grave sin. This knowledge can then be used to tempt others since sin is the devil's goal. I believe that even if people are not directing their thoughts toward demons, they can place thoughts into our minds if we are in serious sin, especially unrepented sins of new age and the occult. Serious sin opens the possibility of going to Hell, Satan's domain, which is exactly where he wants us to go.

This incident happened to my friend on two separate occasions in different parts of a city that was hundreds of miles away from his home. *No one knew that I cried after sexual relations except this one man and me.* That is a fact. I never told anyone and neither did he. So who would know our secrets? God and Satan. Satan and his demons plan their spiritual attacks. We must be watchful at all times, praying the "Our Father," which includes the words, ***and lead us not into temptation, but deliver us from the evil one.*** (These are the correct words found in Matthew 6:13 (NIV).

Good Versus Evil Clairvoyance, ESP, Precognition, and Mental Telepathy

As I mentioned earlier, clairvoyance can also be called ESP, precognition or mental telepathy. The three experiences I related involving this phenomenon demonstrate a diabolical source. I believe that the phenomenon is a spiritually-based experience. All of the experiences I related above were influenced by sin. My own sin was consulting a psychic, and one of the first symptoms of unusual phenomena in my life was clairvoyance, something that I had never experienced before. In the case of Ann's sister, she was actively involved in the occult. In the situation I related about my friend in Washington, D.C., the sin was sexual in nature. All of us opened ourselves up to demonic influence.

Conversely, we may conclude that telepathy could be connected with Godly telepathic communication. For example, often I will be thinking of someone and that person will call me shortly afterwards also thinking about me. We may connect for a reason; for example, to give each other encouragement. My personal belief is that today too much emphasis is being placed on psychical research and parapsychology instead of discerning their moral import—either as a malifice of Satan or as grace stimulated by God.

The document, *Jesus Christ the Bearer of the Water of Life: A Christian Reflection on the New Age,* says ***despite fierce criticism from scientists, parapsychology has gone from strength to strength, and fits neatly into the view popular in some areas of the New Age that human beings have extraordinary psychic abilities, but often only in an undeveloped state.***[29] If we participate in sins of new age and the occult or any other serious sins, it can only be the beginning of serious spiritual problems.

29 *Jesus Christ the Bearer of the Water of Life: A Christian Reflection on the New Age.* www.vatican.va/.../pontifical_councils/interelg/documents.rc_pc_interelg_doc_20030203_new-age_en.html - 216k - 2033-02-20 (Section 7.2).

If our spirit within us is Godly, we will have Godly thoughts. If our spirit within us is demonic, we will have demonic thoughts. Although our lives are a struggle between good and evil, we should strive to cultivate a life of holiness and prayer in order to protect ourselves. I also think general knowledge of the spiritual dangers of new age and the occult is extremely important today to avoid the traps Satan is setting for all of us. Confession of any past serious sins is necessary to close the door opened by our offenses to prevent further demonic interference.

In the Bible we read: ***For who knows a person's thoughts except their own spirit within them? In the same way no one knows the thoughts of God except the Spirit of God. What we have received is not the spirit of the world, but the Spirit who is from God, so that we may understand what God has freely given us. This is what we speak, not in words taught us by human wisdom but in words taught by the Spirit, explaining spiritual realities with Spirit-taught words.*** (1 Corinthians 2:11-13 NIV) The Holy Spirit can help us discern and lead us to truth.

Angels of Darkness

I frequently heard singing which I thought was from angels. I often heard classical music, too. I thought it was all from Heaven. One day I was in church praying alone after Mass when I began to hear crystal clear classical music. I looked around the entire church, but there was no radio, sound system or other source where the music could have been coming from. In fact, there were only two people left in the building. I was listening to the music, fascinated. I think it was demonic because I had to be somewhere and I was being detained by staying to listen to that music. The devil is clever. Also, I should have been praying.

One night a demon lay on me with his arms around me, squeezing me. I was distraught and prayed silently in my mind for his hold to ease until I could pray, *Begone in the name of Jesus Christ.* Then I saw a vision of what appeared to be an angel because it was white and had wings, but before my eyes it became a black face of a demon—it was a fallen angel. This experience had a distinct message. Satan tries to imitate things of God. Satan came to me as an angel of light, but in reality he was an angel of darkness. We must be careful and discerning. Test the spirits during any apparitions you may encounter. If the spirits are evil, they must leave. If they are good spirits, they will remain.

Demonic "Angels" Disrupt Prayer Group

One night at a prayer group, a couple wandered in that our group did not know. The woman claimed she received messages from an angel. She and her husband had left the Catholic Church, and this was a Catholic prayer group. We were meeting at a Catholic shrine, and they just happened to be going past it and came in. I sensed many evil spirits with her. She ended up disrupting our entire lesson plan that night and argued about the tenets of Catholicism. This couple began to come back each week for awhile before we just had to ask them not to come. This was obviously Satan's way of infiltrating our group to take us away from our normal prayer and scripture lesson.

I suggested to this woman that the "angels" with her may be demons, which really upset her. Many people do not test the spirits. If you test the spirits, you will know if they are demons or not. Just say: *If you are not from God, begone in the name of Jesus Christ.* The criterion for judging such phenomena from a moral perspective is the primary principle of discernment: Jesus' norm, ***by their fruits you shall know them.*** (Read Matthew 7:17-19). The charism of discernment of spirits is most helpful (read 1 Corinthians 12:10), when used with the cautionary advice of John: ***Dear friends, do not believe every spirit, but test the spirits to see whether they are from God, because many false prophets have gone out into the world.*** (1 John 4:1 NIV) Because this woman disrupted our group, her "angels" were definitely not from God because it did not bear good fruit.

The Angel Workshop

Angels began to be the subject of many books, TV programs and workshops in the mid 1990's. The TV show, *Touched by An Angel,* aired for many years (1994-2003). I loved that show, and it was good entertainment because it had a positive message, unlike most of today's TV shows. One day, I attended a local angel workshop. It turned out to be more than I expected, and part of it contained new age. The instructor asked us to meditate (blank out our minds and try to channel our angels). I was very uncomfortable and did not do it. There are still workshops around the world like this, even online. I did express my concern to the instructor after the workshop. Later on, I discovered she had written a book containing new age and occult beliefs.

We do not need to channel our angels nor should we meditate to get in touch with them. All we have to do is pray! It's that simple. Our angels are always with us. Personally, I think the prayer to our Guardian Angel is a great way to start the day.

Prayer to Our Guardian Angel

Angel of God, my guardian dear, to whom God's love commits me here, ever this day be at my side, to light and guard, to rule and guide. Amen.

Demonic Noises

Demons and disembodied damned human souls often disrupted my sleep with various sounds for many years. I heard almost every sound imaginable so I will only list some examples. One night Satan woke me up by a sound like air coming out of a big balloon. Then he laughed. I have also heard the sounds of a pig grunting, a mouse squeaking, a phone ringing (not mine), a doorbell, the rustle of papers, a door chime, a belch. One night Satan blew a whistle in my left ear. On another night Satan played a radio for me. It was very loud, blasting endlessly. Then he fought with me. He finally pinned me down by holding my wrists. Jesus rescued me after I commanded that he leave in Jesus' name. I believe these noises were for my ears only, a diabolical form of harassment.

When I was writing this book, there was a demon who began hammering on the walls in my apartment building. This noise was audible; in other words, other people could hear it. People were complaining about it, but I realized it was demonic. My neighbors heard the hammering in the late hours of the night, and no sensible person would be hammering at that hour on a regular basis. No one knew where the sound was coming from. This is called poltergeist activity. It finally stopped after a week or two.

One day, also during the course of writing this book, there was loud banging going on inside the walls of my apartment in more than one room. At first, I thought my neighbor was moving. But that wasn't the case. When the banging went on most of the night, I realized it was a poltergeist spirit. A poltergeist is "a ghost that manifests itself by noises, rappings, and the creation of disorder."[30] Although the definition in this dictionary calls the poltergeist a ghost, it can also be referred to as a demon, an evil spirit, or a disembodied damned human soul. This happens nightly to me now in varying degrees. It also happens while I am in Adoration. These noises are audible and can be heard by others. I believe it is retaliation for the book I am writing because the demons with me are very upset about this book and often talk about it. They do everything they can to put obstacles in my way so I do not write.

Demonic Voices

Demons and disembodied damned human souls have spoken to me for most of the past 20 years. It used to occur only at night, but now it occurs around the clock. I can hear their voices, both male and female, but I am sure that other people cannot hear them because no one has ever said anything to me. It is a demonic form of harassment and a particular form of suffering intended for me based on my personal sins. Here are just some examples.

One night at 3:30 a.m., I heard a female voice singing like a broken record, *It's 3:30, it's 3:30, it's 3:30…* on and on. It woke me up, disrupting my sleep. I had trouble going back to sleep. When I did, I had a dream of a sexual nature, which was another form of harassment.

On another occasion, I heard the voice of what sounded like a young man who had gone to Hell say to me, *Hey, Judy!* to disrupt my sleep. I also heard the voice of an older man who had gone to

30 *The Free Dictionary of Farlex*, www.thefreedictionary.com.

Hell say my name in a gruff tone. There are people in Hell of all ages. The youngest disembodied damned human soul I ever saw was about eight years old. Once we have the use of reason, we can sin and sin seriously.

My nights were filled (and still are) with demonic harassment. On another occasion, I was awakened in the middle of the night by the sound of someone vacuuming. Then the evil spirit spoke into my right ear at which time I commanded him to leave in Jesus' name.

Today, demons speak to me day and night. They tempt me, they talk about me, they talk about the book I am writing, they try to distract me from doing anything good and to cause mishaps and accidents. They particularly try to keep me from getting to Mass and Adoration. However, Jesus has given me the grace to endure it. Although I know that this harassment is the consequences of my personal sins, I look forward more than ever to the place of peace; namely, Heaven.

Satan and Evil Spirits Imitate Voices of Living People

One night Satan came to me and paralyzed me. After this I distinctly heard the voice of one of my two sons say: *Hi, Mom.* The voice sounded exactly like my son's voice, yet no one was with me at the time. It was the middle of the night. I grabbed my crucifix and said, *Begone in the name of Jesus Christ.* Satan left. I had just gotten to sleep. It was 3 a.m., which is Satan's hour because it is the opposite of 3 p.m., the hour that Christ died. Many demonic experiences occur at that hour.

Another time I heard a demon imitate the voice of an elderly person I had been visiting on a regular basis. The evil spirit imitated her voice exactly. Both of these people whose voices I heard were living. Remember this if you live through the Three Days of Darkness, which is going to happen in the end times. During those days, people will be in their homes with the windows covered with blessed candles lit, praying. Evil spirits will imitate the voices of loved ones in order to entice those in the home to open the door. Do not be deceived; they are evil spirits.

Do not let them in. The three days of darkness are spoken about in Revelation in the Bible and also by many saints and Blesseds. Some of the saints are St. Faustina, Blessed Anna Maria Taigi, and St. Gaspar del Bufalo.

Animals, Beasts and Bugs

Demons came in the form of hideous beasts or creatures quite often. The beasts would be repulsive; it is hard to describe them. Demons would also take the form of animals, such as ugly black cats, dogs, pigs, cows, mice, and many other creatures that do not exist.

Evil spirits would place bugs on my body. For example, Satan put a huge, crawling bug on my back one night. I could actually feel the bug on me, crawling on my back. I had been asleep, but woke up. I could even feel the bug crawling on my back when I woke up. When I got out of bed, I felt it crawl off. This happened more than once.

Possession of Animals

In the Bible, we read the story of the demoniac who was possessed by many demons who called themselves, "Legion." Jesus was going to cast them out, but they begged him to go into a large herd of pigs who were nearby. He gave them permission, and the demons entered the pigs. The herd, about two thousand in number, rushed down a steep embankment and drowned. (Mark 5: 1-13)

I believe that animals can become possessed. I witnessed one such incident years ago. I was visiting my brother, who had a cat. The cat had been a family pet for several years and was accustomed to having people around the house. We were eating lunch one day around the kitchen table. The cat was lying nearby. All of a sudden the cat screeched and went absolutely berserk. It attacked my niece, who was about seven years old at the time. It jumped on her head and bit her all over her head. Her head was dripping with blood and she had several wounds. My sister-in-law took her to emergency where she had stitches put in the worst wounds. The cat had to be put to sleep.

I believe a demon entered this cat. This was a friendly cat who had been in the home and with the same people for many years. What could have caused it to attack my niece—and so viciously? We forget there are invisible spirits around us.

Electrical Problems

I began to have strange electrical failures and problems with electronic equipment. For example, I had purchased a brand new VCR, tape recorder, and TV, all of which failed to work one day. There were no apparent reasons for this to happen. There were no storms, power outages, or wire or connection problems. The circuit breaker worked fine and other parts of the room on the same circuit breaker had electrical power. I believe that evil spirits can manipulate electronic equipment and electricity. It is manipulation of energy. If these electrical failures were a one-time occurrence, I could understand it. But over a period of many years, I noticed a pattern of unusual and untimely electrical failures. The equipment would begin to work again without human intervention. Prayer helps!

Once two light bulbs in my overhead kitchen fixture both went out at the same time. It was a Friday, and I made a mental note to change them. However, over the weekend, I completely forgot about it. Every time I went into the kitchen, I would automatically turn on the switch and then when the lights did not go on, I would remember that I had to change the bulbs. I did this several times during the course of the weekend out of sheer habit. On Monday, I once again turned on the switch, forgetting the bulbs were burned out, but they both worked. What's more, they continued to work. I thought it was strange that two bulbs would burn out at the same time, although it wasn't impossible. But it did not make sense that they were only out for a weekend. All of the other lights in my home worked.

One day three of my burners on my electric stove did not work. When I used the one burner that did work, a fire started. I quickly had to get water to pour on it. That was scary. My stove was newer, and I had no previous problems with it. Once again, everything worked fine quite unexpectedly, and I did not have any further problems.

Once EWTN aired a special TV program which took place at the World Apostolate of Fatima. It was a seven and a half hour special prayer service for peace and the end of abortion. The evil spirits blacked out the program not once, but twice! Once it said, "pause" on the screen, but the TV control was not in my hands. I got the control and pushed "pause"and the picture resumed. When you push "pause" on a control, it just stops the picture momentarily; it does not cause the picture to disappear with a totally blank screen. I had no other problems with the remote.

Computer and Printer Problems

One day when I was going to use my computer the words "Hi" were typed by themselves on it. It was demonic. Also, the printer broke down completely and I had to replace it. Luckily, it had a few more days under warranty and God sent me a brand new printer! Often, while doing volunteer projects for church over a period of several years, my computer, printer or power would fail. Every time I was doing the Lord's work I had these kinds of problems.

Another time, I put on a new Windows upgrade and completely lost my sound system. I had been playing religious music using the computer's CD drive. I had also listened to Catholic radio using the web, but who wouldn't want me to do that? Satan and demons, of course. These things happen a lot, and too frequently to be explained by natural causes.

Another time my computer completely locked up. I couldn't even turn it off. The On/Off button would not work. I said a prayer and it turned off and then I was able to restart it again. I had no further problems.

When I was writing this book I had power failures and equipment failures. I have two printers and one day both of them would not work! One was an inkjet printer and the other was a laser printer. My internet went down more than once. My phone did not work. My TV didn't work, but I gave it up as penance. You can turn your trials into blessings! For me, it's all in a day's work.

Sleep Paralysis

Medical professionals always attempt to explain unusual physical phenomena using a medical explanation. Sleep Paralysis is the medical term used to explain a type of paralysis that occurs in the dream state. Usually, people wake up unable to move, swallow, possibly choking, or barely able to breathe. Some people hear strange sounds. Others report seeing a black, shadowy figure or figures by their beds which will try to inflict harm. Sometimes they feel someone touching them, characterized by a strange sense of energy running through their bodies. I believe all of these experiences are caused by demons and disembodied damned human souls.

I, too, have had these experiences. Demons would frequently paralyze me so I could not reach for my crucifix. I also could not speak. At these times I would think about the image of the crucifix in my mind and say the words *Satan, begone in the name of Jesus Christ* in my mind. It worked and the paralysis would end every time.

Based on the thousands of diabolical experiences that I've had, my opinion is that this disorder called "Sleep Paralysis" is a spiritual problem. I believe that demons and disembodied damned human souls attack us while we are sleeping. These attacks can happen to anyone because we are all subject to the struggle between good and evil. It is very important to say, *Begone in the name of Jesus Christ!* This is true if you are paralyzed, have a feeling of negativity, nightmares, or any signs of demonic activity.

I read several accounts of sleep paralysis on the internet. One story is particularly enlightening. It was written by a man who had been having the experiences for 20 years. After doing a lot of reading, he concluded the experiences were diabolical. Now, when he senses the presence and his anxiety builds, he recites in his mind the instruction to all Christians in time of need of defense, the phrase: *Begone in the name of Jesus Christ.* He says it works every time. I, too, have found this simple rebuke prayer to work every time in all of the thousands of incidents I have had. At the time of this writing, I no longer have sleep paralysis. The demons gave up. If you are a victim of sleep paralysis, try this rebuke prayer. Use your spiritual weapons!

Panic Attacks

I began to have panic attacks one night as I was travelling home from Madison to Milwaukee, WI after a visit with my mother. When she had Alzheimer's, I went to visit her quite often. She lived at a group home in the Madison area. I would always pray with her, usually the Rosary. I would also play religious music for her and the other residents on a keyboard I brought along.

On this particular night, I was three-quarters of the way home when all of a sudden, I felt really weak. I got off the freeway and pulled into a parking lot where I tried to rest for a few minutes. When I got back on the freeway, extraordinary fear gripped me to the point where I couldn't drive. I pulled over to the side of the road quite often, but nothing helped. I literally inched my way home on the freeway, which luckily did not have a lot of traffic because it was very late. That was the first episode of many panic attacks which occurred for about three to five years.

I believe these attacks were demonic. First of all, Satan did not like it that I was praying with my mother and also visiting with others who didn't have company. In fact, my frequent visits with the residents in this group home are what led me to become a caregiver after my mother passed away.

I had a very difficult time during the years I was getting panic attacks. I could not drive at night unless I took city streets. I couldn't take freeways at all or I would "freeze." There were times I just had to call out to God for help. It was only God's mercy and the angels who helped me avoid many accidents. When I went to Madison, I had to travel during the day time and come home during the day. The attacks only happened at night.

I see a link between these panic attacks and the attacks I had as a trauma survivor. When I was going through PTSD, I would have panic attacks at night, which the doctor told me were hidden memories trying to come to the surface. I think it was a spiritual problem because I was hit in the center of my forehead, which was unusual. I personally believe that Satan caused the panic attacks I had when I was having symptoms of PTSD and the ones I had when I was driving. After years of prayer and reparation, I have only had a handful of other occurrences of panic attacks while driving, but I did not give into them. I said the St. Michael prayer over and over. They happened when I was on my way to religious events. I arrived safe and sound.

However, I have had a few panic attacks during the course of writing this book. I find this fact significant. I have not had panic attacks for years. Today I had a bad one when I lay down to rest before writing. There is absolutely no doubt in my mind that these attacks are demonic. I have demons with me, and they do not want this book published. I am in a great spiritual battle, and they will stop at nothing to prevent this book from being written. I am literally in God's hands.

Materialization

During the course of writing this book, I began to see dozens of people on an almost daily basis when I closed my eyes briefly. They looked like real people with corporeal bodies, not apparitions. I usually saw just their faces. None of them looked happy. They were men, women and young people. I didn't really know what to make of it. One day when I was on the internet, I came across the term, "materialization." I looked it up in a reference book I got a few months into this project, and it said it was a form of Spiritism (seeing dead people). The definition in the book said that often it happens that only faces appear to people. The book stated that it usually happened at séances, but what is happening to me could be a derivative of it.

I had purchased a used reference book as a source of definitions of new age and occult words, which I planned to use in this book. Ironically, it was a reference book footnoted by a Catholic author in her book. However, in reviewing the reference book after a couple of months, I saw that it was actually written by someone who was actively participating in new age and the occult and is now deceased. I decided to throw the book in the dumpster, which I did. However, occult books should always be burned. Because I live in an apartment building, I couldn't burn it. Consequently, I still saw faces of deceased people for awhile, but less often. Over the past few months, however, God has mercifully limited this experience because He understands I tried to do the right thing.

Conclusion

We are all under demonic attack in one way or another. Be strong! God is infinitely more powerful than Satan and evil spirits. I have survived thousands of demonic attacks. It would be impossible to record them all. However, I trust in Jesus. Jesus helped me cope and even assisted me in battling the evil spirits I had brought into my life. We may fall, but we can rise again. Never give up. God will never give us more than we can handle. At the end of our lives is the promise of eternal salvation. As it is written: *What no eye has seen, what no ear has heard, and what no human mind has conceived the things God has prepared for those who love Him.* (1 Corinthians 2:9 NIV)

Chapter Five

Dreams, Visions and Locutions

A dream is *a series of images, ideas, emotions, and sensations occurring involuntarily in the mind during certain stages of sleep.*[31] REM sleep is *the stage in the normal sleep cycle during which dreams occur and the body undergoes marked changes including rapid eye movement, loss of reflexes, and increased pulse rate and brain activity.*[32] The REM stage of sleep is said to be the deepest dream stage, usually the first two hours.

A vision is the experience of seeing with the eyes a scene enacted which is similar to watching a movie. A person can see heavenly or demonic beings in the experience.

A locution consists of words spoken into your mind from outside yourself. I have had experiences with all of these types of spiritual phenomena, and I am going to give you some examples in a summary. You will notice that some of my experiences include a combination of dreams, visions and/or locutions.

Reprint of Book on Miracles

After I wrote the book on miracles, which was published in December 1997, I began to read about new age and the occult from a Christian perspective. Although at the time, I still lacked adequate knowledge about this subject, eventually I did recognize two stories in the book I'd written in which the healings were connected with a new age or occult practice. In March of 2002, I replaced them with two orthodox miracle stories and made other minor changes to the book. I destroyed the remaining books from the first printing (approximately 9,000 copies), and reprinted 10,000 copies of the revised version of the book. I then set about

31 *The Free Dictionary of Farlex,* http://www.thefreedictionary.com.
32 *Ibid.*

trying to sell the books, but had little success.

The reason I did not hesitate to reprint the book is because I'd had a dream that I was making some changes to the book I had written and reprinting it. Between 1994 and 2002, I had literally thousands of dreams, visions and locutions, usually several each day. Although I did recognize some of these experiences as demonic, I thought I was able to discern all of them, most of which I thought were from God. Consequently, I took this dream literally as coming from God to reprint the book. Looking back, by this time, I was in the grips of Satan.

I discovered that I was not accurately discerning these spiritual experiences. Slowly, the Holy Spirit began to teach me discernment because I realized that many of the experiences that I thought were from God were actually from the devil. Here are some examples of how analyzing these experiences, looking to them for help in making decisions, and lack of proper discernment affected my life.

Types of Dreams

When I began to write the book on miracles, I began to have vivid dreams. By vivid, I mean that they were clear, detailed, lucid and memorable. I had never had many dreams in the past that I remembered up to this point in my life. Now, I would see the past, the future, and people I would actually meet in the future. I had messages in dreams. Some of my dreams were also coming true.

Although I take the responsibility for not adequately discerning my dreams, a factor that reinforced my belief that we should look to dreams for answers was a class I took at a local Catholic School of Theology shortly after my contact with the psychic. It was a class called "Dream Therapy." I had signed up for this class because I was starting to have a lot of dreams.

In the class, we were taught how to analyze dreams, relying on the teachings of Carl Jung. We were taught about archetypes or symbols in dreams and what they meant, how to interpret dreams, and that they were spiritual experiences designed to comfort us, give us direction, or to heal us. The teacher taught us to look to dreams for answers to our problems and understanding ourselves. We were not taught how to discern dreams, but we were taught that all dreams were a supernatural experience designed to help us in our lives. I did this, and began to look to dreams for direction. It is actually a mortal sin. We are not to rely on dreams for answers to all of our problems or to get too dependent on them for help in our lives. We are called to trust in God.

Looking back, this class only brought more demons into my life. One important thing the teacher neglected to say was that all dreams are not from God. Dreams from Satan do not help us in any way!

I did some research on Carl Jung. However, I do not recommend that you read any books on Carl Jung because he was working for the devil. The teachings of Carl Jung are completely contrary to Catholicism and Christianity. This is not surprising considering how he lived his life. He was a Spiritualist (someone who communicates with spirits), and in his younger days, he attended séances and used a Ouija Board. A séance is "a meeting at which spiritualists attempt to receive messages from the spirits of the dead."[33] A Ouija Board is a "game" that consists of a board with the alphabet on it that is used with a planchette (a triangle shaped pointer) to spell out messages given by evil spirits. Of course, people do not realize they are contacting evil spirits, which makes it a deadly occult tool. I had a friend who played this "game" once and a Russian spirit began to speak through her. It scared her so much that she never played it again.

Carl Jung did automatic writing, an occult experience whereby the person is used as a conduit for a demon that pens the writing of an individual. He was visited by a spirit guide. Many of his experiences and his teachings are in essence ones of an occult nature. I cannot understand how Catholic psychologists and schools can offer dream therapy courses and promote his teachings! As I write this in 2014, Catholic schools, some retreat centers and colleges still offer these classes. In fact, they are prevalent all over the world now in many other settings as well.

Dreams come either from God, Satan, or our own human

---

33 *Ibid.*

nature. Dreams from God can provide healing, comfort, hope, instruction, warnings, prophesies, or messages. They are often uplifting. At times they can provide information that will lead us or someone we know closer to God or be helpful to us in handling a specific situation. For example, you might have a dream about someone who needs prayers. Most of all, dreams from God will never lead you into sin.

We have many examples of dreams in the Bible. Dreams were given to believers from God. For example, Joseph was shown in a dream to take Mary as his wife because she was pregnant by the power of the Holy Spirit. *Joseph, son of David, Do not be afraid to take Mary as your wife; for the Child who has been conceived in her is of the Holy Spirit.* (Matthew 1:20 KJV) This was a dream of instruction. Joseph is later warned by an angel in another dream to leave Bethlehem and go into Egypt because Herod and his men are coming to kill the child, Jesus. *Arise, and take the young child and his mother, and flee into Egypt, and be thou there until I bring thee word: for Herod will seek the young child to destroy him.* (Matthew 2:13 KJV) This was a dream of warning.

We have another example of dreams from God in the Bible in the story of Daniel. Daniel had a gift of interpretation of dreams. In fact, Daniel gained favor with King Nebuchadnezzar (634-562 BCE), the greatest king of ancient Babylon, because he was able to interpret the king's dreams. King Nebuchadnezzar had a dream of an image with a head of gold, his breast and arms made of silver, and his belly and his thighs of brass. His legs were made of iron, his feet part iron and part clay. Then he saw a stone cut out without hands, which smote the image upon his feet that were of iron and clay and broke them into pieces. Then the iron, clay, brass, silver, and the gold were broken into pieces and became like chaff which the wind carried away, and the stone that smote the image became a great mountain and filled the whole earth.

God gave Daniel the interpretation of this dream. Daniel explained to the king that he was the head of gold. After his reign, Daniel said that another inferior kingdom would arise and still another third kingdom of brass, which would rule over all the earth. The fourth kingdom would be strong as iron, but it would break into pieces and bruise. The feet and toes of part iron and part clay meant the kingdom would be divided, partly strong as iron and partly broken as clay. The two parts of the kingdom would mingle themselves with the seed of men, but they would not cleave one to another as iron is not mixed with clay. And in the days of these kings God would set up a kingdom which would never be destroyed. This kingdom would not be left to other people, it would break into pieces and consume all these kingdoms and it would stand forever.

For interpreting his dream, King Nebuchadnezzar *made Daniel a great man, and gave him many great gifts, and made him ruler over the whole province of Babylon, and chief of the governors over all the wise men of Babylon.*(Daniel 2:48 KJV)

God also gave messages to his prophets in dreams. Jeremiah was one of them. *The prophet that hath a dream, let him tell a dream; and he that hath My word, let him speak My word faithfully. What is the chaff to the wheat? saith the Lord.* (Jeremiah 23:28 KJV)

Dreams from Satan are given to us to mislead us, confuse us, cause anxiety or lead us into sin. These dreams are often accompanied by a feeling of negativity. For example, once I dreamt of floods all around the area in which I was living. I saw myself drowning. This dream caused a great deal of fear and negativity, and I believe it was from Satan. It was rather detailed. However, Satan can give us dreams where negativity is not present, too. For example, the dream I had to reprint the book on miracles did not have any negativity associated with it. In the dream, I merely saw that I was changing parts of the book and reprinting it. Sometimes there are no clues in a dream that it is from a demonic origin. That is why discernment and prayer are necessary.

Dreams from what I call our own human nature come from our personality, fears, or phobias. For example, I had recurring dreams all my life about flunking tests at school. This is because I always had apprehensions before taking exams beginning in early childhood. The irony is that I was a good student and got good grades. Other natural dreams may occur if you are worried about something, which may cause you to dream about the problem. Food can also be a factor, and if you sleep after a big meal, you may dream more.

My mistake was that I did not adequately discern the many vivid dreams I began to have after I began to have unusual phenomena in my life in 1994. I began to analyze my dreams and used them to make decisions on what to do next. They became my focus. Our focus should be on God. I didn't confess this until 2002, and at that time many demons left me. I had a lot of peace in my soul. At the time of this writing, I still get a few dreams, both good and evil, but very, very few. (I am writing this book from a prompting of the Holy Spirit which I had during Eucharistic Adoration over a period of a couple of years.)

It is so important to give dreams the test of time and pray to the Holy Spirit. Never act abruptly from information in a dream unless you are called to pray for someone else or you have a good reason to believe the dream is from God, as it was with many prophets and patriarchs in the Bible. Satan can use dreams as temptations, so prayerful discernment is advised. This same caution is true for visions or locutions.

Life is a struggle between good and evil. Although God does speak to us in dreams at times, it is not something we should expect. These dreams are purely spontaneous I believe. I have had dreams in which God spoke to me to get me back on track or to help me in times of great need. However, looking continually and actively at dreams for answers to our problems or to know the future is a serious sin. We should not analyze dreams either. If God wants to speak to us through dreams, He will in His way and time.

SAMPLE DREAMS FROM GOD

Dream about the Miracle Book

One night shortly after I began to write the book on miracles in 1993, I had a dream of a black cloud over my computer, and it came to me that it meant trouble for the book. That was true; the book was not from God. However, I did not realize it at the time. To me, the dream did not necessarily mean that I should discontinue writing. Works of God are always under attack, and I realized this, so I continued to write. Looking back on this dream, it was God trying to tell me not to write the book. I should have done more research on psychics so I knew more about them instead of just assuming that the psychic was sent to me from God.

Messages to Pray for People

On occasion, I have had dreams from God showing me people who need prayers or they may go to Hell. Many people are not following God's commandments. Sometimes I knew the person and sometimes I did not. Sometimes, I was led to know who I was praying for.

One night I was shown three men in a dream that were destined for Hell unless they changed their lives. One of them I knew and the other two I did not. Within a few days, I knew who the two men were that I didn't recognize. One of them was my girlfriend's brother. My girlfriend confided to me that her brother needed prayers because he was in serious sin. He had received three warnings already from God and still had not heeded them. His home had caught on fire three times, each fire causing increasingly worse damage. The third fire had completely destroyed his home, but he and his family managed to escape just in time. Ironically, I think the fires were symbolic of the fires of Hell if he didn't repent and change his life. God gives us all warnings, but sometimes we just don't pay attention.

On a separate night during this time frame, I was awakened at 2:30 a.m. Then I heard voices, and I just laid there awake listening to them. It was a man and a woman arguing. The man was yelling at the woman, and she whimpered. Then I heard the sounds of low voices, unhappy ones. "Hell" came to me.

I knew who the people were that were arguing. I'd gotten a phone call from someone I didn't know in another state. She asked me to be a guest on a radio show to discuss my book, which had been printed. While we talked, she confided some things to me about her husband, who she said often yelled at her. She asked me to pray for him. This man had suffered three heart attacks, his own warnings, still unheeded. He was the second man I was asked to pray for. Sometime later, I discovered he was into new age. I knew that if he continued on the path he was on, he might go to Hell. Sometimes intercessory prayers can help someone to have the grace to repent and change their lives. Intercessory prayers can help save souls.

Messages About My Mother

Once I saw my mother in a dream, starving, but I was told she was starving for prayers. The message was to pray for her in earnest. This happened about a year before her death. My mother was being bothered by Satan near the end of her life. She would be distraught and tell me, "They're telling me all my sins." On the other hand, she would hear, "We love you, Virginia," which was probably from people she knew who had passed on or saints in Heaven.

I had asked our Lord to show me when my mother was dying so I could go to be with her since she lived out of town. I was the only practicing Catholic left in my family and still am, and I wanted to be sure to give her prayer support. One night, I had a dream where I saw my mother slumped over in a wheelchair, dying, and no one was helping her. I immediately got up and prepared to drive to Madison to be with her. Unfortunately, I locked my keys in the car and had to call a locksmith (through AAA). I was in a spiritual battle. However, after the locksmith came out and opened my locked car door, I left for the one and a half hour trip from Milwaukee to Madison, WI.

When I arrived at the nursing home and went into my mother's room, she was just as I had seen her in the dream, slumped over in a wheelchair, dying, and no one was helping her. I took care of the situation. I was at the nursing home day and night for three days. My mother had the Sacrament of the Anointing of the Sick. The priest from her parish came to do it when he heard about her condition. He knew her well because she always attended daily Mass and had been the organist in the parish for about 25 years.

When my mother died, I was with her, praying the Rosary and reading Scripture out loud. Although I was exhausted, I did the eulogy at her funeral. In a dream, I saw people in attendance who loved her and had also died: friends, relatives, and neighbors. I felt their presence. This was one of several supernatural experiences I've had which were from God. I have often felt the peaceful presence of my mother's spirit with me. I feel presences of deceased people, both good and evil, even to this day.

The spiritual battle is more intense near the end of someone's life because Satan is running out of time to win that soul for himself. It is precisely at the end of our lives that our prayers and sacrifices help us to resist the devil. It is also helpful to have prayer support from other people. Many times family members come to be with the person who is dying, but they just converse and do not pray for the person who is dying. Even if the person is unconscious, they can still hear. It is the last of our five senses that fails. The dying person needs prayers more than ever because you can't see the spiritual battle they are in. Pray for them! Someday it will be you on your deathbed.

Dreams from Satan

I have found that often I saw people in dreams that were having problems in their relationship with God. They were committing serious sins, whether knowingly or unknowingly, which most likely made them a greater target of the devil. I was off track in my relationship with God, too, so we were all in the devil's camp. The closer you become in your relationship with God, the more protection you will have, although you can never let your guard down. It is essential to pray, pray, pray.

A Famous Talk Show Host

I had several dreams about a famous talk show host coming to my home. I had sent this person a copy of my first book and asked to be a guest on her program. I actually prepared a meal for her when I thought she would be coming on more than one occasion, but she never came. This person had frequent guests on her program who spoke about new age and occult topics. Over the past several years, she has become immersed in new age concepts, practices and beliefs. She has been influential in spreading the New Age Movement. Satan has rewarded her with fame and money, and she probably sincerely believes she is helping people. The truth is, however, that although she is helping people with her works of charity, she is also exposing people to demonic influences that may cause them to lose their soul. When this talk show host did not come to my home, I just dismissed the matter and went right on believing my dreams were from God.

Dreams of a Near-Death Experience

The psychic suggested I read the book, *Embraced by the Light,*[34] by Betty Eadie in which she details her near-death experience. Eventually, I purchased her book and read it. Betty Eadie claims that she died and visited the afterlife. Betty Eadie's mother was a Sioux Native American and when Betty was young, she attended a Catholic boarding school. She eventually became a Mormon and was exposed to new age paganism.

Betty's book is full of moral errors. In speaking about her near-death experience, she says she learned many things. For example, she states that we helped God create the earth, that spirits from the other side help us learn lessons in this life, and that there is no judgment. We judge ourselves. She also states that Hell is not forever and in the end we are all saved. Of course, all of these statements are against Scripture. Demons want us to believe these things and many demonic near-death experiences are misleading many people. While there are some genuine near-death experiences from God, those that are false contain moral errors.

Betty blurs the distinction between good and evil. In her book, she states that there is no right or wrong; our choices are personal preferences. We are one and divine—beings here to make spiritual progress toward our full potential as a god or goddess. We all have divine beings that assist us, according to her story. The truth is that there is nothing Christian about these writings. These are the tenets of new age and occult philosophies.

Betty never mentions the crucifixion or the need to make reparation for our sins. In fact, none of us needs redemption! Betty claims she met Jesus, but which Jesus did she meet? I believe she met the devil who took on the form of Jesus. There is no mention

34 Eadie, Betty, *Embraced by the Light,* Bantam, September 1, 1994.

of the victory of Jesus Christ over sin and no resurrection. All of these teachings are unbiblical and against Christian and Catholic teachings. Basically, Betty's new age worldview consists of *1) All is one; 2) All is God; 3) Man is God; 4) All is changing; 5) Man is changing; 6) All is relative; Self is the Judge; 7) The gospel is unnecessary.*[35] The book she wrote is a mixture of Mormonism, eastern religions and the occult.

Scripture says: ***Watch out for false prophets. They come to you in sheep's clothing, but inwardly they are ferocious wolves. By their fruit you will recognize them.*** (Matthew 7:15-16) In other words, whatever comes from God will be in line with Holy Scripture. Good "fruit" will come from it, meaning that it will lead others to God, not to Satan or sin. The messages will not lead us down the wrong path or misuse of God's creation. Jesus says, ***I am the way and the truth and the life. No one comes to the Father except through Me.*** (John 14:6 NIV)

The psychic worked for the devil, and the devil wanted me to believe the lies in this book. When I first read it, I didn't see the errors. But after I did some investigating, I found her writings to be erroneous teachings not in line with Scripture. It shows the need to really learn our faith and what is in the Bible. Here is one area where Catholics falter compared to other Christians. Many Catholics do not know the Bible, and that can get us into trouble. I suggest using a Catholic Study Bible and reading it as often as possible.

Sometime after I read Betty's book, I met her personally when she came to my hometown and signed books in a local bookstore. Immediately after this meeting I began to have dreams of having a near-death experience. By that time, I had published my book on miracles. The dreams spanned several months. For example, in one dream, I saw myself on a hospital bed. There were some doctors and a nurse in the room. I was having surgery, and during the procedure, I clinically died. After a few minutes, I came back to life. The doctors thought I was dead and were amazed when I opened my eyes. Although these dreams could have been from God, I am certain they were from the devil. Why?

I believe the devil wanted me to become fascinated by near-

35 Wise, Russ, Probe Ministries, *Embraced by the Light of Deception*, http://www.leaderu.com/orgs/probe/docs/eadie.html.

death experiences so I would read more about them. He most likely wanted to lead me to other false (demonic) near-death experiences that would contain moral errors. In fact, I did read other books on near-death experiences which I thought were from God, but learned later on were not from God. One reason the dreams occurred could have been to entice me to write a book on the subject. This would make sense because in my first book on miracles, I had included some information on near-death experiences. Unfortunately, the information led people to read unorthodox and spiritually dangerous books on the subject. This was because, as I discovered years later, the books and people I referenced in my book were actually spreading demonic (false) information on the subject. If we read something influenced by demons, we open ourselves up to temptations. I would not recommend these same books to anyone today. After I dismissed these near-death dreams, the dreams stopped. Satan will give up if we resist him.

My "Dream Home"

Once I had finished writing the book on miracles, I looked around my 1300 sq. ft. condo and began to think it was too small. This was a temptation to materialism, although I did not recognize it at the time. I had written the book on miracles out of a closet. I had taken the doors off of my bedroom closet and put a desk, computer and printer in it. Now that I was a writer, I thought I needed more space. So, I began looking for other places to live.

I found a 3,000 sq. ft. condo in a more upscale neighborhood. It was a brand new construction. It was huge. There were three levels in this condo, and it was actually much more than I needed. But, at the time, I rationalized that it would be a good investment. It was my "dream home," the perfect home that I thought would make me happy. Satan is good at helping us rationalize our poor decisions.

I put my small condo up for sale. But, to my surprise and the surprise of my neighbors, it did not sell. I had kept it well maintained, and it was like new. I had bought it new, and it was only about six years old. When it did not sell, I had to make a decision. Should I let the other condo go or should I take out a bridge loan? I remember that I agonized over this decision. This is one way you know whether something is from God or not. With a decision from God, you get peace. If you have to agonize over a decision, have fear or anxiety, then it is a sign that it is not from God. I learned this as I went along, but at the time I did not know this.

Unfortunately, I made the decision to take out the bridge loan. I did this because of a dream. I had presumptuously purchased Venetian blinds in advance for the new place so I could get them on sale. There were 16 windows in the new condo. I only had one window left for which I needed to purchase a blind. In the dream I had before I made the final decision to get the bridge loan, I saw that I was putting up the blind on the window I just mentioned. This led me to believe that I was supposed to buy the new condo. So I took out the loan and kept waiting for a buyer.

A buyer was not forthcoming. Actually, this was God's way of allowing me to reconsider my decision to buy the other home. I did not pay attention. After an entire year, the place I was living in finally sold. I made one of the biggest mistakes of my life buying that larger condo. I suffered monetarily, and it brought nothing but misery. I have always regretted it because the smaller condo that I sold was the perfect size for me, even if I was going to write more books. I could have made it work easily by converting my second bedroom into an office.

The larger condo cost me a fortune to decorate. Because it was so much larger, I bought a lot of new furnishings to fill the rooms. I also painted and decorated it to the hilt. It was like a home out of Better Homes and Gardens magazine. I always enjoyed decorating and spending money. It took six months and $10,000 to complete the work.

One night just after I had finished the work, I had a locution from God the Father. (A locution is words that come into your mind from outside yourself). God the Father said, *Sell what you have and give it to the poor.* I got down on my knees and realized that I had made a big mistake. I told God I was sorry, and I asked for more time because I was exhausted from moving and doing all the work in the new place. He didn't say anything. Shortly after that, I had a dream that my possessions were dragging me down.

Nevertheless, I did call a realtor and put my home up for sale. I had a buyer come and offer me $5,000 more than the asking price. I wavered in my decision to sell it, however. I admit this was really wrong. Despite my fatigue, I should have trusted in God.

I had gotten a new job, but lost it after a few months for talking with people about the book on miracles at work. I did not have money to pay the next month's mortgage.

I had a dream to rent out my home, so I put an ad in the paper. I rented it out within three days to a family. In another dream, I saw a roommate, a girl with blond hair. In the dream, I saw some of the rooms in her condo. I called the only female roommate in the paper and went over to see her place. As soon as she answered the door, I recognized her as the person in my recent dream. She was an ex-Catholic who was looking for a Christian roommate. She had a condo about the same size as the smaller one I had sold, and she was renting out a room, 10′ x 12′. Of course, I would have use of the kitchen and living room also. I took the room on the spot. My roommate and I got along well.

I moved out of my large condo and in with my new roommate immediately. I left all of my possessions behind and only took immediate necessities. I applied for a job as a cashier at a grocery store within walking distance of my new home and got the job on the spot. Praise the Lord—I was able to pay the mortgage without missing a single payment!

For the next several months, I lived with old, dilapidated furniture that I purchased used and I lived out of boxes. There was not enough room for my belongings in the small closet in the room. But I learned that I could live on less. I didn't miss my possessions.

During that time, I had a huge cross. I met a man at the grocery store who I began to date. Inexplicably, after only a few days, I felt I was in love with him. It didn't make any sense at the time and was out of character for me. From that experience, I learned that the devil can manipulate our emotions. After only a few weeks, the man broke up with me. I was completely devastated and aghast at how I could be so emotionally involved after so short a time. I turned to God in prayer, walked for exercise to keep the stress at a minimum, attended daily Mass, wrote notes in a diary and did volunteer work. I did everything I could to put him out of my mind. I finally succeeded with the grace of God. However, it was one of the hardest things I have ever done.

About six months later, my mother passed away. In her later years, I became very close to her and mourned her passing, but she had a happy death with absolution by a priest. Since I was going to get an inheritance, I asked the Lord if I could move back to my large condo and sell it. My prayer was answered. The family who rented my condo gave notice that they were moving, and I moved back into the condo and put it up for sale. I did not get a realtor, but decided to sell it myself. I had met a Christian woman who was a realtor who offered to give me the paperwork. I know God put her into my life.

I decided to sell my new furniture and decorations (such as mirrors, lamps, clocks, and pictures) for whatever I could get for them. I had a rummage sale for two solid weeks for eight hours a day and sold most of my new possessions at a substantial loss. I'll never forget the first day of the sale. People came and bought small items for a quarter. I said a prayer and asked God if someone would come and buy some furniture—I had a lot of new furniture and was also selling some older furniture that was in great condition. Immediately after this prayer, a woman came and asked if I had a bedroom set for sale. I did and I showed it to her. She bought it on the spot for $3,000. I almost fell over when she pulled out $3,000 in cash and gave it to me to hold the furniture for her! I sold everything that I needed to within two weeks. I made several thousand dollars, however, I did not give it all to the poor, which I regret.

God was good and sent me a buyer within a couple of weeks who purchased the condo for the asking price. It was the highest sold condo ever in the complex. I was able to completely pay off the mortgage. God richly blessed me.

Dream of "The Home from Hell"

I had a dream before I sold my "dream home" about moving to a condo in another suburb. I wasn't shown the condo itself in the dream, just the name of the suburb. When I did research,

I found only one condo for sale in that suburb, so I figured that was the one I was supposed to purchase. I was convinced that God wanted me to move there. So, without a home inspection of the premises, I bought it for cash from the inheritance money. It turned out to be what I began to call "the home from Hell."

I called it "the home from Hell" because things went wrong every day from the time I moved in. Unlike my previous condos, this one was much older. The toilets didn't work, the living room had never been painted, water leaked into the rec room downstairs so the ceiling tiles needed to be replaced, the front door molding was not stained, some of the woodwork needed to be replaced and stained, the ceiling in the hallway leaked when it rained, the bathroom towel bar fell off the wall, the closet shelving was falling down because the screws were stripped, the chain on the garage door opener was taped together with cellophane tape and fell apart, the garage door needed a splash guard, the water heater had a gas leak, and it needed a new tile floor in the kitchen. I also purchased a new stove and refrigerator. It also needed window treatments. I purchased new carpeting for the rec room. I spent about $7,000 in repairs and improvements over the course of seven months in addition to doing some of the simpler work myself, i.e. washing windows and some painting and caulking. Needless to say, I didn't get anything else done. Most of all, I wasn't happy or comfortable there.

At the end of seven months, I asked God if I could please sell the condo. I prayed that I would be able to place only one ad in the paper, sell it "by owner" for the asking price (which would include the amount of money I paid for the condo plus all of the money I had spent fixing it up) and that I would sell it to the first prospective buyer that walked in the door. That was a tall order, but the Lord answered my prayer! The first person that came to see the condo purchased it for the asking price! It was a miracle because no other condo in that older complex had ever been sold for such a high price. Of course, I had spent thousands of dollars in improvements. But, I felt guilty and voluntarily lowered the price before the sale. I had added a small amount of money to the price so I would come out ahead, but I decided to break even was sufficient. I moved into another condo which I rented.

Nightmares

Nightmares are some examples of dreams and visions from Satan. Satan can use dreams and visions to frighten us. Sometimes nightmares may be caused by watching a television show or movie with a demonic, occult theme. Nightmares may also be caused by reading a sinful book, such as one full of sexual innuendos, murders, or ones with new age or occult themes. In addition, nightmares could be given to us by demons if we are not in the state of grace. Satan has access to our dreams by our choices. If we are sinning and not right in our relationship with God, the devil has full access to all of our senses and our dreams. Sometimes, however, Satan simply wants to disturb our peace. This is especially true if you are leading a good life!

If your child has a nightmare, try to find the source, especially if it is a repeated experience. It may be caused by reading a demonic book such as Harry Potter, playing a Satanic video game, watching a new age TV sitcom, or even a cartoon, which is not immune from demonic influences today. It may have been a result of playing a demonic board game, especially a Ouija board. There are many sources. Our Catholic schools usually sell publications by Scholastic Books, most of which contain new age and occult themes which go over the head of both parents and children. Satan is very active in the world today. Protect your children and monitor what they do. Be sure they are praying and leading good lives.

When I was in the grip of Satan, I dreamt that a little stuffed life-size doll that I had began to walk on its own. I also dreamt that my house was going to be haunted by someone I knew after he died, who I saw roaming the halls. I had dreams that the walls in my home were crumbling. Since I used to put credence in all of my dreams, I actually thought these things would happen, but they were all from the devil. Here are some other nightmares I had.

A Horrible Dream of a Murder

One night I had a dream about a murderer—he was insane. He killed a young boy. I watched him do this from inside a car. The windows were down. He came past the car, but I had covered myself with a blanket so he couldn't see me. He didn't. I was wishing I had the windows up and locked. Then I saw me in the car outside a house. I was still under the blanket watching the murderer, scared stiff! The murderer was standing outside someone's door. On the door was my son's name. Then I woke up, filled with fear. I thought my son was going to be murdered. The dream had so much detail. I kept notes so everything I have written is exactly what I dreamt. But, praise the Lord, it never happened. It was demonic.

The Plane Crash

Once I was on a trip out East. I had gone to a conference for the weekend. On the night of my arrival, I went into a deep sleep. I had a very vivid dream. I dreamt that the plane that I was on during my return trip home crashed. I could actually feel the descent as it plummeted to what I knew would be certain death for all of us. When I awoke, I was really scared. I decided to stay an extra day and hopefully avoid being on the plane that crashed.

I called my airline and changed my itinerary. It cost me a fee and also another night's stay in the hotel. When I traveled home, all the flights were delayed. It caused me considerable stress, although I tried to be patient.

This dream was from Satan to scare me, cause me to spend money unnecessarily, and to keep me from doing things at home that were required. Also, look at the delays I had on the new flight I chose. The flight that I was supposed to be on in the first place arrived safely and did not crash. That is proof that the dream was from Satan. In this case, because the dream stressed me out, I did not pray about it. Be sure you pray whenever you have a dream that is scary or unsettling.

Locutions

Locutions are words that come into your mind spontaneously. They are usually complete sentences. Locutions from God can provide direction, give counsel, console us, or lead us to truth. On the other hand, locutions from Satan will lead us to sin.

Locutions from God

On various occasions, I had locutions to go to Confession. This was a real grace given to me and during the past 20 years, I have had this prompting several times. Sometimes, I was reminded of serious sins that I had forgotten to confess. I know other people who have been prompted to also go to Confession through something they read or just knowledge that came to them. It helps to pray fervently and consistently on a daily basis. It also helps to attend Adoration and sit in silence before Jesus and listen. Write down your thoughts. At times, I also had locutions to pray for the Holy Souls in Purgatory. These locutions were obviously from God because they had a good objective.

My first supernatural experience with Mary was when she came to me during the song, *Let It Be,* that led to my healing. It was a powerful experience. Often, I feel her presence with me just as I did back in February 1994. Mary has always been with me, although I didn't really know her. I made my formal Consecration to Jesus through Mary by St. Louis de Montfort in 2001 and renew it yearly. I started to do First Friday and First Saturday devotions. I began to pray the Rosary. I joined the Blue Army and other Marian organizations. I went to Marian shrines and apparition sites. I started to wear the brown scapular and medals of Mary. I say many other prayers asking for Mary's intercession, especially under her title of Our Lady of Perpetual Help. Mary led me to all of these Marian devotions through locutions and divine inspiration.

God the Father spoke to me a few times. In 1998 after I had published the book on miracles, I heard Him say in a locution: ***Love the Lord Thy God above all else...*** He said He had sent His Son who was born of the Virgin Mary. He mercifully was trying to get me to re-analyze my life and get my priorities straight. He relayed information to me, but also chastised me. But I am grateful because I love Him, and do not want to offend Him.

One time a scripture passage was placed into my mind: 1 Corinthians 14:1. I looked it up in the Bible and read: ***Follow after charity and desire spiritual gifts, but rather that ye shall prophesy.*** I took this to mean that I should write this book to help build up the Body of Christ for the welfare of God's people. Specifically, it meant to me that I should help bring people back to God through the sharing of my story. I say this humbly, dear readers, for I am a sinner. But, I also love you and want all of you to save your souls and beware of the traps Satan sets for us. In a very true locution from God I heard, *The book is a grace given to you.* This is the book He was referring to and I praise the Lord for it! I have indeed received abundant graces!

Locutions from Satan

Conversely, locutions from Satan can lead us to sin. Once I had a locution that I should *take an enrichment course.* This sounds like something good, right? Subsequently, I signed up for an enrichment course at a local Catholic college. I wanted to become closer to Jesus. When I went to the class, I was in shock. The enrichment course ended up to be a new age class given by a nun who distorted the teachings of the Catholic Church on the Trinity. This "Catholic" class encouraged the students, mostly Directors of Religious Education from Catholic parishes, to read the writings of a dissident nun who had re-written the Creed!

The course promoted use of archetypes, symbols and metaphors which are concepts that come from Carl Jung and other new age teachers. Truths in the Bible were distorted and twisted into symbolic and metaphorical ideas, not the facts we are taught in the Catholic Catechism. In other words, the Bible became interpretive for the reader. A person picks and chooses what they want to believe when reading it.

The teacher actually questioned the fact that Christ rose from the dead in a glorified body. She also told the class that she did not believe in the Ten Commandments! Her commandments were integrity, trust, stillness, inclusivity, generativy, and faithfulness. This boggled my mind! The question of going to Mass on Sunday was brought up and this nun would not say we should attend Mass. I raised my hand and asked her if it is not a commandment to keep holy the Lord's Day and doesn't the Catholic Church say we are to go to Mass on Sunday, especially to receive the Eucharist? She ignored my question and went on to the next one! When I spoke to her about this during the break, she was just silent. Even worse (if you think it can get worse) is that she questioned Jesus' divinity. Need I go on? This class really upset me, and this is what is happening in our Catholic parishes and colleges and retreat centers today. Catholic teachings are being distorted into new age teachings all over the world.

All locutions are just another form of spiritual experiences which must be tested. The message is the key factor. Does the message lead you to God or to sin?

Visions

Visions are very similar to dreams. Like dreams, they can happen in your sleep. However, unlike dreams, visions can also happen when you are awake or when you shut your eyes momentarily. They are similar to watching a movie and can be in black and white or in color.

Visions from Demons

Demonic Visions of the Life of William Randolph Hearst and His Mistress

The first vision I had happened as a result of reading a book in 1995. On a trip to California, where I went to get miracle stories, I had some free time. I decided to make the trip a combination of "work" and leisure activities. Hearst Castle in San Simeon had been recommended by someone I had asked for sightseeing information.

As I pulled into the castle's visitor parking lot, the song, *Let It Be,* came on the radio. I wondered about it. I remember the thought came to me that maybe I was not supposed to tour the castle as I planned to do. Upon reflecting on this later, I see that it was a warning from the Blessed Mother not to take the tour of Hearst Castle. But I didn't listen.

To me, this tour was just an excursion; however, it ended up to be a lot more than I bargained for. To tell the truth, I really did not know anything about Mr. William Randolph Hearst, although I do now. Mr. Hearst (1863-1951) was the owner of 28 major newspapers and 18 magazines before his death in 1951. He was one of the richest people in America.

However, Mr. Hearst did not leave a good legacy. He was known for his investigative reporting, but also for lurid sensationalism and fraudulent journalistic methods. He was pro-Nazi in the 1930's and a staunch anti-Communist in the 1940's. It is believed by many that Mr. Hearst initiated the Spanish-American War of 1898 to promote sales of his newspaper. He also advocated political assassination in an editorial shortly before the assassination of President McKinley. He turned Americans against many nationalities, including Spaniards, Japanese, Filipinos, Russians and Mexicans. This was not a man living the Gospel message.

In Mr. Hearst's private life, he had married Millicent Willson in New York City and had five sons with her. Eventually they separated and Mr. Hearst moved to his mansion on 240,000 acres in San Simeon, CA. When he lived there, he had a mistress, Marion Davies, who moved into the mansion with him. His affair was well known and continued until his death (almost 30 years). Mr. Hearst's wife would never consent to a divorce. After Mr. Hearst's death, Marion wrote a book about her life with Hearst. I purchased it and read it when I got home. It was called *The Times We Had: My Life With William Randolph Hearst.*[36]

As a direct result of my reading this book, I began to have vivid visions of Marion and Mr. Hearst in the mansion. It was like watching a movie. I saw little glimpses of their lives, including an explosion that actually took place when they were living. These visions were frequent and lasted for the duration of the time I read the book. I saw excerpts of the book re-enacted through my visions.

At the time, I didn't realize these visions were demonic. I didn't know what to think. However, I learned as I went along. In this case, Marion and Mr. Hearst led sinful lives. The book was not moral, and just exploited and sensationalized their life of adultery which spanned many years in the lives of this couple. The book was spiritually void of any remorse on Marion's part and really was not a wise choice in reading material. I learned we should not read about the sins of others for pure entertainment

36 Davies, Marion, *The Times We Had: My Life with William Randolph Hearst*, Ballantine Books; 1st edition (March 12, 1985).

value. Deceased people who lived sinful lives and did not repent can be damned souls. Damned souls want to lead us to Hell. The visions stopped after I finished reading the book which shows that reading the book itself was allowing evil spirits to come into my life.

Dear readers, do not read anything sinful, impure, suggestive, or that makes evil appear to be good. Even if you don't see visions, have dreams or see demons, it does not mean that reading these types of books is not harming you. Most people cannot see the demons that become attached to them.

Visions of Solving Murders as a Psychic

One night I had a vision that a classmate I had gone to grade school with was murdered. The next day I got an invitation to a grade school reunion, and my classmate's name was on the list of missing people they could not find. This coincidence, of course, was all part of Satan's plan. I prayed for her soul. I also asked God to see her murderers or to know how she was murdered. Over a period of a year, I had visions of bits and pieces of the alleged murder, but it was not from God but only *allowed* by God.

The first vision began three weeks after I began to pray to see the murder. Initially, I was told in a locution that my classmate was in the National Guard. Then I saw a cabin in the mountains. I was looking through an open door into the living room. In the living room was an old over-stuffed contemporary couch, two chairs and a coffee table in the center. There was a TV on the back wall of the room. I saw three men in the room. An older man was sitting close to the TV, watching a program. Two younger men sat on opposite sides of the coffee table. I saw a dog and he sensed my presence. He began to bark viciously—it was a Dalmatian. As he barked more and more vehemently, there was an invisible shield put between the dog and myself so he couldn't harm me.

The men got up and went outside. They had guns. I knew they were murderers. There was an earthquake, and as they ran outside, the ground underneath them was breaking up. The two young men slid down a hill and escaped into the woods. I saw rocks falling all around them. Then the vision ended. The state of California came to me and that these were my classmate's murderers. The vision began in black and white, but ended in color. It wasn't until much later that I realized this entire vision was demonic after I was led to read about visions and dreams from a Christian perspective.

In a separate, but related vision, I was meeting with people to "develop my psychic ability" to solve murders. I knew by that time that this type of message in a vision was from Satan. We are not called to develop our psychic ability.

At the time, Sylvia Browne was appearing on many television shows. She claims to be a psychic who solves murders. An article by Ryan Shaffer and Agatha Jadwiszczok on Sylvia Browne, "*the most extensive study of alleged psychic Sylvia Browne's predictions about missing persons and murder cases, reveals a strange discrepancy: despite her repeated claim to be more than eighty-five percent correct, it seems that she has not even been mostly correct about a single case.*"[37]

Psychics work for the devil. Do not have anything to do with them. In my case, Satan used the psychic temptation sin again, but with a little different twist.

Message in a Vision from Satan

One night in a vision I was sitting at a table with some "people" who actually seemed more like animals. The Blessed Mother was speaking, but she had an animal-like form. I had a message: *Your mission will begin. Look to Heaven for your strength. You will be allowed to perform miracles like the disciples if you choose and you will go public with these miracles.*

I knew that this message was from Satan. The Blessed Mother would not take the form of an animal. Also, I was not seeking to perform miracles, which seems like a temptation of pride.

Visions of Jesus from Demons

When I had finished writing the first version of the book on miracles and it was ready for printing, I had a vivid vision of

---

37 Shaffer, Ryan and Jadwiszczok, Agatha, *Psychic Defective: Sylvia Browne's History of Failure*, Skeptical Inquirer, Volume 34.2, March/April 2010, www.csicop.org.

a shower of roses coming down from Heaven, and I saw what looked like fireworks—flashes of one image after the other, which continued for quite some time. It was a real mix of images, including Jesus, Mary, flowers, and even humorous cartoon characters. I saw this vision while I was awake with my eyes open. It was overwhelming and made me think that I was really being blessed by the Lord.

I had another vision after rewriting and reprinting the book on miracles a few years later. While I was sitting on my sofa in the living room, I had a vivid vision of Jesus standing right in front of me. I had my eyes open. He showed me His hands. He took a ring and placed it on my finger. I was moved to tears. The ring looked like the illustration of a ring I had included in my book. I thought this was really Jesus because this vision was so real. It was very detailed. However, both of these visions were from Satan.

I learned that Satan can take on the very person of Jesus Christ to deceive people. People can become false visionaries easily because they automatically think they are really seeing Jesus, but they may not be. Once a Catholic man handed me a picture of Jesus he said was taken at Necedah, WI. There were alleged apparitions by the Blessed Mother there to Mary Ann Van Hoof in the late 1940's and early 1950's. However, the seer had a history of practicing spiritualism and attending séances. The apparitions were condemned by the local Bishop due to errors in the messages on faith and morals. Therefore, the photo this man had, which really looked like Jesus, was an apparition by Satan. Satan is allowed to mimic things of God, including appearing to others as Jesus Christ. All of us have to be very cautious. Be sure to pray to the Holy Spirit for discernment.

Dream and Locutions from God

I discovered that my vision of Jesus after I reprinted the book on miracles was from Satan by means of a dream and a locution from God.

In a *dream*, I saw an excerpt of a story towards the back of the book that I had just reprinted and I had a *locution*: "errors in the book." Then I was told, "Do **not** reprint it." The word not was emphasized.

I looked for the excerpt I had seen in the dream and researched the nature of the miracle, which involved a healing of a Native American who was a medicine woman (a shaman). After reading some information on Native American spirituality and shamans from a Christian perspective, I understood the error in the story. I'll discuss this more in the next chapter of this book.

I destroyed all of the books once again in 2003 because I realized there were other errors in the book, too. I finally realized that the psychic was not someone who worked for God, not a "prophet" like I referred to her and, therefore, the entire book was never God's will.

I went to confession, and then I picked up the pieces of my life. I destroyed the books I had printed. With the destruction of the books, I lost the majority of my savings and my inheritance, about $100,000, which was the cost to travel, write, print, store books, market, and ship the books. But I am so glad I did this. It is better to be poor and in the state of grace than to be rich. I've never had any regrets and I thank the Lord for all of His patience and His Divine Mercy.

God has provided for my every need despite the fact that I spent my money foolishly on material things and on a book that was from the devil. But at times, my faith was put to the test. Once I had a full time caregiving job working for one client, which was not through a company, but private employment. I lost the job because the family placed their elderly relative in a nursing home. I had difficulty finding other work.

The only way I could survive was to charge everything I could on my credit card. I did have a good credit rating. I ended up $10,000 in debt. I did not know how I was going to pay it off, but I prayed to be able to do it. My priority was getting to daily Mass, and the Lord honored that desire. After several months, God sent me two part time jobs which still allowed me to get to daily Mass. I paid off the entire $10,000 debt within a year and a half.

When I needed a different car, the Lord helped me again. I was able to get a loan from my bank, which had a special loan program going on. The interest rate was only 1.9% and you could take as long as you needed to pay off the loan, even 20 years if you needed to. However, I made extra payments and paid it off within three years or so. It was not specifically a car loan, but a loan where you could use the money for any reason. During that time, I still worked at my two part time jobs. From these experiences and the many other ones I have had, I began to trust in Jesus more. We should have faith in times of trouble.

Dreams, Visions and Locutions about the End Times

The prophesies for the End Times include a Warning, Miracle, Chastisements, Reign of the Anti-Christ and The Three Days of Darkness. Prior to the reign of the Anti-Christ there will be a world wide warning where people will see the state of their souls. It will be given so people have some time to repent, although they will not have long. The warning will be followed by a miracle that people will be able to see if they go to the sites of the miracle (Garabandel, Spain and Medjugorje, Yugoslavia).[38] Then there will be chastisements which can be lessened if people repent in response to the warning and the miracle.

The Anti-Christ will reign for three and a half years and be an instrument of Satan. The Three Days of Darkness will take place after the reign of the Anti-Christ. The earth will be purified of Satan's influence. Then there will be an Era of Peace until the Second Coming of Christ, which is the end of the world.

I had messages in dreams, visions and locutions about the End Times beginning in 1998. In the first vision, I saw Jesus in the sky. I received a locution about the Second Coming of Christ. I didn't know what the Second Coming of Christ was and had to ask people. Subsequently, I had many dreams and visions about other parts of the End Times.

I saw apostasy in the Catholic Church. People were going

38 I did not see these two apparition sites of the Blessed Mother in my spiritual experiences about the End Times. I am only mentioning them because today (2014) these are two sites where alleged messages of the Blessed Mother have stated there will be a miracle for all to see in the End Times. Since they are yet unapproved apparition sites, this information is based on private revelation. The apparition sites cannot be approved until the messages come true.

to Masses in private homes because they could not go to the churches. It seemed to me that there were no longer valid Masses and faithful Catholics and Christians were being persecuted. I saw an explosion in the sky. I saw many natural disasters. These included earthquakes, torrential rains, a tidal wave, and I saw storms with winds as high as 200 mph. I saw what looked like a barren wasteland. I saw famines, and fish dying. Water was contaminated.

In a vision, I saw a Spanish woman by a hill with her hands raised in the air pleading to God for mercy. She was wailing and crying for devastation was upon all the earth. ***And they said to the mountains and to the rocks, Fall upon us and hide us from the face of him who sits upon the throne, and from the wrath of the Lamb; for the great day of their wrath has come, and who is able to stand?*** (Revelations 6:12)

I saw the Anti-Christ. Everyone was supposed to worship his image, but some Christians refused to do so. The government required a mark to be placed on people's hands or forehead as a means of identifying those aligned with the Anti-Christ. Those who did not worship his image were arrested and put into detention centers. (At the time I had this dream, I met a military man who talked to me about their existence. He had seen them.) I also saw Catholics in underground caves. It was pitch dark in the caves. I saw people going from place to place to find refuge. (During this time I met some people who had set up refuges in preparation for these times. I met them on pilgrimages.) In a dream, I saw a refuge, a home, with people sprawled all over the house. I also saw people living underground. Whether they were Christians or apostates I do not know.

I saw a Monarch, a French King. (I had to ask a priest who this was.) He said that the Monarch will work with the Pope to defeat the Anti-Christ. The French King comes towards the end of the world and works with the Pope to rebuild the Catholic Church. At the time I saw this Monarch, I did not know anything about End Time prophesies and had not read the book of Revelation. Here is a prophesy from Blessed Catherine of Racconigi (1547 AD) about the Monarch:

The Great Monarch and the Great Pope will precede Anti-Christ. The nations will be in wars for four years and a great part of the world will be destroyed. All the sects will vanish. The capital of the world will fall. The Pope will go over the sea carrying the sign of redemption on his forehead, and after the victory of the Pope and the Great Monarch peace will reign on earth.[39]

St. Cataldus of Tatentino (500 AD) prophesied:

The Lion Monarch shall he made famous unto all and shall subvert kingdoms, peoples and nations. Then God shall send a King from the sun, who shall cause all the earth to cease from disastrous war. He will take away the intolerable yoke of slavery which is placed on our neck, and he will do away with impious laws and violent chains. When He shall come there shall be fire and darkness in the midst of the black night. [40]

I saw the three days of darkness. I saw a home with a few Catholics in it. The windows were covered. They had lit blessed beeswax candles and were praying. Outside the home I heard the voice of someone who wanted to come in. It was a demon pretending to be someone they knew in order to get into the house. Demons will use the voice of a loved one or friend in order to fool people. So do not let them in. After the Three Days of Darkness, the earth will have been purified of evil and there will be an Era of Peace.

As a wretched sinner myself, I urge all of you to repent as I have. These are such evil times, but there is hope. While we are still living, we can repent and change our lives. God brings good out of evil. Don't be caught off-guard. The devil wants your soul, and he will entice you with every reason why you do not need to go to church on Sundays and to continue in your complacency and sinful behavior. He will try to get you to put off to tomorrow what you should do today. Demons are real, and so is Hell. God is real, too, and so is Heaven. The time to repent is now while you

39 Unity Publishing, *Book Two: Prophecy and References*, http://www.unitypublishing.com/prophecy/ARK2the%20great%20monarch.htm.
40 *Ibid.*

still have time. None of us know the day or the hour of our death. It could be today.

Conclusion

And it shall come to pass afterward, [that] I will pour out my spirit upon all flesh; and your sons and your daughters shall prophesy, your old men shall dream dreams, your young men shall see visions. (Joel 2:28 NIV) However, be aware that not all dreams, visions and locutions are from God.

We live in a time when many people are having many supernatural experiences from God, but also many experiences that are coming from demons. People must be aware that because of the presence of so much evil in the world, we are all in a great spiritual battle. The devil will use many tactics to deceive us. Learn as much as you can about spiritual warfare.

Chapter Six

Déjà Vu

Déjà Vu is "the feeling that you have already experienced something that is actually happening for the first time."[41] I was often in situations and with people who I was sure I'd met before and the situation would seem very familiar. This happened to me several times.

I used to think that all déjà vu experiences were demonic. The first experiences I had with déjà vu were demonic, but then I also began to have déjà vu experiences that I believe were from God. Unlike the demonic déjà vu situations that I had experienced, these déjà vu experiences were works of charity. I will give examples of both déjà vu experiences I believe were from Satan and the ones I perceive were from God and let you draw your own conclusions. However, they may also come from the human spirit, although I think this is probably not common because most people are not thinking of déjà vu when they are going about their daily lives. In fact, like me, they don't even know what it is. I didn't know what deja vu was until I was writing this book. It came from the Holy Spirit.

I do suspect that these experiences, whether good or evil, are spiritually based. I know psychology approaches déjà vu as a mysterious anomaly of the memory. But it is the nature of psychology to analyze the mind in a scientific way without the spiritual element that is inherent in all of us as children created by God. I believe much of psychology is merely subjective and using hypnosis, altered states of consciousness, and other spiritually dangerous practices may lead to fallacies in regards to the conclusions. I urge caution.

In his book, *The Demonic Roots of Globalism,* Gary H. Kah asks (after quoting from the book, *Personal Theories: An Introduction*), *Is it any wonder that so many of our sons and daughters, who go off to*

41 *Merriam-Webster Dictionary,* http://www.merriam-webster.com/dictionary/d%C%A9j%A0%20vu.

the college campus, find their faith challenged and often shattered by this pseudoacademic atmosphere; when in reality modern psychology, presented as a science, is a bankrupt "religion" with no real capacity for helping people? Under the guise of psychology, spiritual/occultic concepts have gained acceptance as being legitimate scientific principles. Hence, occultism is increasingly going forth in the name of psychology and the "human sciences."[42] His comments are related to the teachings of Carl Jung, a psychologist who lived in the latter part of the 1800's, who has influenced many intellectuals towards acceptance of new age and occultic psychology.

Even the document, *Jesus Christ the Bearer of the Water of Life*: A Christian Reflection on the New Age, points out: ***The tendency to interchange psychology and spirituality was firmly embedded in the Human Potential Movement as it developed towards the end of the 1960s at the Esalen Institute in California. Transpersonal psychology, strongly influenced by Eastern religions and by Jung, offers a contemplative journey where science meets mysticism. The stress laid on bodiliness, the search for ways of expanding consciousness and the cultivation of the myths of the collective unconscious were all encouragements to search for the God within oneself. To realize one's potential, one had to go beyond one's ego in order to become the god that one is, deep down. This could be done by choosing the appropriate therapy – meditation, parapsychological experiences, and the use of hallucinogenic drugs. These were all ways of achieving peak experiences, mystical experiences of fusion with God and with the cosmos.***[43]

Indeed, I have personally discovered some intellectuals living today that are teaching moral errors due to Carl Jung's influence and their own obsessions with new age ideas connected with psychology. The devil works subtly today and deceives even the elect.

---

42 Kah, Gary H., *The Demonic Roots of Globalism,* Huntington House Publishers, Lafayette, LA 70505, 1995.

43 *Jesus Christ the Bearer of the Water of Life: A Christian Reflection on the New Age.* Pontifical Council for Culture, Pontifical Council for Interreligious Dialogue, (Section 2.3.2) www.vatican.va/.../pontifical_councils/interelg/documents. rc_pc_interelg_doc_20030203_new-age_en.html - 216k - 2003-02-20.

Demonic Déjà Vu Experiences

I discovered that déjà vu can be connected with dreams. I believe that Satan gives us dreams which come true in some cases, causing the feeling of déjà vu. Often people do not remember the dream right away, but they do later after the incident has happened. Satan's motive may be to get us to rely on dreams instead of God or perhaps to think we have psychic ability. Demonic déjà vu experiences also may lead us into temptation or into sin. Here are some examples of my demonic déjà vu experiences.

The Woman on the Staircase

I went to a Catholic religious conference and wanted to go to confession. Dozens of people were lined up along the railing of a spiral staircase which led to a room at the top where the priests were hearing confessions.

While waiting in line, I began to speak to the person in front of me. At the time, I was writing the book on miracles, so I started to tell her about the book and how it came about. Before I knew it, she was telling me her own miracle story. As she was speaking, I began to have the feeling that I knew this woman and had met her before. Also, I recognized the story she was telling me! I asked her if we had met before. She said no. Then she told me that she had never told this story to anyone before.

For the rest of the weekend, I pondered how I knew this woman and her story. It really stumped me. After a few days, I remembered that I had dreamt about this entire scene a year earlier. Wouldn't this freak you out? Today, I know it was a tactic of the devil. In this case, Satan placed the thought to go to this conference in two people (this woman and myself). Satan knew I was writing a book on miracles which he had the psychic tell me I would do. He knew that wherever I would travel, I would be asking strangers for miracle stories because I had made the decision to do just that. He also knew this woman had a miracle story. So he gave me the dream, and then put thoughts into both of our minds to prompt us to go to the conference and end up on the staircase where we discussed our miracle stories.

Satan used déjà vu to try to convince me that the dream was from God, which is actually what I thought. It was one of the first stories I got, and it spurred me on. I was anxious to get more stories for the book, a book that was actually instigated by a psychic. I naturally thought that this was a miracle—seeing a scene in the future an entire year in advance! Satan probably is successful using this tactic a lot, but I am sure he fails, too. Don't let it happen to you.

The Teacher

I had a dream about meeting a man who was a teacher. I saw we met in a restaurant. During this time in my life, I was placing personal ads in a magazine in an attempt to find someone to date. One day a few months later a teacher called me in response to the ad. We decided to meet in a restaurant. During our conversation over a cup of coffee, the feeling of déjà vu came over me. Everything seemed so familiar, almost as if I had met this man before in this very place! Even his name seemed familiar.

It was then that I remembered the dream I'd had months earlier. It was now coming true. This made me think that we were supposed to meet, and maybe he was my future husband. Therefore, I readily agreed to date him. Eventually we discontinued the relationship. However, it put both of us into a source of sexual temptation, which was Satan's motive all along. Satan used this déjà vu experience for the express purpose of trying to get us to sin.

Dream of a Future Husband

In August of 1994, I had a vivid dream about a man in the publishing field, and the word, "marriage," came to me. He was about 5'5" tall, slender, about 50 years old with graying hair. I shrugged this dream off, but a year later I actually met him.

A man I had met through the course of my job invited me to meet his out-of-town guest one night. His guest, whom I'll call Matthew (not his real name) was in the publishing field and, coincidentally, he wrote articles on religious and spiritual topics. He had also written a book of his own. At one point in our conversation, I began to think Matthew looked familiar. I kept thinking, *Where have I seen him before?* Then I remembered the dream I'd had an entire year earlier. He was indeed the man in the dream, down to the last detail. I couldn't believe it! Also, he happened to be single!

Actually, Matthew had asked to meet with me because he had heard about my unusual spiritual experiences and the book that I was writing on miracles from my friend. After our conversation, he said he would try and help edit the book I was writing. Two years went by (1995-1997), but it never happened. We talked on the phone a few times, but that was the extent of it.

Then in August 1997 I had another dream. In it, a man was courting me and we were falling in love. We were sitting next to each other on the sofa in my home. I did not recognize the man, and I thought maybe God had chosen someone else for me instead of Matthew.

Two days later, the phone rang. It was Matthew. He said he was in town and asked me if I'd like to go to church with him. We agreed to meet in the back of my local Catholic parish. As I was waiting in back of church, a man came up to me. He shook my hand, saying, *Hello, Judy!* It was the man I'd seen in the recent dream just two days earlier! It was Matthew, but I didn't recognize him because he had gained a little weight and combed his hair differently. As I sat next to him in church, I thought, *Well, Lord, I really believe I'm going to marry this man now! But he lives in a different state and I live in Wisconsin. How are we ever going to get to know each other with that much distance between us?*

A few days later Matthew called and told me that he had put a deposit down on an apartment in downtown Milwaukee. He had decided to move to Milwaukee! In November of 1997, he took me out for my birthday, and we had a good time. During subsequent months, we were both very busy and did not have any contact.

In January of 1999, quite unexpectedly, I met another psychic, a home health aide who took care of my mother, who was in an assisted living facility in Madison, WI. This worker said she had a "gift" of seeing the future. She told me things about myself, and

I became obsessed with hearing more and would call her often. She didn't charge me money, and I thought she had a gift from God. However, she was sent by Satan.

This worker told me to call Matthew and invite him over for a spaghetti dinner. She suggested that I serve garlic bread, a salad and chocolate mousse for dessert. I rarely ate chocolate mousse, but I happened to have a box of it in my pantry I had purchased. She told me there was another woman in Matthew's life, who she said had been sent by Satan. She suggested that I act immediately, so the day after our conversation, I called Matthew and asked him to come to dinner. He accepted.

The meal was perfect; it was all of his favorite foods. Then I told him about the first dream I'd had alluding to our marriage. He told me that he had been deliberately avoiding me because he knew about the dream. (I had told his friend about it and he had told Matthew about it.) Matthew said he had no interest in dating me or marrying me. I could feel negativity and the presence of demons during that entire conversation. They were with me, not Matthew.

That night I prayed. During the night, Satan attacked me fiercely. In fact, several demons pounded on my body. When I went back to sleep, a demon twisted my left arm. Satan physically and violently attacked me. I could feel the blows physically even though there were no outward signs of the attack on my body. Satan traced a cross on my back as a mockery of the Cross of Jesus Christ, but it was also a reminder to me of the cross I had brought on myself through sin.

Matthew and I did see each other again, but it was during the course of a Bible Study I had in my home. I had an excellent Catholic apologist conduct the study, and Matthew enjoyed discussing Scripture with him. However, Matthew and I never dated or saw each other outside of that Bible Study.

These déjà vu examples show how Satan can influence our future, although he does not have control over it. However, he can use people, places, things, circumstances, our weaknesses, our sins, our desires, our dreams and visions, to manipulate the future. The stories about the teacher and Matthew show how Satan uses our past sins to tempt us in a similar way. The teacher was sent to tempt me sexually and the home health aide was a psychic. I had succumbed to both of these temptations in the past and had opened myself up to demonic influence because of my sins. Satan figured that if I had committed these sins before, I may commit them again.

The Priest

One day in 2013, in a combination vision and locution, I saw many saints praying for me and then a date came into my mind emphatically. I actually prayed and tried to get rid of this locution, but it did not work, perhaps because God wanted me to pay attention to it. To me, the message was to be careful on the date I was given. I must say this experience was unusual because I usually am never given dates.

A few days after this message, I received a return call from a priest who I had called to see if I could meet with for spiritual advice. A friend had told me about him and that he received locutions from Jesus. I surmised that if he was hearing from Jesus, I would be in good hands. The priest set up the appointment and he chose the date, which happened to be the date I had been given in my supernatural experience. I remembered the supernatural experience with the saints, but went ahead with the meeting. In retrospect, I should have cancelled it.

When I met with the priest, he began by making "small talk." I asked him about his locutions. His answers did not give me confidence. I became suspicious about his "gifts." I asked him if he tested the spirits when he got locutions. He said that he didn't need to. He honestly confided to me that he knew some of his locutions were from the devil because they were not in line with Scripture, but he said that, since he was a priest, he could discern them. He refused to test the spirits, and, therefore, I could only conclude that he may be in the grip of evil and his locutions may come from the devil. No one working for God will refuse to test the spirits. I reminded him it says to do this in the Bible: ***...do not despise prophesying, but test everything; hold fast what is good, abstain from every form of evil.*** (1 Thessalonians 5:20-22 RSV) To add to my concern, I experienced déjà vu. Déjà vu can come from either God, from Satan or the human spirit, but I believe that this time it was from Satan.

My sense was that the devil had a real hold on him, and I sensed this to be true in other areas of his life as well. I detected other evil spirits with him, too. After our meeting, I had trouble with demons the rest of the day, and I think demons became attached to me that were with him. This can happen to people. It was one of the worse days that I'd had in a long time. I was under demonic attack all day. I had horrible temptations all day to commit a sin that I knew this priest himself was committing. This visit produced bad fruit, which is a sign that the entire meeting was from the devil.

This priest wrote to me after I sent him a letter honestly telling him about my apprehensions that he was having demonic experiences. Among his feeble efforts to convince me that he could discern was his statement, *Demons cannot say that 'Jesus is the Lord.'* However, that is not true. I had evil spirits tell me to say *Jesus is the Risen Lord* for four hours one time. They can say that, but they cannot say, *Jesus is MY Lord.* (A retired exorcist explained this to me years ago when we spoke by phone. Although I asked this exorcist for help and advice on a few occasions, he told me not to call him anymore. I believe he passed away about two years later. I think he was under demonic attack himself. No one is immune from the battle between good and evil.)

Even priests can be duped by Satan. The priest that was getting locutions obviously did not understand spiritual warfare. I am not trying to be overly critical because demonology is not taught in most seminaries. However, I believe it should be. By demonology I mean that priests should be aware of how demons tempt people and the capabilities of demons. Priests should also be taught how to recognize new age and occult practices. Classes need to be held for all priests and religious in the world so that the Catholic Church can be purified. This information should then be taught to the laity.

DÉJÀ VU EXPERIENCES FROM GOD

The Stranger at Mass

One day I went to a Catholic Mass at a parish near my home. It was not my usual parish, but I started to attend Mass there once in awhile because it fit into my schedule better. Before Mass, the Rosary Group usually prayed the rosary and anyone could join in. In the narthex I happened to encounter a woman who was looking for a brochure which contained the prayers of the rosary so she could join the group. I usually had extra pamphlets with me, but I couldn't find any that day. I even went to my car to see if I had an extra one there, but couldn't find one.

While I was looking for the pamphlet, the Rosary Group began to pray the rosary and we both missed a large part of it. So I told the woman if she wanted to pray the rosary after Mass with me, I'd stay and pray it with her. After Mass we both went into the crying room, which was a room adjacent to the main church that was quiet so we would not disturb other people who were still praying.

By this time, I actually found a pamphlet on how to pray the rosary I had tucked into a prayer book in my purse. I gave it to her to use. As she was praying, I noticed she had a lot of fear of forgetting the words of the prayers even with use of the pamphlet. She kept saying that she was afraid of getting the words wrong. Finally, I stopped praying and told her she had demons of fear with her. I rebuked Satan and demons of fear and taught her how to do this on her own, too. We continued praying and she did better. I began to get the feeling of déjà vu in the middle of the recitation of the rosary.

When the woman said she couldn't kneel anymore because of a large scar on her knee from an injury, everything seemed very familiar to me. I looked at the scar, which was very large, and the feeling of déjà vu came over me very strongly. After we said the rosary, I taught her the Divine Mercy Chaplet and gave her a pamphlet on how to say it. This was also familiar as was her departure. She said she had to leave to meet her husband because they were going camping, and when she left, I was certain this was a déjà vu experience. But it baffled me because I'd always thought these experiences were demonic. This one seemed to be from God because it was all positive. In fact, she said she was really grateful for my help and would continue to pray.

An Old Man Needs Help

One day I went downtown to go to Mass and confession. I didn't realize that the church parking lot was being repaired and was closed. I had to park in a parking structure a few blocks away from the parish. After Mass I was walking back to my car when an elderly man on the sidewalk asked me how much bus fare was. I didn't know because I never ride the bus so I couldn't answer his question. I continued on, but then it occurred to me that maybe I could drive him to his destination if it wasn't too far out of the way for me. I needed to work that day and didn't have a lot of time.

I retraced my route looking for the man. I found him asking someone else how much bus fare was. These days you need exact change to get on a bus in Milwaukee unless you have a pass. The young woman he asked didn't know how much the fare was either. I went up to this man and asked him where he was going. He said he needed to go to the IRS office because he had a problem with his taxes. The IRS office was only a few blocks down the street, but he had trouble walking because he had diabetes in his right foot. He had been in a nursing home for the past three months receiving treatment. However, although he was better, he still had trouble walking and was using a cane. He was taking medication, too. I would guess this man was about 75 years old.

I told him that my car was parked in the parking structure but if he could wait a few minutes, I would get my car and come back to drive him to the IRS office. I found him along the sidewalk waiting for me when I returned. When he got in and started telling me the story about his stay in the nursing home, the feeling of déjà vu came over me very strongly. This entire situation seemed familiar. He told me he lived in an apartment close to his daughter who helped him when she could, but today she was busy. I think this déjà vu experience was from God because it involved a work of charity.

As I have discovered, life is really a struggle between good and evil. Experiences from God are imitated by Satan so proper discernment is very necessary at all times. Déjà vu is just another example.

Chapter Seven

Elemental Spirituality
(Nature Spirits)

Today, Elemental Spirituality has become a very common new age belief among many people in all walks of life. Elemental Spirituality is the belief that everything in nature—for example, plants, animals, water, air, mountains, and inanimate objects—possesses a spirit (a soul). This is referred to as "animism." Therefore, all of creation becomes sacred and nature is considered a god. This heresy also regards each creature (especially each living creature) as a kind of god. Humans are considered gods, too, because they are living creatures. While it is true that people reflect something of God, we are ***made in the image and likeness of God.*** (Genesis 1:26-27 NIV). However, we are still creatures and not gods. There is only one sovereign God. ***I am the Lord, and there is no other; apart from me there is no God.*** (Isaiah 45:5 NIV)

Animists believe that we must be in harmony (in balance) with nature on both the material level and on the spiritual level. Therefore, we have a connection with the divine and with nature. Thus, it is believed that we must integrate the earth with body, mind and spirit.

This concept of interconnectedness comes from Carl Jung (1875-1961), a well-known psychologist who has contributed to the spread of new age thought. It is a Pantheistic view (all is god). *Pantheism is the belief that the universe* ***(or nature as the totality of everything)*** *is identical with divinity, or that everything composes an all-encompassing immanent God.*[44]

Pantheism is especially prevalent amongst Native Americans (both Christians and non-Christians), many of whom still follow traditional native pagan beliefs and practices. American tribes still have their own set of pagan spiritual beliefs, rituals, festivals, myths, forklore, dances, vision quests, ceremonies and

44 Wikipedia, *List of Pantheists*, http://en.wikipedia.org/wiki/List_of_pantheists.

sacred creation concepts which have been difficult for them to abandon. These practices include such activities as connecting with the spirit world using visualization; trying to find a spirit guide for help with the daily challenges of life in such places as a sweat lodge; worship of nature, creatures and inanimate objects; worship of "Mother Earth," and the elements (earth, air, water, fire); and communication with the dead through rituals like the Ghost Dance or the Sun Dance. Rituals, ceremonies and beliefs vary between different tribes.

Evil spirits of the occult and new age are some of the strongest evil spirits, and it is not easy to detach from them. Since Native Americans have persisted in pagan beliefs and practices for many years, the predisposition to commit the same sins exists in every generation. Although I am pointing out these truths, I am only using them as an example. I am not judging them. I, too, have Indian blood in me on my father's side of the family. Everyone in the world is one family, one body in Christ. The truth is that we all have sins that have been passed down to us from our ancestors.

According to Fr. John Hampsch, C.M.F., with whom I consulted while I was writing this book, God's mercy allows the generational progression of ancestral sins and their effects to be stopped. God's gift of family healing can be obtained by arranging to have Masses celebrated for all members of one's family tree—past, present and future. To learn more about generational healing, you may want to order Fr. Hampsch's book, *Healing Your Family Tree*, from Queenship Publishing. You can order it by calling 1-800-647-9882 or online at www.queenship.org.

Wicca

People encounter Elemental Spirituality in many places today, such as books, retreat centers, colleges, TV programs, churches, psychology, health fairs, the internet, and more. Satan's goal is to turn the entire world and its people into his followers. Therefore, we see in the world a rise of paganism in general among individuals and in many religions. However, it seems to me as if Elemental Spirituality is growing in popularity.

Wicca is a pagan religion which has Celtic roots. It falls under the general category of Neo-Paganism, which goes back to ancient times before Christianity began. It is based on the practice of witchcraft. Wiccans present themselves as "good witches." There is no such thing as a "good witch." It is a contradiction because you cannot mix good with evil and call it good. A witch is always someone who is not obeying the First Commandment because a Wiccan or a witch is worshipping false gods through practicing and living "the craft."

The Wiccan motto is: *An it harm none, do what ye will.*[45] In other words, live and let live as long as no harm is done to oneself or others. Today we often advocate "tolerance" when it comes to how people live their lives. While loving one another is a moral truth, when it comes to loving God, the parameters must be in line with God's commandments. Unfortunately, Wiccans do not obey God's commandments and, therefore, are not in conformity with God's ways. Therefore, the Wiccan's seemingly great motto does not absolve them from sin.

Wiccans twist their beliefs into something innocent. God must be placed first in our lives and pagan beliefs should not be twisted into something that is acceptable. This is how Satan works: He presents sin as something good when it is actually not. Wiccans revere nature and support peace. However, their concept of safeguarding peace comes from being in harmony with nature and not mistreating Mother Earth. This has led the world to worship of ecology, which reveres nature in all its forms. They believe that only ecological balance can sustain freedom.

In the document, *Jesus Christ the Bearer of the Water of Life: A Christian Reflection on the New Age*, we read: ***The warmth of Mother Earth, whose divinity pervades the <u>whole of creation</u>, is held to bridge the gap between creation and the transcendent Father-God of Judaism and Christianity, and removes the prospect of being judged by such a Being. In such a vision of a closed universe that contains God and other spiritual beings along with ourselves, we recognize here an implicit pantheism.*** [46]

---

45 Wikipedia, *Wiccan Rede,* http://en.wikipedia.org/wiki/Wiccan_Rede.
46 *Jesus Christ the Bearer of the Water of Life: A Christian Reflection on the New Age.* Pontifical Council for Culture, Pontifical Council for Interreligious Dialogue, (Section 2.3.1) www.vatican.va/.../pontifical_councils/interelg/documents/rc_pc_interelg_doc_20030203_new-age_en.html - 216k - 2003-02-20.rc_pc_inte

Most Wiccans believe in a female and a male god. The feminine god is called a mother goddess because she represents motherhood, creation, fertility, nature and the earth. The mother goddess can be called by different names. For example, the goddess associated with the earth, called "Mother Earth," is also known as "Gaia." Feminists seem to gravitate to this sect due to worship of a feminine goddess. The male god is called, "the Horned God." The Horned God is typically associated with hunting, the wilderness, sexuality and the life cycle. He is *the personification of the life force energy in animals and the wild....*[47] Although the belief in two deities is the most common amongst Wiccans, some Wiccans believe in polytheism (many gods) and even monotheism (one god).

What is truth in this "religion"? This is an example of how people in the world are making up truth as they go along without any basis for it! It is called moral relativism, whereby we determine our own beliefs. This is probably what is most appealing about this "religion," which is how it is described in many sources. Wiccans also do not believe in Satan, therefore, there is nothing to fear. Therefore, unlike Christians, they have no fear of the consequences for sin or eternal damnation. I suggest they pray to the one, true God to discover the truth. If anyone really wants to learn truth, read the Bible. You will see that paganism was the downfall of many in the Old Testament.

Wiccans perform occult practices such as casting spells and performing magic. They sometimes do this by going into altered states of consciousness. They do this as part of a coven or sometimes they do this alone. The five pointed star (the Pentagram) is used for casting spells and performing magic. I found a Pentagram in a Catholic cemetery while I was writing this book. I prayed about what to do. I was led to rebuke the evil spirits using holy water, blessed salt and holy oil. Armed with these sacramentals, I rebuked the evil spirits of the occult, magic and any spells or curses connected with the Pentagram, commanding that they leave in the name of Jesus Christ. I then asked Jesus to cover me with His Most Precious Blood. Then I dismantled the Pentagram and disposed of it. Satanic objects like

47 *Horned God,* http://en.wikipedia.org/wiki/Horned_God.

this should be burned.

Unfortunately, Wiccans do not realize that they can become possessed. In an article entitled, *Dispelling the Charms of Wicca,* by Mary Zurolo, she states that she found an online posting where a writer identifying herself as Britt said: *'I was talking to my friend Dave...and he is quite a devout Christian...I just found out...that he used be Wiccan. He said that he got so deeply into it, that he was nearly demonically possessed'.*[48]

Wiccans believe in such new age concepts as reincarnation. Reincarnation is *the belief that the soul, upon death of the body, comes back to earth in another body or form.*[49] It is believed that we do this as long as it takes to achieve spiritual perfection or "karma."

Wicca has become a popular religion. An article entitled *Why Wicca is a Major World Religion in 2012* states: "*The importance of Wicca as a new religion is probably most obvious from its current size and rate of growth. The movement has been doubling in size about every two years since Ray Buckland brought the first officially Gardnerian coven to America in the early 1960s. In 1999, according to a survey sponsored by the Covenant of the Goddess, there were about 600,000 initiated Witches in America and therefore probably about 6,000,000 practicing Pagans—and it has been growing just as fast since then... this religion is clearly meeting some needs in American society that are not being met as well by other religions.*[50]

People do not really understand what they really need. We do not need "religions" like Wicca! We need God in our lives! That means we should worship Him and Him alone. Instead, we seem to think that we can do as we please without any consequences. You, dear readers, may believe that there are no consequences for sin, but don't tell that to me. I have demons in my life because I made the wrong choices. It can happen to you, too. Our goal is pleasure without any inhibitions or limitations. Anything that makes us happy is acceptable. We are losing our

48 Zurolo, Mary, *Dispelling the Charms of Wicca,* Catholic Faith & Family, Circle Media, Inc., Hamden, CT 06514, as seen on http://www.catholicculture.org/culture/library/view.cfm?recnum=1289,2014.

49 Reincarnation, *Dictionary.com,* http://dictionary.reference.com/browse/reincarnation.

50 Kelly, Aldan, *Why Wicca is a Major World Religion in 2012,* http://www.patheos.com/blogs/aidankelly/2012/06/why-wicca-is-a-major-world-religion/#ixzz3CUYm5pz6.

sense of right and wrong, becoming slaves of the devil. We are listening to his temptations and carrying them out. His goal is to rid the world of worship of the one, true God. One way he is succeeding is through Elemental Spirituality (including Wicca) and a fascination with new age and occult beliefs and practices.

My Wicked Wiccan Experience

In the early 2000's, I signed up for a class at a local Catholic College called "Elemental Spirituality." The class was under the heading, "Spiritual Growth" in a brochure I had received. I signed up for this class because I wanted to grow spiritually and become closer to God. I had no idea what it entailed, but I thought that it was a basic course on Christian spirituality. It turned out to be a class in Wicca.

Coincidentally, I had just read about Wicca two days before attending this class. After I sat down in the classroom, I felt the Holy Spirit prompting me to leave, but I didn't do it. This was a critical error in discernment. Even though I was taken off-guard, it was a big mistake to remain in the class. I participated in the class doing the minimum of what was expected.

The teacher was working as a spiritual mentor at a company in my locale. According to the information I kept on her, she instructed students in *Wholistic Changes for Healthful Living*. In the description of the class in the brochure, it stated, *As the human Jesus incorporated the elements of nature into his living and teachings, let us reclaim our incarnational spirituality by celebrating the inner and outer dynamism of this four-fold connection of wholeness where the four are One.* The four stated in the brochure were soil, fire, water and air, the elements of all life. Unfortunately, at the time, this description was beyond my comprehension.

Many Directors of Religious Education attended the class I was in as a means of ongoing education. DREs take what they learn back to their parishes and implement it. This is just one way that new age and the occult has entered the Catholic Church.

Before the class began, we were given a series of handouts. One handout contained information on chakras, a new age Hindu belief. Another handout listed a series of prayers for us to recite to the "Great Spirits" of the four directions: East, North, South, and West. Notice that the word "spirits" is plural. Native Americans and Wiccans pray to the **spirits** of the directions. Each spirit is invoked by name, i.e. "Spirit of the East," "Spirit of the West," etc. Even though some Native American tribes believe in a Great Spirit (whom they consider to be God), they also believe in other deities. Therefore, in this class, we were being introduced to multiple gods. This is idolatry, divinizing what is not God. (CC 2113).

The first thing we were asked to do in the class was meditate. I prayed instead. Then the instructor put representations of the four elements in the center of the room: water (in a bowl), fire (a candle), air (a fan), and soil (earth). We were informed that there is also a fifth element called "spirit." Spirit is not one of the physical elements. There are different, elusive definitions of the fifth element, but in this class it was called "ether." However, another definition of the fifth element by Wiccans is that it is *a force that unites all things.*[51]

Our next assignment in the class was to walk around the representations of the elements in a circle, doing spiritual chants. We were instructed to integrate earth with body, mind and spirit, and to feel the connection with the divine and nature, focusing on the ways these elements helped us. I discovered later that these elements are considered by Wiccans as sacred creation concepts. Each of these elements is believed to possess a spirit of its own—they are spirits of nature. We were worshipping pagan gods in a Catholic setting!

Later, we were asked to divide into four groups and prepare a short skit. Each group had to focus on one of the four elements and use it as the basis for the skit. Using the element we were assigned, each group had to do the following: 1) Give their skit a tribal name. 2) Use words, gestures, song, sound, and movement to tell about their element. 3) Describe their element's qualities/characteristics in nature. 4) Tell how their element sounded, looked, tasted, felt, smelled, and moved. 5) Describe the gifts their element offered. 6) Explain what their element lacked. 7) Explain the message their element had about women and spirituality. 8) Describe what their element needed from women leaders. It was

51 WitchesLore,*The Five Elements*, http://witcheslore.com/bookofshadows/witches-workshop/the-five-elements/4683/.

very impromptu and again, I was simply not into it. I only said one line. I kept waiting for some explanation of how this all fit into Christian beliefs, but it was not forthcoming.

That night I was visited by disembodied damned human souls who identified themselves as Native Americans. I knew immediately they visited me because of my participation in the class. They identified themselves as "No Name" spirits. I wondered what the significance of "No Name" was. I discovered that many Native Americans believe that all forces and power have their origin in a larger force (of which they are continually a part) for which there is no name. It is based on superstition. This is actually Monism, a new age belief. Monism is the belief that there is only one universal being (or force) of which every thing and every person is a part.[52]

The demonic entities tormented me and I suffered from a form of demonic oppression. I could not do anything and had no energy. It felt like a heavy weight was on my body. I asked the Lord how to get rid of these spirits from Hell, and Jesus told me that ***some spirits can only be cast out by prayer and fasting.*** This is actually in the Bible in Matthew 17:21. So I fasted and prayed, and they left a few days later. Praise the Lord! I would never have known what to do. Jesus helped me so many times when I got myself into trouble. He is so merciful.

The Third Eye

After taking the class in Wicca, I saw the "Third Eye." The Third Eye is a Hindu belief which refers to the mystical experience of seeing the spiritual world with a Third Eye. It is believed that this Third Eye is in the center of the forehead. Perhaps many of you have seen Hindu women wear a red dot or a piece of jewelry (which is called a bindi) on their foreheads between their eyebrows. They wear it in this location because it is believed that the sixth chakra (ajna), the seat of divine wisdom, is located in

52 *Jesus Christ the Bearer of the Water of Life: A Christian Reflection on the New Age.* Pontifical Council for Culture, Pontifical Council for Interreligious Dialogue, (Section 7.2) www.vatican.va/.../pontifical_councils/interelg/documents/rc_pc_interelg_doc_20030203_new-age_en.html - 216k - 2003-02-20.rc_pc_interelg_doc_20030201_new-age_en. html _ 216k - 2003-02-20

this area.

One night shortly after attending the Wiccan class, I had my eyes closed when all of a sudden I saw a HUGE eyeball staring at me in the center of my line of vision. The Holy Spirit gave me knowledge that it was the Third Eye, which is connected with chakras. *Chakras are said to be centers for cosmic energy in the human body that are aligned to allow the Kundalini energy to proceed from the base of the spine to the top of the forehead.*[53] In our Wiccan class, you will recall we were given a handout on Chakras, which explained this Hindu belief.

I believe that my experience with the Third Eye was a direct result of taking that class. It was evil, a new age and occult concept, and caused by demons of Elemental Spirituality. However, God, in His mercy, did not allow this experience to be drawn out, so I did not see it again.

Reflections

I want to say that if I had evil spirits come into my life from an hour and a half participation in a class on Wicca (a form of witchcraft), they must be strong evil spirits. Right now this chapter is causing me a lot of demonic attacks. The demons are furious with me for writing on Wicca and have been trying to stop me from writing this for months now. Many times, something would happen to prevent me from writing it. Last night, after I had finally made some headway writing this section, the demons hit me forcefully in the center of my forehead, and it took awhile for me to stabilize. It happened at 3 a.m., Satan's hour because it is the opposite of 3 p.m., the hour Christ died.

I think Wicca and witchcraft are extremely spiritually dangerous forms of new age and the occult. You could have demons come into your life. Trust me, you do not want that to happen. The more often you participate in pagan practices such as Wicca, the more demonic entities will tempt you and eventually may possess you.

53 Watchman Fellowship, *Index of Cults and Religions*, Chakras, www.watchman.org.

Spiritism

In general, Spiritism is an attempt by the living to contact spirits of the departed. In a broad sense, it is termed "paranormal" activity. Contacting the dead is done, for example, through such practices as séances, use of Ouija boards, visualization, seeking spirit guides in Native American practices such as vision quests and the Ghost Dance, contact with mediums (psychics), Transcendental Meditation, use of crystal balls, mirror gazing (which was used by Nostradamus), and more. Sometimes people use such things as drugs and rituals to conjure up a spirit. Unfortunately, all of these and related practices are very prevalent today in the world and are forbidden by God. The First Commandment is: ***I am the Lord your God: You Shall Not Have Strange Gods Before Me.*** (Traditional Catechetical Formula, Catechism of the Catholic Church).

As I have just mentioned, contacting the dead can be done by use of demonic tools by an individual. However, Spiritism is also accomplished through use of a medium (also called a psychic or channeler), who acts as an intermediary between a person seeking information and the spirit world. There are two types of mediums. The mental medium tunes into the spirit world by use of the senses. Therefore, spirits are contacted through listening, sensing a presence or even seeing evil spirits. The medium makes a conscious choice to do this.

On the other hand, a physical medium conjures up "noisy" evil spirits which use such noises as raps, creaking, banging, ringing of doorbells, flying objects, and other discernable noises and phenomena in their manifestations. Spirits are also contacted in a variety of other ways. Some of these ways can include mental telepathy, going into an altered state of consciousness and channeling.

Of course, some psychics are actually just amateurish fortune tellers that use trickery and scams to provide a credible atmosphere for gullible clients. If they can trick a client once, they may be able to get follow-up business. However, all contact with any psychic, fortune teller or channeler is forbidden, since it is against the First Commandment.

Channeling

Channeling falls under the category of Spiritism and is part of the occult. Channeling is "*the act or practice of serving as a medium through which a spirit guide purportedly communicates with a living person.*[54] Today going to psychics or mediums to contact the dead seems to be accepted as the norm. There are psychics everywhere, set up in small shops interspersed with other types of businesses. Psychics and mediums have also been invited to colleges, parties, and health fairs. However, from a spiritual perspective, it is very unhealthy to use the services of a psychic or medium to channel an entity. When a psychic or medium channels an entity, they go into an altered state of consciousness. An evil spirit actually takes temporary control of their body and their faculties. Some channelers even see images of the spirits they contact.

When people attempt to contact the dead, they are easily deceived. Satan convinces them they are contacting a saint, an apostle, an angel, a spiritual master, guru, a deceased loved one, a spirit of an animal, a famous person in the past, or even Jesus or Mary. Evil spirits will pretend to be whoever you are trying to channel. Demons can masquerade as people whom you have known in this life, so remember you are actually speaking with a demon during channeling, not your Aunt Millie, whom you wanted to ask a few questions. Demons can also mimic the voice of a departed person through a medium. Remember also that demons know about events and circumstances that have already occurred (even though you may not be aware of them) and they can use them as bait to get you to continue to use a medium to get more information.

The psychic who directed me to write a book on miracles told me she heard voices, who gave her answers to my questions. I thought they were people in Heaven, but they were demons. These demons were with her and provided her with information when she asked them for it. <u>They were attached to her.</u> She told me her psychic abilities were in her family tree. Today, I realize that she needed prayers of deliverance. She also needed to say

54 *The Free Dictionary by Farlex*, http://www.thefreedictionary.com/channeling.

prayers for healing of her family tree.

Because Satan succeeded in duping me by seeking information from a psychic, he tried to tempt me in a similar manner a few months after my initial contact with her. If we commit a sin, Satan will tempt us in similar ways because it worked for him before. It helps to make a good confession, but we must always be on our guard because Satan does not give up. He just bides his time. Here are some examples of other temptations Satan gave me after I succumbed to the temptation of consulting a psychic. However, God gave me the grace not to succumb to them.

A Woman Channels St. Peter

One day I got a flyer in the mail from someone who was promoting a spiritual workshop. I called to find out more about it and to discern it. I discovered the young woman was channeling St. Peter. In other words, St. Peter spoke through her. When I asked her what St. Peter was saying, she said he spoke a lot about reincarnation.

I explained to her that reincarnation is against biblical teaching. The Bible says ***Just as people are destined to die once, and after that to face judgment so Christ was sacrificed once to take away the sins of many; and He will appear a second time, not to bear sin, but to bring salvation to those who are waiting for Him.*** (Hebrews: 9:27-28 NIV) The Bible clearly states here that we die only once, and we do not come back in another body or in another form. We have but one life, one chance at eternal salvation. Therefore, we should do our best to do God's will.

I told the young lady that it was not St. Peter speaking to her, but the devil. She refused to consider the fact that she was in error. She justified and defended her position and wouldn't give it up. I suggested that she test the spirits by saying: *If you are not from God, begone in the name of Jesus Christ.* She made a lot of excuses why she did not need to do this. She was convinced the entity was really St. Peter. Also, she had been channeling this entity for several years and believed the messages. Satan had a grip on her.

I think the longer we engage in a demonic activity, the more power Satan has over us. This woman had built a business around the channeling, charging people for newsletters that she wrote in connection with the messages she was getting. If she accepted the fact that she had been duped by Satan, it would have meant a drastic change in her life, and one she was not willing to accept. However, it is a spiritual work of mercy to point out other people's moral errors if we recognize them.

Since I myself was in error at the time because I was following messages from the devil, I want to say I do not condemn others who are also in error, but we are reminded to pray for them. It is extremely humbling to realize that you have been wrong, to repent, and then pick up the pieces of your life. But we must do it if we love God and want to get to Heaven.

Other common lies given by demons during channeled communications include the teaching that humans are gods, that Jesus Himself lived past lives, that Jesus was only a wise teacher and that man creates his own destiny. Don't fall for these tactics of the devil.

The Channeled Book, *A Course in Miracles,* by Marianne Williamson

Because I was writing a book, I took a class in writing and met another classmate there who was going to become a minister in an interdenominational church. She was a Catholic and was leaving the faith. We became friends and she invited me to her ordination. I attended the service because I knew her. What a mistake, not only because by my presence I was silently condoning her decision, but, as I discovered, her church did not use the Bible, but a book called *A Course in Miracles.*[55]

I was outraged that they were using this book even though I did not know anything about it at the time. But, I did know that the Bible alone is the source of God's Word. When I researched *A Course in Miracles,* I found out that it is actually a new age book. The material was channeled to Helen Schucman, a Columbia University Professor of Medical Psychology, in 1965. It was

55 Schucman, Helen, *A Course in Miracles,* Original Edition Perfect Paperback, A Course in Miracles Society, January 1, 2009.

supposedly a new revelation given to her by Jesus Christ.

Schucman began hearing an inner voice who requested that she take notes. After seven years, the information Schucman received became the book *A Course in Miracles.* The messages in the book are contrary to Scripture and directly contradict it. Therefore, we can safely discern that the information was relayed by demons. Messages from God do not contradict Scripture.

Many people have been and are being duped by the book *A Course in Miracles.* The channeled messages contain doctrinal errors, and are dangerously deceptive. The following lists of sins (without the comments which are mine) are from an online article called *A Course in Miracles EXPOSED.*[56] In the work, *A Course in Miracles,* the writings state that:

- *There is no sin…* (p. 9) Of course, we know this is incorrect. Ever since the first sin of Adam and Eve, mankind has continued to sin. When we look around the world, it is very easy to see that this statement is a grave error because sin abounds everywhere.
- *The journey to the cross should be the last "useless journey."* (p. 11) The Christian Bible states: ***Then Jesus said to His disciples, "Whoever wants to be my disciple must deny themselves and take up their cross and follow Me."*** (Matthew 16:24 NIV) Actually, the journey to the cross is what God asks us to do. ***For whoever wants to save their life will lose it, but whoever loses their life for Me will find it.*** (Matthew 16:25 NIV) Suffering is part of life. Just as Jesus suffered for us, we all have to suffer, too. However, Jesus said it would never be more than we can handle.
- *Do not make the pathetic error of clinging to the old rugged cross.* (p. 12) This is simply a reiteration of the same moral error stated above.
- *The name of Jesus Christ as such is but a symbol… It is a symbol that is safely used as a replacement for the many names of all the gods to which you pray.* (p. 13) This is not

56 Jesus is Savior.com, *A Course in Miracles EXPOSED,* http://jesus-is-savior.com/Wolves/a_course_in_miracles.htm.

true. Jesus is the only true God, therefore, He cannot be lumped together with other false gods. His name should be praised above every other name. In the Christian Bible, it states: ***Therefore God exalted Him to the highest place and gave Him the name that is above every name.*** (Philippians 2:9 NIV)

- *God is in everything I see.* (p. 14) This is pantheism (all is god), a new age belief.
- *The recognition of god is the recognition of yourself.* (p. 15) We are not gods, and we should not divinize ourselves.
- *The oneness of the Creator and the creation is your wholeness, your sanity and your limitless power.* (p. 16) The concept that all is one is Monism, a new age belief.
- *The Atonement is the final lesson he (man) need learn, for it teaches him that, never having sinned, he has no need of salvation.* (p. 17) This statement is against Scripture, which teaches that we are all sinners and need salvation. Jesus Christ opened the door of Heaven for us by His Passion and Death on the Cross, but we must obey the commandments and repent of our sins to get there.

New age and occult practices have steadily gained in popularity for the past 50 years. As you can see, *A Course in Miracles* is filled with lies, new age beliefs, and moral errors. No Christian should read it. Since it was published, there have been many other new age books that have piqued people's interest. However, they are spiritually dangerous. Learn as much as you can about the subject from a Christian perspective so you, too, are not duped.

Jesuit Father Mitch Pacwa, who is very knowledgeable on the topic of new age, sees *A Course in Miracles* written in a manner that can dupe Catholics and others, luring them to study the course. *The key problem is the [course's] pseudo - Christian vocabulary and ideas,* said Father Pacwa. *People don't know the Catechism, they don't know their faith.... The course strongly rejects the use of reason and thinking.... This is precisely what makes the course feasible. Once you get rid of reason, you get rid of discussion.*[57]

The good news of Jesus Christ is that there is a better place after death for those who love and serve God. This should be a source of strength to all of us. I encourage all of you to read the Bible, obey the commandments, and love one another. Be sure you always only worship and pray to the one, true God. Be sure to renounce all Satanic practices you have participated in by saying prayers of deliverance.

Final Remarks

Deliberately contacting the spirit world is extremely dangerous because once you begin to contact the spirit world on a regular basis, evil spirits will attach themselves to you. Initially, they may not openly manifest themselves. But if you continually and repeatedly engage in any occult or new age practice, you will have evil spirits in your lives. Eventually, stronger demons come in. **This is true of any sin you repeatedly commit.** As time goes on, these demons may begin to manifest themselves through speaking (either audibly or in a manner which other people cannot hear), frequent accidents, raps, noises, electronic equipment failures, apparitions, mishaps and accidents, nightmares, and the like. Often, it isn't until someone becomes seriously oppressed or possessed people that they realize they have been under demonic influence and need to seek deliverance or an exorcism.

I personally think we need many more deliverance ministries and exorcists today because I think new age and the occult is so widespread that it is spiritually affecting many, many people. There is a fascination with new age and the occult in our modern world. I believe institutions need to be built where people can go who are having spiritual problems. I believe that the staff should include doctors of medicine to screen people who may have physical or mental problems. However, I also believe there should be Catholic and Christian deliverance ministers and exorcists on staff. I think these institutions should be built all over the world.

57 Moran, Tracy, *A Course in Brainwashing*, http:/www.ewtn.com/library/newage/brainwas.txt.,1996.

I recommend that you never contact the spirit world. Also, remember if you ever do have any paranormal experience, be sure to test the spirits. Say *If you are not from God, begone in the name of Jesus Christ.* Even if you have not attempted to contact the spirit world, evil spirits in your family tree may be just waiting to deceive you, too. Even children can be susceptible to demonic influences from ancestral evil spirits—a situation that places them in very great moral danger. Parents have an obligation to keep their homes free from every occultic influence.

Truth comes from the Holy Spirit and from much prayer. Always pray to the Holy Spirit for guidance. The Holy Spirit will help you through divine inspirations and infused knowledge when you pray. Praying to the Holy Spirit is not a technique, but prayer to God from the heart. A good place to pray to the Holy Spirit is during Adoration of the Blessed Sacrament in the Catholic Church.

Chapter Eight

The Spiritual Dangers of Alternative Therapies

Today more than ever before, I see people who want quick fixes for their health problems. Suffering is looked upon as something to avoid at all costs. This is apparent with such immoral choices today such as euthanasia. While it is good for us to obtain help for physical, emotional and mental problems, today people are seeking solutions through many new age pagan remedies, which are actually spiritually dangerous. Sometimes there are no cures for our health problems, and perhaps it is God's will that we offer up our suffering to help save souls or to shorten our stay in Purgatory.

Suffering is no longer considered something of value. Indeed, if Jesus Christ did not suffer and die for us on the Cross, none of us would be able to enter Heaven because of our ancestors' sins (Adam's and Eve's). We must trust in God for all our needs. We can pray for a good physician, and we should do what we can to prudently take care of ourselves; *i.e.* getting enough rest, proper nutrition, exercising, and so forth. But the rest is in God's hands.

During the past several years, more and more alternative healing therapies have been introduced to the general public. Alternative therapies are often referred to as holistic, nontraditional, complementary, mind/body, new age, or unconventional. In other words, they are not based on science or proven methods. Once we have been to doctors of medicine, had tests, and exhausted all standard medical procedures, I do not believe we should desperately seek out alternative therapies. If we add a spiritually contaminated practice to our existing health problems, the results can be catastrophic.

I do acknowledge, however, that parts of some therapies may be morally acceptable and beneficial to some people. For example, forms of chiropractic care that include standard medical practices such as massage, corrective exercises, ice packs, bracing, bed rest, moist heat and massage are morally acceptable. It would not be sinful to go to a chiropractor for this type of help. Also, a 12-step program to quit drinking would be morally acceptable if we did not rely on ourselves to accomplish the goal, but on God's grace. If we pray to God for healing, this is in line with Holy Scripture. We cannot do anything without God. However, in general, I believe that all alternative therapies are new age and spiritually dangerous despite the fact that parts of them could be considered acceptable.

There are many varieties of new age alternative therapies. According to the Pontifical document *Jesus Christ the Bearer of the Water of Life: A Christian Reflection on the New Age,* ***...New Age covers a wide range of practices as acupuncture, biofeedback, chiropractics, kinesiology, homeopathy, iridology, massage and various kinds of bodywork (such as orgonomy, Feldenkrais, reflexology, Rolfing, polarity massage, therapeutic touch, etc., meditation and visualization, nutritional therapies, psychic healing, various kinds of herbal medicine, healing by crystals, metals, music or colors, reincarnation therapies and finally, twelve-step programs and self-help groups. The source of healing is said to be within ourselves, something we reach when we are in touch with our inner energy or cosmic energy.***[58]

The principles of holistic medicine are based on the belief that a person is ultimately responsible for his or her own health and well-being. Other principles of holistic medicine include the following: 1) All people are divine and can heal themselves; 2) The "whole" patient should be healed, including body, mind and spirit; and 3) Treatment should include supplements and/or alternative therapies. These are often used in conjunction with one another. For example, if someone is depressed, holism would look for bodily nutritional deficiencies, mental problems, or spiritual problems that may be causing the depression.

While the premise of treating the whole person; namely, the

---

58 *Jesus Christ the Bearer of the Water of Life: A Christian Reflection on the New Age.* Pontifical Council for Culture, Pontifical Council for Interreligious Dialogue, (Section 2.2.2) www.vatican.va/.../pontifical_councils/interelg/documents/rc_pc_interelg_doc_20030203_new-age_en.html - 216k - 2003-02-20.rc_pc_interelg_doc_20030201_new-age_en. html _ 216k - 2003-02-20

body, mind and spirit, appears to be good, we must be cautious because the devil can trick us very easily into becoming dependent on alternative therapies rather than standard medical practices. We do not want to make an error in discernment only to discover we have not only the physical maladies to contend with, but evil spirits, too.

Herbal Remedies (Botanicals)

Herbal remedies, also called botanicals, are remedies derived from plants or plant extracts and include extracts, tinctures, capsules, tablets and teas. They were used in ancient times. They are very popular today as people seem to want to incorporate what they consider "new" remedies into their lives instead of traditional medicine. Perhaps people think there may be fewer side effects than standard medication or that they will cost less money. In any event, these remedies have become accepted and are commonly used today by people of all ages.

In and of themselves, herbs are not intrinsically evil. Some herbal remedies today reportedly contain medicinal properties and are used by doctors in medical treatment. The problem is that many herbalists who make these concoctions from plants are incorporating spiritual beliefs with the material aspects of the products. They may also use hallucinogenic plants that can induce an altered state of consciousness. In my research, I discovered that herbal remedies have Native American pagan roots. From a spiritual perspective, the cost could be deadly.

Native American Herbal Remedies

From personal experience, I can tell you that demons can cause illness and infirmities. Since they can cause sickness, they also can lead people to demonic cures. We find some of these "cures" in Native American spirituality. If we look carefully, we can see the connection between Native American herbal remedies and new age tenets today.

In general, Native American healing practices go back thousands of years and include many treatments using herbs, roots, and natural plants. Native Americans used these sources to heal various illnesses. However, they also incorporated spirituality into their beliefs. Kathy Weiser, a writer on Native American Legends, states: *...most tribes believed that health was an expression of the spirit and a continual process of staying strong spiritually, mentally, and physically. This strength, as well as keeping in harmony with themselves, those around them, their natural environment and Creator, would keep away illness and harm. Each person was responsible for his or her own health and all thoughts and actions had consequences, including illness, disability, bad luck, or trauma. Only when harmony was set right, could their health be restored.* ***Herbal remedies filled an important role within these healing practices, stretching beyond the body's aches and pains and into the realm of the spirituality and harmony.***[59]

If we look closely at Weiser's report, we can see a number of similarities between Native American healing practices (including herbal remedies) and new age beliefs today. First, we see their focus on body, mind and spirit. Second, we see the new age concept of being in harmony with nature and the belief that everything needs to be kept in balance. Third, we see that Native Americans held themselves responsible for their own health. New age is nothing more than a revival of old paganism. Why would we want to go backwards instead of relying on Christ?

Native Americans see a connection between the spirit world and natural herbs, which they believe are sacred. They believe that everything (both material and spiritual) is animated by spirits (gods). Formulas in many herbal products we have in stores today have come from Native Americans. According to a Cherokee Legend, Cherokee medicine men would go to caves at least once a year where they would meet for seven days. During that time, they would chant sacred songs, dance, tell stories, invoke animals such as deer and bear, and participate in drumming. Spirits called "Little People" would give them secret knowledge about herbal remedies. Remedies were given to them for such common health problems such as asthma, diarrhea, inflammation of the stomach, gout, jaundice, worms, cracked hands, and almost every common ailment we have today.

59 Kathy Weiser, owner/editor, *Legends of America*, http://www.legendsofamerica.com Native American Medicine, 2012.

Secret knowledge is called "Gnosticism," and is part of the occult. These secret remedies would then be passed onto other Native Americans. From these secret remedies came herbal medicines. Native Americans passed them down from generation to generation and to us. In fact, *more than 200 botanicals, derived originally from Native Americans, have been or are still in use in pharmaceuticals...The major difference between Native American's healing and conventional medicine, both in the past and present, is the role of spirituality in the healing process. Native Americans believe that all things in nature are connected and that spirits can promote health or cause illness. Therefore, it is necessary to heal not only the physical parts of an individual, but also their emotional wellness, and their harmony with their community and the environment around them.*[60]

The process of assigning a spiritual power to an herbal remedy is also called "potentization." The process of potentization supposedly releases the hidden healing powers or healing force from inside a product. *A potency is a preparation consisting of a substrate, usually inert, upon which a specific energy pattern has been imprinted either electronically or mechanically in order to correct dysfunction in the subtle energy fields that underlie a physical state of existence. The most widely used potencies are those created through traditional homeopathic processes.* [61]

Homeopathy is *a system for treating disease based on the administration of minute doses of a drug that in massive amounts produces symptoms in healthy individuals similar to those of the disease itself.*[62] In other words, it is based on the principle "like cures like." Homeopathy was popularized by German physician Samuel Hahnemann in 1810. However, the cure was based on energy. According to George Vithoulkas, author of two textbooks on homeopathy, greatly diluted remedies *contained no detectable material trace of the original substance. It followed, therefore, that their curative effect was not material, but involved some other factor—energy ...Hahnemann concluded that (illness) was nothing other than a*

60 *Ibid.*, 2012.
61 Oregon Herbalist, *Potentizing and Homeopathy,* http:/www.kellyresearchtecch.com/articles/potentizer.pdf.
62 *The Free Dictionary* by Farlex, http://www.thefreedictionary.com/homeopathy.

derangement in the life force of man.[63] Homeopathy and energy fields are warned against in the Vatican document, *Jesus Christ the Bearer of the Water of Life: A Christian Reflection on the New Age* as are *various kinds of herbal medicine.*[64]

Another problem with herbal remedies is that they are often untested. There is a tendency in herbalism to ignore scientific facts, pursuing something which is perceived to be good but that can actually be physically dangerous to the user. Many herbal and holistic remedies are simply quackery. Doctors and proponents of herbal medicines claim that herbal remedies help those with various illnesses, but I believe people should be wary of them.

According to Stephen Barrett, M.D., *Herbal advocates like to point out that about half of today's medicines were derived from plants. (Digitalis, for example, was originally derived from leaves of the foxglove plant.) This statement is true but misleading. Drug products contain specified amounts of active ingredients. Herbs in their natural state can vary greatly from batch to batch and often contain chemicals that cause side effects but provide no benefit.*

When potent natural substances are discovered, drug companies try to isolate and synthesize the active chemical in order to provide a reliable supply. They also attempt to make derivatives that are more potent, more predictable, and have fewer side effects. In the case of digitalis, derivatives provide a spectrum of speed and duration of action. Digitalis leaf is almost never used today because its effects are less predictable. Many herbs contain hundreds or even thousands of chemicals that have not been completely cataloged. Some of these chemicals may turn out to be useful as therapeutic agents, but others could well prove toxic.

Dr. Barrett adds: *Even when a botanical product contains ingredients that are potentially effective, it may not be practical to use. Garlic, for example, has been demonstrated to lower cholesterol. However, prescription drugs are more potent for this purpose, and garlic has anticoagulant properties. No data are available to indicate the risk of combining garlic with other widely used products (vitamin E, ginkgo,*

63 Vithoulkas, 1978, 89 as seen in Hoyt, Karen, *The New Age Rage*, Spiritual Counterfeits Project, Fleming H. Revell Company, Old Tappan, NJ 07675, 1987.

64 *Jesus Christ the Bearer of the Water of Life: A Christian Reflection on the New Age.* Pontifical Council for Culture, Pontifical Council for Interreligious Dialogue, (Section 2.2.3) www.vatican.va/.../pontifical_councils/interelg/documents/rc_pc_interelg_doc_20030203_new-age_en.html - 216k - 2003-02-20.rc_pc_interelg_doc_20030201_new-age_en. html _ 216k - 2003-02-20

fish oil, and aspirin) that can interfere with blood clotting.[65]

In the early 1900's, Native Americans began to use modern medicine, but in recent years, their herbal products have been making a comeback and have been popular with many people who have never been exposed to them. Therefore, even though we view these products as a new trend, they are not really new. Herbal products are powerful supplements so they should be taken with caution. They can cause health problems, so you may want to consult your doctor before purchasing them. Also, buyers should be aware of the spiritual factors that may be connected with some of these supplements.

A Miracle from Satan Through A Shaman

As I have mentioned earlier in this book, I was shown in a dream and through a locution from God that there were still errors in the reprinted version of the book I wrote on miracles. The specific error I was shown was a story about the healing of a Native American through a medicine woman, also called a shaman. (Shamans can also be men).

Among Native Americans, shamans were considered to have more power than others in the tribe. Typically, shamans believe that everything in nature has a spirit. Their primary role is to obtain help from the spirit world, especially the "Great Spirit" to facilitate healing. Some shamans have ancestors who have been shamans. (Sins commonly run in families). Other shamans may have received their calling in a vision. *In some cases, the healer would go into a trance state and seek the help of spirit guides.*[66] In the document, *Jesus Christ the Bearer of the Water of Life: A Christian Reflection on the New Age,* we read, *The shaman is often seen as the specialist of altered states of consciousness, one who is able to mediate between the transpersonal realms of spirits and gods and the world of humans.*[67] Thus, going into altered states of consciousness contacts

65 Barrett, Stephen, M.D., *The Herbal Mindfield,* http://ww.quackwatch.com/01QuackeryRelatedTopics/herbs.html.

66 Weiser, Kathy, owner/editor, *Legends of America,* www.legendsofamerica.com, *Native American Medicine,* 2014.

67 *Jesus Christ the Bearer of the Water of Life: A Christian Reflection on the New Age.* Pontifical Council for Culture, Pontifical Council for Interreligious Dialogue.

evil spirits and demons (other gods).

Even though shamans and Native Americans may believe in a "Great Spirit," it is not typically God. To most Native Americans, the "Great Spirit" is considered a being which is the source of power in the spirit realm. This "Great Spirit" is also believed to be one with spirits of nature. This is a pantheistic view (all is god). Therefore, their concept of the Great Spirit is **not a separate and distinct being.** It is not the Judeo-Christian concept of God although some people erroneously think that this particular concept of the "Great Spirit" and God are synonymous. Although some tribes believe in a Great Spirit, they also believe in other deities. There is only one, true God, so belief in other gods is incompatible with Christianity.

The one, true God is a separate and distinct being. The God of the Bible is the Trinity: Father, Son and Holy Spirit, who are three persons in one God. God the Father created all things. He sent His Son, Jesus Christ, to redeem us after Adam and Eve's sin of disobedience in the Garden of Eden. The Holy Spirit, who is the love between the Father and the Son, guides us through divine inspirations which come to us in prayer. God the Father, Son and Holy Spirit had no beginning, and they will have no end. We should pray to only the one, true God for our needs. All other created things were given to us by God for our use, but they are not divine and do not have a spirit.

During the course of writing my book on miracles, the psychic suggested that I call a Catholic priest in a Catholic mission church in Arizona to get miracle stories from his parishioners. She had known this priest for a long time. She gave me his phone number and I contacted him. He agreed to let me come and interview some of his parishioners who had miracles happen to them. Sadly, this priest was pastor of a parish where some members of his congregation, who were Native Americans, were under the influence of evil spirits and he didn't realize it. I didn't realize it either at the time, and I thought this parish would be a good source of stories for me. It certainly seemed like it was from God.

I did get some miracle stories there which were from God. However, often Satan mixes evil with good, and that's what happened in this case. The story about the shaman I was shown in the dream involved a woman who had been diagnosed by a doctor with cancer and back pain. The doctors were giving her shots, but her pain was unbearable. Finally, a relative suggested she consult a medicine woman (a shaman).

When the shaman met with the patient, she could "see" that the patient had an infection in her stomach, which was the source of her pain. She gave her some water with a yellow powder sprinkled on top of it and had her drink it. She told the patient that the infection would leave her body in four days. She then instructed the patient to bring her an abalone shell, which the shaman said she would boil with a root she knew where to find to cure her of cancer. They would do this on Sunday because it was a holy day. She also gave the patient an herb, which she instructed her to boil and add to her bath water.

The patient was healed four days later, but it was through the power of the devil. Satan used pagan and superstitious practices to bring about this healing through the shaman, who used divination and pagan herbal and naturopathic remedies. Part of this healing practice was done on the Lord's Day, which I'm sure greatly offended Him. Later, after the patient was healed, she had a surge of energy go through her. Knowing what I do now, this flow of energy was from evil spirits. New agers believe that a vital life force energy flows through the body. It is believed that illnesses are caused by this flow of energy not being in balance.

The flow of energy the patient had was probably a result of her participating in "cures" through pagan practices forbidden by God. Satan loves to dupe people, and without adequate knowledge, many people are susceptible to his wiles. I have read other accounts of energy going through bodies of individuals involved in new age and the occult. People think it is from God, but it is from demons. When I received this story, I did not understand that the cure was from evil spirits. Jesus led me through a long journey to truth. Praise the Lord! I thank Him with all my heart, and He has given me this book to help all of you.

In the "miracle" I relayed in my book, the herbal remedy came from evil spirits who conveyed the information to the shaman, who was similar to a psychic, because she looked to the spirit world for answers. Abalone shells (which were used as part of the healing) have a strong elemental bond with the Earth and its healing capabilities. Abalone shells are connected with spirits of water, and it was believed by Native Americans that they were cleansing properties. Native Americans assign a pagan spiritual power over water and other natural "elements." It is pagan because they believe that all things found in nature have a spirit. Consequently, it becomes a false god. Conversely, priests in the Catholic Church assign a spiritual blessing through prayer over natural things such as water, salt and oil, which assigns a blessing upon them from the one, true God.

Abalone shells were also used to heal anxiety, joint disorders, muscular problems, the digestive system, and more. Ironically, it was also believed that Abalone shells helped to stimulate psychic development. In this I see a connection with the psychic who persuaded me to write my book and one of the "miracles" in the book—a miracle the psychic led me to!

Just prior to receiving the message from God about the error in my book in the miracle story I've mentioned, I happened to be doing more research on Native Americans and their beliefs. Most likely, it was the Holy Spirit preparing me for the knowledge I would be given.

My Experiences with Herbal and Holistic Supplements

In this section, I am going to discuss herbal and holistic supplements and my own experiences with them. Some supplements may be morally acceptable. However, one of the problems with taking supplements is spiritual contamination. Another one is <u>indirect</u> sin, which is sin related to taking the supplements. I will give you some examples in my own life in this summary.

I began to take basic vitamin supplements when I was 30 years old. Beginning in 1993, at age 46, I increased the number of supplements, but it was still within the normal range. These supplements included a Multiple Vitamin, Vitamin C, Vitamin B Complex, Vitamin E, Calcium and Zinc. These are vitamins that help alleviate stress.

Eventually, I learned about alternative holistic and herbal supplements through some new Catholic friends and began to add them to my diet. I joined a co-op recommended to me by one of my friends. However, it was a trick of the devil. This particular health food store was comprised of shoppers who signed up and paid a yearly fee to get a discount. By signing up, the new member automatically became part owner of the store.

The co-op sold organic groceries, including a wide selection of fresh produce. It also sold fresh juices made to order at a juice bar and organic meat, chicken and seafood. God made everything "organic" but man has manipulated God's creation and created his own version of food known as "GMOs (genetically modified organisms). We do not know how safe they are. Personally, I believe God will not honor this blatant act of pride! I believe that God may be punishing us for this through health problems connected with these genetically modified foods. Cancer, for example, is becoming so widespread. Man is making himself a god by re-creating such basics as food and drink!

In addition to organic foods, the co-op also sold herbal, holistic, and homeopathic supplements and held classes that taught spiritually dangerous new age practices. Therefore, it was a sin to participate in supporting this company despite the fact that some good was incorporated with evil. When you are part owner of a company, you are partially responsible for the products sold to customers and the classes promoted to patrons. This was an <u>indirect</u> sin connected with purchasing the supplements at this co-op.

My Experience with IBS

I was diagnosed with IBS in the early 2000s. IBS (Irritable Bowel Syndrome) is common today. Doctors recommend various practical ways to help the condition; such as exercise, stress reduction, and a high fiber diet. These are good ways for all of us in general to improve our health. However, doctors also recommend various problematic solutions (in my opinion) such as psychotherapy and hypnosis. In my opinion, these solutions can be spiritually dangerous. We can enter altered states of consciousness. Other recommended solutions I see as spiritually problematic are acupuncture and biofeedback, which are new age therapies.

Many people who become frustrated with poor results turn to various herbal and holistic supplements for relief of bloating, stomach upset, headaches, abdominal discomfort, and rashes. Some of these products include evening primrose oil, borage oil, fish oil, and probiotics. In my case, I took all of these products without success. I was led to these herbal and holistic supplements through much reading on IBS in various publications. Evening primrose oil and borage oil are herbs. Fish oil is taken from the fatty tissues of fish. Probiotics are "good bacteria," and considered scientifically beneficial to our health.

The fact is that doctors do not know what causes IBS and the various alternative therapies are not very effective. Doctors diagnose IBS through a process of elimination. In today's world of advanced medicine, surely this a clue that its source may not be physical. Since I had IBS, I think it is a spiritual problem caused by personal sin. I took all of the above mentioned alternative remedies for IBS, but I only got worse.

I think there are many illnesses or disorders today that are caused by demons of infirmity (illness). For example, demons can come into your life through personal sins such as gluttony or other food disorders. They may also come into your life from taking potentized supplements. The "punishment" usually fits the crime. You may also be drinking too much soda, coffee or malts. Whatever you do to excess can cause demons of infirmity to come into your lives, especially if it continues for a long period of time.

Today, I personally avoid all holistic supplements and herbal remedies. You should also be aware that if you do use spiritually contaminated supplements, some symptoms may disappear (either permanently or temporarily), but demons are happy to produce some good results in order to get you to depend on the supplements.

My Encounter with the Spirit of Edgar Cayce

Edgar Cayce (1877-1945) is known as the "father of holistic medicine." For over 40 years, Cayce gave psychic readings to thousands of people while in an altered state of consciousness, diagnosing illnesses, and giving advice on **holistic remedies.** He was known as the "sleeping prophet." It was all from the devil. **Shouldn't this tell us something about holistic medicine?**

In his early childhood, Cayce had encounters with evil spirits. One of them advised him that if he could sleep a little, he would receive help. In his twenties, Cayce began his trance sessions advising people of holistic remedies for their illnesses with remarkable accuracy. The devil does provide cures sometimes for the express purpose of leading people to follow him instead of God. Cayce went from being a Sunday school teacher who taught God's word to a "sleeping prophet" who imparted knowledge from demons to people who relied on that information instead of turning to God for help.

God gives us all choices. In the beginning stages of his readings, Cayce actually was worried that his ability was a demonic scheme to take him away from the truths in the Bible. He shrugged this off and after a few years of doing the readings, it seems he never gave it a second thought. The devil had a grip on him. The longer we engage in a sin, the more power the devil has over us.

In addition to prescribing holistic health remedies for people who heard about his readings and came to see him, Cayce's readings expanded to include an outpouring of new age and occult beliefs. Some of these included monism, reincarnation, karma, and universal consciousness. Therefore, we know for absolute certainty that Cayce's trances were demonic because the messages Cayce received contradicted Scripture, something impossible with genuine messages from God.

Cayce also revealed people's past lives and prophecies of things to come. We know that man only lives once. (Hebrews 9:27) I personally know someone who met Edgar Cayce when he was a young man, and to this day, thinks he was instrumental in the past lives of some saints. I can't convince him otherwise. He still has ongoing demonic visions and dreams which influence him to this day from his encounter with Cayce many, many years ago. In my opinion, he needs deliverance. This is how people get duped by the devil.

I had a visit from Edgar Cayce's disembodied damned human soul one night. Cayce's spirit was much stronger than other ones I encountered, probably because of the scope of his sins. He cast a lot of negative energy on me, attempting to immobilize me. However, God helped me when I said the prayer to rebuke evil spirits. Unfortunately, it appears to me that Cayce's estimated 16,000 readings went unrepented even up until the time of his death.

One day, I bumped into a friend I had not seen for awhile at the co-op store. At the time, we were both taking holistic supplements. My friend said she was getting messages from Jesus, Mary and saints and invited me over to her home. For the next few months, we both were immersed in the facade. We got together weekly, and it became an obsession. We couldn't live without the messages. She told me what she was hearing from these spiritual beings, and I just said what I thought the Holy Spirit was telling me. We were committing a mortal sin and eventually, we both realized it and went to confession. However, it is ironic that we began these demonic sessions from a meeting in the co-op store which sold holistic health products. Edgar Cayce also combined holistic medicine and messages from evil spirits.

Dependence on Supplements

Between 1994 and 2003, I began to depend more and more on herbal, holistic and vitamin supplements. Whenever I had a symptom, I would look up what natural or herbal remedy to take for it and add it to my growing list of supplements. I had purchased a book on nutritional healing as a guide. By 2003, I was taking a total of 59 capsules a day. By 2005, I was spending $800 a month on herbal and vitamin supplements. This was a sin. I had succumbed to temptations. This was another indirect sin related to taking the supplements.

In December of 2005, Jesus told me in a dream that I was placing more emphasis on supplements than on Him. I confessed it on December 24th. Praise the Lord that He warned me. Whenever we place more emphasis on a "creature" (anything in this world) more than on God, it is a sin against the First Commandment, which calls us to love God above all else.

I discovered when I gave up holistic and herbal supplements that I actually felt better! This was probably because demons of infirmity began to leave me because it was a spiritually-based problem. Also, confession of our sins heals us, too. In addition, I gave up drinking a variety of teas that I purchased in the co-op. Some seemingly innocent drinks such as teas, may also be spiritually contaminated. I advise you to read the labels on some products, such as teas, that make a reference to or claim to have "spiritual powers." I have found teas from India with this claim on the label. Use of these products can bring physical maladies upon you just by drinking them. If you have used products like this, confess it and any demons that are bothering you should leave. If you still have some problems, I suggest prayer, fasting and penance and prayers of deliverance.

I changed my habits. Since 2005, I only take a small amount of basic vitamins and eat a healthy diet. If I get sick I pray, purchase over-the-counter medication, and go to a clinic if I need to. I have been doing very well since I gave up holistic supplements and also refrain from eating sweets and fast food. It's also good penance, something we all should do on a regular basis. I added fruits and vegetables to my diet at least five days a week and eat good quality whole grain bread and foods with lots of protein. I can't afford to eat organic foods, so I do eat GMOs (genetically modified organisms), but so far God has protected me and my health has been excellent.

Today, I often say the Our Father prayer, which includes the words: ***Thy Will Be Done…*** (Matthew 6:13 NIV). It is not God's will that we should take our health into our own hands.

Satan entices us in subtle ways to solve our own problems. One way he does this today is by tempting us to focus on alternative therapies and supplements. We can forget we should be praying to God and going to doctors of traditional medicine. God works through prayer and through doctors of traditional medicine. Satan works through diabolical new age remedies.

Today I cannot believe people are actually taking a supplement to prevent cancer even though they do not have cancer! How many supplements would we have to take to prevent every illness we could possibly get? We are all going to die of something. If we really know what is good for us we will trust in Divine Providence and use common sense.

I cancelled my membership in the co-op store, and now I trust in God. I threw out all of the holistic remedies I had in my home because God comes first in my life now. The money I spent on them did not matter. God is what matters most. I didn't want to rely on them anymore instead of God, and I didn't know if they were potentized. In addition, I didn't really know how many were actually beneficial. We have to show God that we will follow Him and that means changing our habits and showing Him we really mean it when we renounce evil and choose good.

Although I recommend going to a doctor of medicine when we are ill, be careful. Some doctors are now prescribing holistic supplements and herbal remedies. Some of these treatments may be acceptable and some may not be. Many doctors prescribe them now because their patients ask for them. I believe that the average person is unschooled in the broad range of both physical and spiritual problems that can arise from this popular healthcare trend.

Screen your doctor thoroughly before choosing one. Look at the doctor's credentials. Does the doctor prescribe or recommend any alternative therapies? Does the doctor believe in God; that is, the God in the Bible? Does your doctor believe in abortion or prescribe contraceptives? Does your doctor belong to an organization that recommends or promotes new age treatments? Basically, you want to be sure your doctor is aligning his/herself to adherence to God's commandments within his/her profession.

The spiritual dangers of herbal (and holistic remedies) may not be apparent to you, but, nevertheless, they are present. Unfortunately, there is no proven method to determine whether or not an herbal or holistic supplement is potentized. In general, I recommend that you refrain from shopping at natural food stores or health food stores which tend to carry more products I would classify as spiritually dangerous.

Eat a healthy diet so you can stay well. Eat more salads and fruit. Limit sweets or give them up entirely and you will feel better. I certainly do! Herbs and supplements should not be thought of as a substitute for healthy eating. Besides the spiritual problems that may be connected with these products, the benefits of the nutrients you get through foods in your diet are not necessarily reproducible in a supplement. Try to exercise daily. I walk on my treadmill almost every day for a half hour while saying two rosaries. The rosary is a powerful protection against evil because it's based on Scripture. I feel great after I do this. I highly recommend staying close to God in prayer. If you can't use a treadmill, walk. Most people can walk and it's great exercise. You can also walk and pray at the same time! In addition, be sure to obey the commandments and lead a Godly life.

Energy Therapies

Holistic health practitioners believe that divine energy flows through the body. This divine energy is sometimes referred to as "chi," "qi," "ki," or "prana," and is considered to be a universal energy permeating all things. It is believed that two universal energies called yin and yang must be kept in balance for optimum health. The concept of yin and yang, which represent the two opposite principles in nature, comes from Taoism/Daoism, a Chinese religion and philosophy. Yin characterizes the feminine or negative nature of things and yang characterizes the masculine or positive side.

Practitioners believe that this invisible divine energy flows along 14 main pathways called meridians which are connected to an organ system. It is believed that when yin and yang are in harmony, the flow of chi is unobstructed, so the person is in good health. However, when yin and yang are not in harmony, it is believed that the person becomes ill. Therefore, new age practitioners believe that freeing the person from an imbalance of the universal life force energy will heal the person.

The meridian theory is tied to the Chinese doctrine of the early elements of fire, earth, metal, water and wood and each element is tied into a part of the body. Thus we see new age beliefs at work here: 1) the belief in a divine cosmic energy 2) a connection with earth spirituality with the incorporation of earthly elements. These spiritual beliefs are pagan. The concept of divine energy is not based on medical or scientific studies.

Alternative holistic therapies today come from ancient pagan practices where god is an impersonal life force energy. The basic premise in holistic medicine; namely, that all of us are divine and have healing powers, is immoral. All healing comes from God. Holistic health places the emphasis on ourselves. It is one reason why these remedies are forbidden.

In errant new age reasoning, people believe that for every physical, emotional, psychological or spiritual problem, there is an alternative practice or supplement to help them. We just have to figure out which one to use. In holistic health, this means treating the "whole" person. The remedies and alternative therapies are typically new age practices which can lead to further spiritual problems as well. For example, someone with a problem with anxiety may use spiritually dangerous alternative therapies like TM Meditation that may can cause other physical, psychological, emotional or spiritual problems. It is just one way that the devil is ensnaring souls. Use of holistic health remedies and practices can also bring evil spirits into your life.

On the other hand, Christians believe that God is our Sovereign Lord (Father, Son and Holy Spirit). God is not a universal life force. He does heal, at times miraculously, but through prayer. He can also lead us to orthodox medicines and to doctors to help us with our physical health problems. He is a personal God who answers our prayers and has a plan for all of our lives. We will go to Heaven if we obey His commandments. Following the deceptions of the devil may lead us to Hell.

Using new age therapies and practices can cause spiritual sickness because it leads you into sin which affects your relationship with God. Demons can also come into your lives. They may not openly manifest themselves at first, but if you continue to use these products for a long period of time, you may suffer from oppression. Most people cannot see or hear demons, but that does not mean they are not with them. We all have demons around us daily tempting us in the unseen spiritual side of life.

Some Common Energy Therapies

There are various new age practices that are based on balancing universal life force energy. However, the way they are executed varies from practice to practice. Sometimes parts of these practices are morally acceptable to use. Before you agree to any practice, you really should investigate both how the practice is executed and the belief system behind it. In other words, you will need to determine which parts are morally acceptable to use. Here are some examples.

Acupuncture

Acupuncture is used to treat pain, headaches, ulcers, food allergies, depression, weight loss, arthritis, anxiety, stress, bronchitis, and more. Many practitioners believe that the problems they are treating are caused by an imbalance in the universal life force energy in the body. To correct the imbalance, they insert needles at specific points in the skin along the lines of the meridians, which are considered pathways of energy. This is a new age belief. It is an ancient practice that goes back many years. In fact, *Swiss physician and psychiatric consultant, Dr. Samuel Pfeifer, suggests treating diseases with needles "goes back to the earliest doctors, probably spiritistic shamans. They performed rituals similar to those found in today's Voodoo-cults that attempt to expel evil spirits by sticking needles into the body..."*[68]

An excellent article in 2011 by Susan Brinkmann, provides information on a study of acupuncture by the Oxford-based Cochrane Collaboration. The Cochrane Collaboration is an independent, non-profit, non-governmental organization which was formed to organize medical research information in a systematic way. It is based on random, controlled trials and medical research studies. The purpose is to help people in the healthcare profession, policy makers, and patients make educated choices on health-care related options based on evidenced-based

68 Pfeifer, Samuel, *Healing at Any Price?* Milton Keynes, England: Work (UK) Ltd. (English Edition) 1980, 28 as written by Walker, James, *Watchman Fellowship Profile*, Acupuncture. http://www.watchman.org/profiles/pdf/acupunctureprofile.pdf, 1994.

medicine.

The Cochrane Collaboration's report on acupuncture, states that they *found no evidence that this treatment works for anything but some types of pain and nausea—and even these are not considered to be very strong conclusions...The results were disappointing for acupuncturists. The tests found no convincing evidence that real acupuncture is more effective than a placebo in the treatment of chronic tension headaches, nausea after chemotherapy, and migraine prevention.*[69]

According to Susan Brinkman, she personally spoke with a former acupuncturist who practiced the Traditional Chinese Medicine form of acupuncture. Brinkmann learned that the procedure is routinely used to rid the body of evil spirits similar to the Catholic Church's rite of exorcism. The acupuncturist wears special clothing during the procedures to avoid contamination and opens a window or door to let the evil spirits out of the room! Brinkman warns: *A person needs to be very informed about the acupuncturist who is working on them to be sure they are needling for physical health and not attempting to treat what they perceive to be "spiritual" imbalances.*[70]

There may be instances when it is acceptable to use this practice. According to Watchman Fellowship's Profile on Acupuncture, *Symptomatic Acupuncture, also called First Aid Acupuncture, has been used to treat pain and discomfort associated with injury or disease. The treatment is usually temporary and is not intended to cure the disorder itself.*[71] <u>Maybe</u> this is acceptable, but be careful. Acupuncture should always be avoided if it is connected with a manipulation of energy or if the practitioner supports Taoist dualism or the Chinese version of this therapy.

When I went online to see what people were saying about acupuncture I found scientific studies which concluded it didn't work. I also found people who claimed that it was effective. The real question we need to ask is: ***Is the manner of treatment and the belief system of the practitioner in line with morality?***

---

69 SBrinkmann, *Acupuncture Remains Scientifically Unconvincing*, http://womenofgrace.com/newage/?p=463, 2011.
70 *Ibid.*
71 Watchman Fellowship Profile, *Acupuncture*, http://www.watchman.org/profiles/pdf/acupunctureprofile.pdf.

Acupuncture is controversial because if you cannot discern whether or not the practice is morally acceptable, do you want to risk the consequences of using this type of treatment? When it comes to morality, I can tell you the devil will do good in order to achieve his goal of drawing us away from God. I am not personally comfortable with using acupuncture as a remedy for any problem.

People who are terminally ill and the families of loved ones who are going into hospice care need to be careful because acupuncture is now being used on dying people. I personally do not recommend it, especially in someone's final hours on earth when their eternal reward is close at hand. I believe that acupuncture and other alternative therapies may bring demons into dying people's lives at a time when they need to be close to God.

For example, someone told me recently that when a dying person had acupuncture, he mentioned that he was shown a "spiritual path" to take. This sounds like new age to me, and my discernment is that it was the wrong spiritual path. The reference to spiritual paths is commonly used in new age language. You do not want your loved one to be deceived at the moment of death. At the time of death, demons and angels are working in an unseen battle between good and evil, each vying for that soul. It is Satan's last attempt to get that person into Hell.

In addition, let's not forget the value of suffering. Suffering may be taking time off that person's Purgatory. However, it is not immoral to use standard "comfort measures" approved by the Catholic Church for those of you who are Catholic and reading this. These usually include low doses of morphine.

It is better to pray for the dying person (especially the Rosary and Divine Mercy Chaplet), read the Bible out loud, and play religious music. People who are dying can still hear until the end of their lives. Also, be sure to use sacramentals, *i.e.* holy water, blessed salt, and holy oil, which keep evil spirits at bay. If possible, attach a blessed St. Benedict medal to the person's clothing or pillow, as this can be a powerful source of protection from evil. However, the most important thing is to make sure that if the dying person is Catholic that he/she receives the Last Rites, which should include the Sacraments of Reconciliation and the Eucharist (if this is possible) and the Anointing of the Sick with the Apostolic Pardon.

Chiropractic Care

Chiropractic care is an alternative healing therapy involving manipulation of the spine. According to the Christian Medical Fellowship (CMF), an organization formed in 1949 which disseminates information to Christian UK doctors and medical students, *the majority of consultations from patients seeking chiropractic care are for musculo-skeletal problems, particularly of the back, neck, and shoulder.*[72]

Chiropractic care was started by David Palmer (1845-1913), a Canadian grocer and a student of AT Still, the founder of osteopathy. According to an article on Susan Brinkmann's New Age Blog, *It is widely believed that Palmer invented chiropractics on September 1895 when he adjusted a bump on the spine of a deaf janitor and restored his hearing. This led to his conclusion that misaligned bones (known as "subluxations") interfered with the body's expression of Innate Intelligence, a kind of universal energy or life force. The concept of Innate Intelligence came from another popular healing technique of his day known as magnetism (a/k/a animal magnetism), which was a revival of an ancient idea that the planets exude invisible rays of energy that affect our bodies. Palmer believed Innate Intelligence was comprised of this and other spiritual forces.*[73] Unfortunately, Palmer's son, Bartlet Joshua, who also believed in this type of chiropractic care, was involved in the occult and encouraged the idea that he was a Christ figure. His friends included Freemasons and members of the Illuminati. Thus, we see chiropractic care has occult roots.

In the concept of Innate Intelligence, God becomes a universal energy or life force. Healing is based on this energy. This is against the First Commandment in which we are called to love God before all else. That is why this type of chiropractic care and universal energy are on the list of new age practices in the Vatican document *Jesus Christ, the Bearer of the Water of Life: A Christian*

72 Christian Medical Fellowship (CMF) *Chiropractic*, 6 Marshalsea Road, London SE1 1HL. http://cmf.coruk/publications/content.

73 Brinkmann, S, *Chiropractics*, posted on the New Age Blog, June 8, 2010, at http://www.womenof grace.com/blog/.

Reflection on the New Age.[74]

At one time I had back pain and went to a chiropractor. The spinal manipulations were extremely painful. The practitioner said that I would probably need treatments the rest of my life. We began with one or two days a week. However, after every treatment, I was in constant pain. After a few weeks, I discontinued treatments, and I have not had a problem since then. That was about 15 years ago. Perhaps it was a spiritual problem caused by demons of infirmity because at the time I was actively involved in new age and the occult.

According to CMF, *consistency and reliability of specific chiropractic diagnostic methods and a credible and verifiable scientific basis have not been shown, and in controlled trials results are inconsistent for back pain and not demonstrable for other disease.*[75] CMF states that both minor and serious complications can result from chiropractic care, including stroke, spinal injury, thrombosis and joint dislocations. Although these are results from the late 1990s, I believe they are still true today.

From a spiritual standpoint, I can tell you that any practice based on new age or the occult should be avoided. Christians need to use discernment. CMF agrees. *Contact or involvement with dubious alternative therapies or New Age practices may lead to spiritual ill health, manifested as anxiety, depression, fear, lack of Christian assurance or interference with prayer life and Bible reading.* Who wouldn't want us to pray or read the Bible? Satan, of course!

On the other hand, some of today's chiropractors now use conventional physical therapy instead of Innate Intelligence's energy-based practices. Conventional methods include corrective exercises, ice packs, bracing, bed rest, moist heat and massage. As I mentioned earlier, it would not be sinful to go to a chiropractor for this type of help. However, I would still be cautious in choosing who works on you. Screen the chiropractor to see what his actual beliefs are.

---

74 *Jesus Christ the Bearer of the Water of Life: A Christian Reflection on the New Age.* www.vatican.va/.../pontifical_councils/interelg/documents/rc_pc_interelg_doc_20030203_new-age_en.html - 216k - 2003-02-20

75 Christian Medical Fellowship (CMF) *Chiropractic,* 6 Marshalsea Road, London, SE1 1HL, http://www.cmf.org.uk/publications/content.asp?context=article&id=1554.

Kinesiology

In 2004, someone I had met during the course of my job as a caregiver had recommended a practitioner who could diagnose a person's deficiencies in nutrition and make recommendations on what supplements to take to help improve one's health. Since I was having health problems and taking supplements, I made an appointment with the woman, who was a Catholic in my diocese.

To begin with, the practitioner took pictures of me with an ordinary camera. Then she put them into a machine. According to the practitioner, the machine would then record what nutritional deficiencies I had and make recommendations on what supplements I should add or discontinue. It did this in the form of a printout. I asked the practitioner how it worked. She said it was based on energy. I thought that it was strange. After the diagnosis, the practitioner would sell her clients the recommended supplements. I purchased some recommended supplements and left.

After I left and pondered what had occurred during my visit with this woman, I did not have a good feeling about what had taken place. This was the Holy Spirit. I began to do some research to find out more about the practice that the woman had used. It was not easy to get to the bottom of it. I emailed people who knew about new age because I suspected the practice was new age because of the energy part of the process. Most of them could not help me. However, one person finally had some valuable insight. Claire McGrath Merkle, a former yoga instructor who discovered she was teaching a new age practice, thought that it was a derivative of Applied Kinesiology. I did more research on Kinesiology, and I am convinced she was correct.

Applied kinesiology claims to induce proper structural and chemical-nutritional organization in the body, as well as left-and-right-brain hemisphere balance. It claims to evaluate and correct problems of the nervous, circulatory, lymphatic, skeletal-musculature, and meridian systems, thereby maintaining health. Its practices are believed to permit the even flow of cosmic energy throughout the body, thus nurturing individual organs and systems with the proper supply of chi energy.[76]

76 New Age Medicine, http://www.rapidnet.com/~jbeard/bdm/Psychology/newmed.htm.

There are many derivatives of Kinesiology. I believe that the practice used in my encounter with the holistic practitioner who diagnosed my vitamin deficiencies was a derivative of Kinesiology. The concept is clear because the woman used a form of energy (using her own words) to identify the supposed problem of an imbalance in the body. She then made suggestions based on what the machine transmitted to her on how to improve my health. In this case, the machine she used was an instrument of the devil.

I contacted the practitioner I met with after doing research on her method of diagnosing people's problems and told her I felt she was engaging in new age energy work. I suggested that she abandon the practice. However, she didn't listen and went on to take a course in spiritual direction and is now teaching courses (all of which are new age) in a Catholic retreat center in the Milwaukee area. Be careful if you take any courses because most of them have new age in them today. New age practices are not only taught at retreat centers and in spiritual direction, but at parishes, schools, conferences, medical centers, health food stores, and hospitals, to name a few.

Healing (Therapeutic) Touch—Another Energy Therapy

Back in 1994, the psychic I met suggested that I read the book, *Hands of Light: A Guide to Healing Through the Human Energy Field,* by Dr. Barbara Brennan. I purchased the book, but I never read it. However, I did meet people who spoke about it in the course of my journey. Barbara Brennan is a licensed massage therapist, healer, and scientist who has devoted many years of study to the concept of healing energy fields in the human person. Treating the "whole" person is central to her beliefs. Her studies include the areas of philosophy, atmospheric physics, bioenergetics and core energetic work.

Barbara founded the organization Healing Touch International (HTI) in the 1980's, but I found another person online who claimed she was the originator of the idea of the healing touch curriculum.[77] Isn't this just like Satan to duplicate or cause confusion, even within similar ideologies? According to the current BBSH website, in 1982 Brennan founded the Barbara Brennan School of Healing in the U.S. In 2003, she established Barbara Brennan International, Inc., which operates the Barbara Brennan School of Healing Europe.[78]

Brennan became well known for an alternative healing practice called "Healing Touch," a/k/a "Therapeutic Touch." This practice was explained in detail in her book *Hands of Light: A Guide to Healing Through the Human Energy Field.* The method is used to heal people with physical, mental and emotional problems. However, it is considered to be a new age practice by Catholics and other Christians.

Healing Touch is a term that is misleading because in reality practitioners do not actually touch the person. Practitioners believe that a spiritual energy field surrounds the patient and that it can be manipulated to facilitate healing. When administering Healing Touch, the practitioners hold their hands a certain distance from the person's body. As they move around the person's body, they use their hands to remove "bad energy," which they replace with "healing energy." This is an occult technique and similar to that used by witches and psychics.

I remember the psychic who did readings for me once said she would get rid of evil spirits in a house of a friend of mine. We went to my friend's home along with another companion. The psychic went around the house holding her hands at a short distance from the walls and furniture while making sweeping motions of taking bad energy out of the home. It was demonic.

Unfortunately, Brennan received the concept of Healing Touch through a channeled communication with a spirit guide. Moira Noonan, who I met at a conference I attended years ago, writes in her own memoir: *As Brennan herself admits, her ideas are drawn from direct communication with a spirit guide named Heyoan. Her channelings from this entity are regularly published word for word by her institute and offered to the world as expressions of divine*

77 (see. http://www.healingtouch.net/hti.html).

78 BBSH, Barbara Brennan School of Healing, http://barbarabrennan.com.

wisdom.[79] Of course, this alone makes Brennan's book and practice spiritually dangerous. The practice of Healing Touch is based on energy therapy and a channeled evil spirit entity, not on God. It is not in line with Christianity.

There are many new age and occult books available today in bookstores all over the country and also online. Many of them are on new age healing practices such as this one. In the Bible, we read: ***Also many of those who were now believers came, confessing and divulging their practices. And a number of those who had practiced magic arts brought their books together and burned them in the sight of all. And they counted the value of them and found it came to fifty thousand pieces of silver. So the word of the Lord continued to increase and prevail mightily.*** (Acts 19:18-20 ESV). If you have a new age or occult book in your home, burn it. Evil spirits come into your homes and into your lives with these kinds of books.

In my story, you will learn about some of the consequences I had for having new age and occult books in my home. Burn any material connected with new age and the occult, including books, magazines, clothing, etc., and get rid of any toys or games or other occult and new age materials you may have around your house. Then sprinkle your home with blessed salt and holy water rebuking any evil spirits of the new age and the occult and ask Jesus to cover your home with his Most Precious Blood.

Conclusion

I believe that all new age alternative therapies and remedies are spiritually dangerous. Pray to the Holy Spirit for guidance. We are called to prudently take care of our bodies, but we need to do this without sinning.

In addition to the spiritual dangers of alternative therapies, there is also little evidence to prove they are beneficial. Be cautious! We live in evil times where Satan is trying his best to tempt us through a revival of new age paganism. If you participate in one spiritually dangerous new age practice, the devil will lead you

79 Noonan, Moira, *Ransomed From Darkness: The New Age, Christian Faith and the Battle for Souls,* North Bay Books, El Sobrante, CA 94820, 2005.

to another and another. Don't wait until you have participated in or used many sinful new age practices and find demons are in your life. That is what happened to me and others I have met. Close that door through avoidance of all new age therapies and practices, prayers of deliverance, acts of reparation and knowledge. Demons of new age are strong. They will convince you that you can engage in these practices without any problems. It is simply not true! It is a sin of pride. You may not be aware that demons are in your life because they try to remain hidden, but we all have demons around us tempting us daily. Be prudent and stick to traditional medicine with a proven track record, cultivate healthy habits, and pray.

Chapter Nine

Catholic Charismatic Prayer Services

Before Jesus ascended into Heaven, He told the apostles that He would send the Holy Spirit to them. Two weeks later, while they were all together, a great wind began to blow in the house where they were staying. All of them saw tongues of fire above each of their heads. They began to speak in languages they did not know, which was the original gift of speaking in tongues. This outpouring of the Holy Spirit enabled them to begin the work of evangelization. They went out among the many Jews who had gathered to celebrate Pentecost (which was the Jewish feast to celebrate the first fruits of the wheat harvest.) There were about 3,000 Jews who spoke many different dialects, but the apostles were able to speak to them in their own language. When these Jews went back to their own regions, each of them shared the Christian faith with others. This was the birth of the Catholic Church.

In 1962 at the time of the Second Vatican Council, Pope Saint John XXIII led the Catholic Church in praying for a new outpouring of the Holy Spirit. In 1967, some Catholic students from Duquesne University gathered on retreat in Pittsburgh, PA. One of them, Patti Gallagher Mansfield, describes what happened during The Duquesne Weekend, in an online report. According to Mansfield, the students attended a Pentecostal prayer meeting where they encountered the Holy Spirit. Later, they prayed for the grace of complete surrender and an outpouring of the Holy Spirit. They sang the *Veni Creator Spiritus* (Come, Holy Spirit) song. This led to an encounter with the Holy Spirit that deeply stirred them from within. They received the "Baptism of the Holy Spirit," in which they received a new depth of prayer and a strong desire to evangelize. Since her encounter with the Holy Spirit, Patti exclaims that she wants *to proclaim that, "God who is mighty has done great things for us, and holy is His name!"*[80]

After reading Patti's description of the events that occurred during the memorable *Duquesne Weekend,* my only concern was her statement that she and some other people "felt a burning sensation coursing through their hands."[81] What was this burning sensation? Was it energy? Was it from the Holy Spirit? If it was, it is certainly unusual.

In any event, the *Duquesne Weekend* led to the beginning of the Catholic Charismatic Renewal and prayer services that spread across the country within the Catholic Church. Many people who received the "Baptism of the Holy Spirit," at these prayer services felt called to live a life of holiness and conversion with a new emphasis on Scripture, a deeper prayer life, a passion for evangelization, and devotion to the Eucharist.

There was a concern by the Holy See in subsequent years that some Protestantism may be present in the new Charismatic Renewal Movement due to its Pentecostal beginnings. However, in 1993, the Catholic Charismatic Renewal received Pontifical recognition as a private association of the faithful because it seemed to be bearing good fruit. The official organization is called ICCRS: International Catholic Charismatic Renewal Services. According to ICCRS, *the Catholic Charismatic Renewal is currently present in more than 200 countries and has touched the lives of over 120,000,000 Catholics.*[82]

Participants in Catholic Charismatic Services pray in tongues, speak in tongues and sing in tongues. People receive natural and spiritual gifts, called charisms, which are special graces given to people in order to build up the Body of Christ. St. Paul explains the meaning of charisms: ***Now there are varieties of gifts, but the same Spirit; and there are varieties of service, but the same Lord; and there are varieties of activities, but it is the same God who empowers them all in everyone. To each is given the manifestation of the Spirit for the common good. For to one is given through the Spirit the utterance of wisdom, and to***

80 Mansfield, Patti Gallagher, *The Duquesne Weekend,* http://www.ccr.org.uk/duquesne.htm.

81 *Ibid.*

82 ICCRS, *What is the Catholic Charismatic Renewal,* http://www.iccrs.org/ccr.php.

another the utterance of knowledge according to the same Spirit, to another faith by the same Spirit, to another gifts of healing by the one Spirit, to another the working of miracles, to another prophecy, to another the ability to distinguish between spirits, to another various kinds of tongues, to another the interpretation of tongues. All these are empowered by one and the same Spirit, who apportions to each one individually as he wills. (1 Corinthians 12: 4-11)

Charisms during Charismatic Services include messages given to the faithful through the power of the Holy Spirit for them personally or for the whole assembly. However, these messages still require discernment. People need to test the spirits. The apostle John says: ***Beloved, do not believe every spirit, but test the spirits to see whether they are from God, for many false prophets have gone out into the world. By this you know the Spirit of God: every spirit that confesses that Jesus Christ has come in the flesh is from God, and every spirit that does not confess Jesus is not from God.*** (1 John 4:1-3)

One important test that the messages come from the Holy Spirit, not the evil spirit or the human spirit, is that the messages are not contrary to the Commandments. Authentic charisms will not lead Catholics away from the Catholic Church or its teachings or from the practice of the Catholic faith (morally, devotionally or sacramentally). Authentic messages will build up the Body of Christ and cause people to become closer to God.

The Catholic Charismatic Renewal could be beneficial to Catholics, in my opinion, with proper discernment. The Holy Spirit should be a part of our lives, and praying and supporting one another is important. ***And let us consider how we may spur one another on toward love and good deeds, not giving up meeting together, as some are in the habit of doing, but encouraging one another—and all the more as you see the Day approaching.*** (Hebrews 10:24-25).

The Holy Spirit is very active in these times. This chapter is not meant to downplay or detract from the important role of the Holy Spirit or this movement within the Catholic Church or in other denominations. However, because the focus of this book is on my experiences with demons and to show you how demons operate, I am going to present to you some problems I had with the Charismatic Services I attended because our adversary, the devil, tries to contaminate every work of God.

My Experiences in the Catholic Charismatic Renewal Movement

Over a period of years, I attended a few Catholic Charismatic Prayer Groups and Services. When I was writing the book on miracles, I went to one or two Charismatic Prayer Groups in California where I interviewed some people who had miracle stories for my book. People received "words of knowledge" and would just state what they supposedly "heard." I didn't understand it. They told me that the messages would just come to them through a divine inspiration or a locution. Supposedly, it was the power of the Holy Spirit. I wondered how they knew the messages were from the Holy Spirit.

I began to attend a Charismatic Renewal Prayer Service in my own diocese after I had written the book on miracles. I went about a dozen times. The priest had Mass and after Mass people would line up around the altar and get the priest's blessing with holy oil. Many people were "slain in the spirit," also referred to as "resting in the spirit." They would just fall backwards and lie still for several minutes. There were "catchers" to help guide them down gently so they would not hurt themselves. The phenomenon of being "slain in the spirit" is common in Charismatic Prayer Services. Although most of the participants would be "slain in the spirit," it never happened to me.

After the blessing, people would gather in a separate room for prayer. People would receive "words of knowledge," and shout out the message they were receiving, supposedly from the Holy Spirit. Later some regular members of the group would pray with each person individually in tongues and give them a personal message. (I do not know if this is done in all Charismatic Prayer Groups). I stopped going to these prayer services because I became uncomfortable with them.

Problems with Charismatic Renewal Prayer Services

I. What is the Source of Words of Knowledge Given to Group Leaders and Participants?

Words of knowledge (messages) can come from three different sources: the Holy Spirit, evil spirits or the human spirit (ourselves). In a personal conversation in 2014 with Fr. John Hampsch, C.M.F., the founder of the Claretian Teaching Ministry, who has been very active in the Charismatic Renewal Movement since 1970, he stated that, from his many years of experience attending Catholic Charismatic Renewal Services, in his opinion, about 92% of the messages received by attendees of these services are from the human spirit. I would definitely say this is not very supportive evidence that the Holy Spirit is actually working during these services. Fr. Hampsch stated that the messages often are associated with spiritual pride. I urge everyone attending these services to be aware of this. The devil always wants to interfere with anything that will lead people to a better relationship with God.

I hear demons talk all day and night. I can't help but hear some of what they say, but I dismiss it even though at times it's the truth. They tell the truth sometimes to entice me to listen to them. But I'd rather listen to the voice of the Holy Spirit—that still, small voice that gives us interior promptings, but must always be discerned.

After I had stopped attending my local Catholic Charismatic Prayer Service, a regular member of the same Charismatic Group invited me to come again. I decided to go back. On the way there, I got lost even though I was familiar with the area and had gone to this prayer group before. I began to wonder if I was supposed to go, and later I knew that the Holy Spirit was trying to warn me *not* to go. Often the Holy Spirit gently nudges us in the right direction by a simple thought or inclination. I continued on even though I arrived an hour late.

I arrived just in time to hear the guest speaker, who was in the upper echelons of the Charismatic Renewal Movement in the U.S. During his talk, he said very frankly that the messages he gets for others are not always accurate. He said that once he had a message that the person he was advising was in a bad marriage, but it turned out the person was not even married. I was extremely uneasy during this talk. When evil spirits are present, I often feel negativity, and this was the case this particular night. I felt the Holy Spirit wanted me to leave, but dismissed the thought and forced myself to stick it out.

The statement made by the guest speaker that night shows how much discernment is needed at Charismatic Services. If a leader in the Charismatic Renewal Movement can get a false message, what does that mean for the rest of us? It tells me that a participant can get a message that is bogus, which does not add to the authenticity of the experience. Many people could be harmed by a mistaken "word of knowledge."

Someone prayed over me and I received a message, but it was generic. I felt evil spirits there during the entire night. The next day I went to confession and confessed going to this prayer group and participating in the service. *Then I had peace.* Why did this happen?

First of all, the Holy Spirit was clearly trying to warn me not to go to this particular Charismatic Service that night. I disregarded the promptings of the Holy Spirit and went against His counsel. There were evil spirits present in that group that particular night. I think some of them may have attached themselves to me because I had the sense that demons were with me after I left that night.

Here are the types of demons I believe may have been present that night: 1) Demons of Deception and Confusion. These evil spirits can cause some people to get messages from the wrong source (the evil spirit or the human spirit). 2) Demons of Pride. These are demons who motivate some people to deliberately give messages to the assembly that are not from the Holy Spirit, but come from evil spirits of pride. 3) Demons of Obsession. These demons prey on those who are obsessed with either giving or receiving personal messages at these services and cannot live without them. This could become a serious sin against the First Commandment. 4) Demons of Praying or Speaking in Tongues.

These are demons who pray or speak in "tongues" through people when no one is interpreting. 5) Demons of Subversion. Satan can send infiltrators into prayer groups such as these to undermine the faith, morals and any good that the group is accomplishing. That night there were several people there from other religions and one or more of them could have been an infiltrator sent by Satan. However, people claiming to be Catholics but who are actually working for Satan can also infiltrate prayer groups. They may also place curses on the group.

Confession can release people from evil spirits. This sacrament is so powerful and that is why I recommend it often, even more than once a week for those who are actively having experiences with evil spirits. When I went to confession, the evil spirits who came into my life from attending that prayer service left and I had peace in my soul.

When people get "words of knowledge" at these prayer groups, red flags go up for me. I question whether their words are actually from the Holy Spirit, the evil spirit, or the human spirit. The question is: *How can we discern which spirit people are hearing from?* Fr. Hampsch suggests that the group pray for discernment of spirits at the beginning of the service. He states that people are not being taught how to use charisms or to test the spirits.

Fr. Hampsch suggests that in the case of words of knowledge for the entire assembly, the entire assembly should discern the message. He states that it is not common to have an authentic message for the entire community, but when it is authentic, it is the most reliable of messages. For example, he said that after someone gave a message to the entire community where he was in attendance, it affected everyone profoundly. They all were moved by the message and responded by praising God. The message had a deep impact on everyone. As a guideline, he said that all authentic messages will build up the faith of the community.

In addition, I believe that no one should speak unless the assembly has first rebuked any evil spirits trying to interfere with authentic messages. This can be done by prayer and using blessed salt, holy oil and/or holy water. While using it say: *Dear Jesus, please rebuke, bind and command to leave for all of us in this group any and all evils spirits of pride, confusion, discord, lies, false peace, demonic messages, deceptions by evil spirits, inordinate attachments, envy, obsessions, contamination of the group, and any and all other evil spirits that may be present during this prayer service. Jesus, command that these and all evil spirits leave in Your Precious Name and Cover us with Your Most Precious Blood.* This sample rebuke prayer is just a general guideline and you can name other evil spirits if you wish or change any I have mentioned.

II.
How Do We Know When Speaking In Tongues Is Authentic?

People sometimes speak or pray in tongues at Charismatic Renewal Prayer Services. Quite often, when people speak or pray in tongues, no one is interpreting. It says in the Bible there is a gift of interpretation of tongues. How can these services exist without this essential gift of the Holy Spirit? I think it is dangerous for people to speak or pray in tongues without someone there with the gift of interpretation. The Apostle Paul taught: ***If there is no one to interpret, there should be silence in the assembly, each one speaking only to himself and to God.*** (1 Corinthians 14:28)

Tongues are either interpreted collectively to build up the Body of Christ or are spoken privately for individuals as praise to God. There are many gifts of the Holy Spirit, but the gift of tongues is the only one which places the emphasis on *self-edification.* Therefore, people need to be cautious so demons of pride do not mislead them.

Speaking from experience, I once started to speak in a foreign language that I did not know while I was at home. Looking back on this experience, I believe it was demonic. At the time, the devil was bothering me both day and night, and I had written the book on miracles through demonic influence from the psychic. I actually awoke one night speaking in an unknown tongue, and of course, I thought it was the Holy Spirit at the time, but I do not believe that it was. When I prayed about it and dismissed it, it did not reoccur.

The Enemy Infiltrates A Prayer Group: A True Story

A friend of mine had an enlightening experience with her prayer group which I would like to share with you. My friend is a devout Catholic who readily defends the Catholic faith and stands up for orthodoxy in her parish.

Olivia (not her real name), who belongs to a Rosary Prayer Group, had a stranger join one day. From the very beginning, the stranger was disruptive. She would interrupt prayers and ask if she could pray over people. Then she would go from person to person, praying in tongues. Olivia began to have grave misgivings about this stranger. This was the Holy Spirit trying to warn her that something was wrong. After the stranger had come for a few weeks, Olivia was looking through the prayer intention book. The group would typically pray for all of the intentions that members of the group had written in the book. In the middle of the book, Olivia came upon this sentence: *Satan is our leader.* Olivia knew then that her inspirations from the Holy Spirit were accurate. This stranger was working for Satan and had come to contaminate the group.

While driving home, Olivia saw a bumper sticker with the words, *Pray or become Prey.* She then had a locution, "Be salt and light towards her." This meant to her not to let the group become contaminated (because salt loses its flavor when mixed with other chemical substances; in other words, it is no longer pure.) Light meant that Olivia had to stand up for the truth, the gospel of Jesus. Shortly afterwards, Olivia asked this stranger to leave the group. She believes a curse was put on the group while the person "prayed in tongues." To break it, she said prayers and fasted. Fortunately, Olivia knew about spiritual warfare and what to do in this situation.

III.
Is "Resting in the Spirit" (a/k/a "Slain in the Spirit") Always From God?

According to Fr. John Hampsch, C.M.F. an authentic gift of being slain in the spirit can be a life-changing experience. He states that the person will have a profound sense of peace in his/her soul. Jesus says: ***Peace I leave with you; my peace I give you. I do not give to you as the world gives. Do not let your hearts be troubled and do not be afraid.*** (John 14:27 NIV). He has seen authentic instances of this gift where there were major conversions and children who came back to the Catholic Church. These are called "good fruits" of the Holy Spirit.

Unfortunately, there are also inauthentic instances of being slain in the spirit. Keep in mind that any phenomenon can be caused by God, by Satan, or from our human spirit (ourselves).

Satan and demons can also come to Charismatic Renewal Prayer Services, and I believe that they may even cause some people to be slain in the spirit. One night the evil spirits gave me a feeling of false peace. They called it "resting in the spirit," which is the term for Christians being "slain in the spirit." I think God allowed this experience because He wanted it included in this book. It's certainly not something I would ever think of. Jesus wants us to exercise caution. We assume too much and do not test the spirits. Here is a true story about someone slain in the spirit who was under demonic influence.

Dr. Kurt E. Koch wrote an account of a case of possession he experienced in his ministry.[83] (There is another Kurt Koch who is a Bishop, so be sure not to confuse him with this writer.) Dr. Kurt E. Koch, (1913-1987) received his Doctor of Theology degree from Tubingen University and was a noted German theologian, minister, and evangelist. He pastored and counseled those suffering from the occult in its various forms throughout the world, covering sixty-five countries and five continents.

Dr. Koch tells us the true story about a Christian named Mark who was "slain in the spirit." He fell over as people do

83 Koch, Kurt E., *Occult ABC, Charismatic Movement and Demon Possession,* Kregel Publications, 1978.

when they are "slain" and when he got up he was praising Jesus. While attending a Pentecostal church, Mark also received a gift of tongues. The name of the spirit of the tongue was Domenigaio. Some time later, this spirit, Domenigaio, was cast out of Mark. It was an evil spirit. During the exorcism, the demon said he entered the man when he was slain in the spirit. The evil spirit acknowledged that he was posing as the Holy Spirit.

Another demon named "Jesus" was also inside Mark. When Dr. Koch asked the demon named Jesus, "What Jesus?" the demon answered, "Jesus of the devil," and said that he had entered Mark when he was slain in the spirit. This demon was also cast out in the name of Jesus Christ.

Now, while this story may sound preposterous to you, it doesn't to me. You see, I have evil spirits with me who have claimed to be Jesus and the Holy Spirit. They know that I am aware they are evil spirits now, so they no longer pretend to be Jesus and the Holy Spirit because I am with the Lord despite my present state. But sometimes they pretend to be God the Father and use a very loud, condemning and sometimes lengthy ruse to get me to feel guilty about something. I just pray to St. Michael the Archangel. Also, in the Bible, it is interesting that the notorious criminal Jesus Barabbas was released by Pilate because the crowd wanted Jesus Christ to be condemned to death. Their first names were both Jesus according to some translations of the Bible (NET, NRSV, and NKJV). One was evil and the other good.

The phenomenon of being "slain in the spirit" must be examined. Sometimes, when people "fall over," they seem to go into an altered state of consciousness. Rev. Bob Liichow of Discernment Ministries International, frankly states that he has fallen several times during this phenomenon, however, it was due to a mysterious power that he succumbed to. He describes this power similar to electricity that flowed through his body. This sounds like the work of the devil. A flow of electricity through someone's body is a common new age energy symptom.

Certainly some of the reasons for falling down may also include psychological factors or that people expect it and give into it like Dr. Liichow honestly states. In Susan Brinkmann's new age blog on the Women of Grace website, *Examining the Controversy*

Surrounding Resting in the Spirit, she addresses the possibility of a psychological factor. She states that a priest held a Charismatic Service and warned the people who attended that there would be no catchers while the blessing was given to attendees. Not a single person out of 1,200 people fell.[84] This would be a case of the human spirit causing the phenomenon. Some people may do it just because others are doing it so they do not feel inferior. They may be envious of others who are falling and so they fake it.

The late Leon-Joseph Cardinal Suenens (1904-1996), once a strong supporter for the Catholic Charismatic Renewal and the man believed to be responsible for obtaining Catholic Church approval for it from Pope Paul VI in 1975, wrote a book on the Charismatic Renewal in 1987. In his book, Cardinal Suenens shares this information:

The eighth Annual Meeting of Jesuits of the Charismatic Renewal, held near Paris in January, 1983, studied the topic "resting in the Spirit"and subsequently published its findings under the title, Resting in the Spirit: Principles of Discernment. *The Assembly's general conclusion about this complex phenomenon ends as follows:*

'Bearing in mind the very real danger of deviation, the very prudent attitude of the Church's pastors, and lastly the fact that the Charismatic life is not dependent on 'resting in the Spirit,' we are of the opinion that it would be better not to introduce or encourage this phenomenon in the Catholic Charismatic Renewal.' Cardinal Suenens then states: *I, too, am reaching the same conclusion.*[85]

With the benefit of his theological insight and pastoral experience Cardinal Suenens concludes that 'resting in the Spirit,' not only is *<u>not</u>* *a manifestation of the power of the Holy Spirit but it threatens the authenticity and credibility of the Charismatic Renewal.*[86]

I have noticed in my research that many priests who are practicing new age or the occult either belong to or have belonged to Charismatic Renewal Prayer Groups. Some members of the laity in Charismatic Groups also have participated in new age

---

84 Brinkman, Susan, *Examining the Controversy Surrounding "Resting in the Spirit"* http://www.womenof grace.com/blog/?s=examining+the+controversy+surrounding+resting+in+the+spirit.

85 Suenens, Cardinal Leon-Joseph, *A Controversial Phenomenon,* Veritas Publications, Dublin, Ireland, 1987, p.73.

86 *Ibid,* back cover.

practices. In a powerful statement by Fr. James Manjackal MSFS, a Catholic priest who has preached in 60 countries in all continents, he says: *In my Charismatic retreats, the majority of the participants come with various moral, spiritual, mental and physical problems in order to be liberated and healed and to have a new life through the power of the Holy Spirit. With all sincerity of heart I will say, 80 to 90% of the participants had been to yoga, reiki, reincarnation, etc. of the Eastern religious practices where they lost faith in Jesus Christ and the Church.*[87] I believe these people need a deliverance ministry, and I personally think we need more deliverance ministries and exorcists in the Catholic Church.

As with everything, Satan always gets his foot in the door. Therefore, Charismatic Renewal Prayer Services are no exception. The point is that we should always pray for the discernment of spirits at Charismatic Renewal Prayer Services at the beginning of and throughout the service. Perhaps the Catholic Church also needs to warn the faithful about how deceptive evil spirits can be and set appropriate guidelines for discernment at these services.

---

87 Manjackal, James MSFS, *Yoga in philosophy and practice is incompatible with Christianity*, http://www.jmanjackal.net/eng/engyoga.htm.

Chapter Ten

Watch What You Read

By 2006, I had done a lot of research and reading on new age and the occult from a Christian perspective. I had read a number of books and magazine articles by theologians as well as Catholic and Christian authors. I had a good understanding of the subject matter, both through reading and personal experience. Today, I believe that the Holy Spirit led me to read these articles and books in order to help me recognize new age in my own life and to teach others through my mistakes.

Although I was led into new age and the occult by Satan, God can use our mistakes to evangelize. In 2006, I attended a Catholic conference where I had a locution from Jesus: *tell the story about your involvement in new age and the occult.* Subsequently, I began to write a book telling my story and explaining some common new age and occult practices from a Christian perspective. These were practices I personally had been exposed to.

One of Satan's tactics is trying to distract us from our real mission. It was and is my mission to write about my involvement in new age and the occult and to share the supernatural and demonic experiences God permitted in my life, which I am finally doing after trying for almost ten years. I started writing many other times, but always gave up. I usually had serious doubts about writing once I started to write. I learned doubts are a common way Satan works on us. Because of my past negative experience with writing a book that wasn't from God, but from a psychic, which you remember I also reprinted, I was afraid of making another mistake. I always stopped writing, believing I was actually being duped by the devil.

As I made yet another attempt to share my story in 2006, Satan's influence got me off-track again. The book I was writing had been coming along very well until I decided to include a detailed biography of some of the most influential people who contributed to the spread of new age and the occult in history.

Since I had no previous knowledge on this subject, I purchased some occult books as background material. These were not books written by Christian authors, but the actual books written by the occult authors themselves. I began to read a book written by Madame Blavatsky, the "mother" of the New Age Movement. It was a book on Theosophy. I became very mesmerized and intrigued by it. At the time, I asked my spiritual director, a priest, if I should continue to read the book because red flags were going up. He said he thought it would be okay. Unfortunately, this was the wrong answer. I should have listened to the Holy Spirit.

Madame Blavatsky was a medium and under the influence of an evil Hindu "spiritual master," who instructed her to start the Theosophical Society. Theosophy is a religious, occult philosophy based on esoterical knowledge, which means that it is hidden knowledge supposedly given to select people. Some of its tenets, which come from Eastern religions, are belief in reincarnation, spiritual evolution, and a depersonalized God. New agers believe that they can become gods themselves.

Esoterical demons attacked me at 3 a.m., Satan's hour. I heard a saint say, *Evil. Use holy oil.* I heard the word, "voluntary," which today means to me that I was no longer writing by a prompting of the Holy Spirit, but on my own authority. Saints were trying to help me. I tried to save my writing on the computer one day and this came on my screen: *Errors—Recover.* Now I realize that this was a message for me, but I didn't discern this at the time.

I continued to have increased demonic harassment. One night I fought with Satan all night, hitting him and calling on Jesus. Another time, the Holy Souls in Purgatory prayed for me and told me to *Rebuke the demons…* Disembodied damned human souls came from Hell and tormented me. I had very little sleep.

As I continued to read the book on Theosophy, I began to have visits by the disembodied damned human soul of Madame Blavatsky herself. She spoke to me in a foreign language. I was also visited by an ascended master, who wore a turban. He touched me with his demonic hands on both sides of my neck, one hand on the left and one on the right side simultaneously. Subsequently, I found his photo on the internet. His name was Morya. I discovered that he was one of Madame Blavatsky's spiritual masters.

On another night, I was visited by five ascended masters. I was prompted to write about subjects such as reincarnation, hypnosis, the occult, and holistic healing in my book...topics that were discussed in Blavatsky's book. This indeed tells me that these practices can be spiritually dangerous if demons wanted me to write about them. Of course, they would influence me to write about them in a manner that would bring readers into a source of temptation. Perhaps, for example, my writings would pique the interest of the reader to study them or even use them. **(I am warning you, dear readers, NOT to use any new age or occult practices at all!)** Demons have one goal and that is to get us to sin.

These visitations were unsettling and disrupted my sleep. These entities cast negative energy on me and frightened me. Although I didn't know it at the time, the book I was reading was dictated to Blavatsky by one of her spiritual masters, which meant that I was reading a book written by a demon. Blavatsky's demonic writings influenced Adolph Hitler and the Freemasons. Adolph Hitler is dead, but Freemasonry is still active and it is a Satanic cult.

I continued to write, still trying to warn people about the occult and explain its history. Demonic harassment was nothing new to me. I'd had visits from demons ever since I started writing the book on miracles in 1994. However, I still didn't understand what was happening from a spiritual perspective; namely, that I was becoming obsessed with reading the book by Madame Blavatsky on Theosophy, which was endangering my soul. I continued to read it when I could. I also began to write a lot in my book on Madame Blavatsky.

One night I was writing on Lucis Trust, the publishing company of the Theosophical Society. Lucis Trust is named after Lucifer, the light-bearer, another name for Satan. All of a sudden the whole room lit up brilliantly and then the light bulb in my lamp went out and I was in total darkness. Lucifer was with me.[88]

A few days later, in a dream I saw two demons walking

88 While I am writing this, the evil spirits with me are very upset. It is because I am telling you in this book that even though Lucifer himself and strong evil spirits have been and still are with me, they are not in charge. God is. Lucifer (satan) and evil spirits can only do what God permits. So, I say "Jesus, I trust in You!" I am not afraid.

through my apartment. They were coming down the hall to my the bedroom where I was sleeping, but they did not enter. Immediately, I began to pray to St. Michael, who came and prevented them from harming me.

When I read in the book that Madame Blavatsky had teeth problems and a swollen mouth, I got the same identical problem a few days later. I was led to use holy oil and was healed. I have no doubt that the problem was caused by her demonic spirit.

It reached the point where I was reading late into the night. Then one night, I heard voices making comments on my writing, and on everything I did. They talked non-stop. I had no peace. What had happened is that stronger demons of the occult had come into my life—demons of Theosophy and esoterism. Up to this point, I'd had visits from demons, but the encounters were short. The demons that came into my life at this time began to harass and torment me relentlessly and continuously (24/7) and have not left me.

When these demons first came into my life, they pretended to be God the Father, Jesus, the Holy Spirit and Mary. I fell for it and believed they were who they said they were because I had gotten legitimate messages from all of them in the past. God and Mary had often warned me about a sin I was committing or led me to do something that bore good fruit. The demons knew this, so they duped me in this same manner. If someone is religious, evil spirits will use religion as bait. The demons talked to me incessantly and ordered me to do things. I acquiesced, wanting to obey God and the Blessed Mother. They worked with other demons who had been with me for years.

The evil spirits told me, *Demons are everywhere.* This is true. All of us have demons with us, and we just need to identify them so we can rebuke them according to their specialty. The world is full of demons, especially in these times where evil is so prevalent. There are demons assigned to countries, cities, states, counties, places, governments, churches, and dioceses, to name a few.

The good news is that God (Father, Son and Holy Spirit), Mary, and the saints are helping us, too, in our battle with the powers of darkness. The saints pray for us continually if we ask them. We also have the prayers of the Holy Souls in Purgatory.

In addition, we are all assigned a guardian angel. Other angels, particularly St. Michael, protect us in our daily lives as well. We are also all called to pray for one another. Please pray for me, and I will pray for you.

HOW DEMONS HARRASSED ME

Demons of Infirmity

At the time I was writing the book on Theosophy, demons of infirmity caused many problems. I got one physical problem after another. I had stomach cramps and bloating. I had near fainting spells. I had chest pain, and my heart was erratic. It stopped at times. I also got a really bad cold, laryngitis, a bad cough and severe congestion.

I was moaning in my sleep. I thought I was going to die. I had a dream of dying and a nun praying by my bedside. I quit my job because I thought I was going to die and because I had symptoms of Alzheimer's disease. I had several dreams of having Alzheimer's disease. At the time, I was a caregiver and when I drove my clients around, I forgot where we were going. The symptoms were real, but they were caused by demons. I couldn't find my apartment one night. I got lost when I was driving and had no idea where I was. Quitting my job left me without any income, and I had to rely on my small savings.

Because I was writing a book, the demons woke me up every couple of hours to write. They would say, *Write,* and then after I went to the computer and began to write, they would say, *The book is cancelled.*

They did not allow me to eat adequately or get much rest, and I lost ten pounds the first week. My ability to discern was diminished because I became very exhausted and weak. When I would say, *Jesus I trust in You,* I would hear *sleep,* but I couldn't sleep. The demons made such a racket, the only sleep I got was when I played religious music on a CD using headphones. I listened to the CD, *Heal Us Lord, Songs of Mercy,* by Still Waters, over and over. I loved the words to the song, *More Precious Than Silver,* speaking of Jesus being more precious than silver or gold.

As soon as the music stopped, the demons would harass me again so I could not sleep more than an hour at a time. I also began to play the CD of the sung version of the Divine Mercy Chaplet. I started to pray the chaplet often. I am playing CDs with religious music as I write this book because religious music really subdues the demons.

Their tactic was to weaken me physically so I would be more receptive to their temptations. They may have also wanted me to get into a serious accident to keep me from doing my real mission, which is to write this book.

Demons of Problems with Electronic Equipment

My computer would lock up, words would appear to be raised within the same paragraph, fonts would suddenly change, and my printer broke. Of course, what I saw on the screen was only due to demonic influence because perhaps someone not suffering from demonic oppression would not see the same things I saw.

Demons of Confusion

When I would go to Mass I would hear some different words in the Gospel and readings. The demons actually changed the words for my ears only, but which I am sure were read correctly. I recognized the changes because of my familiarity with Scripture because by this time, I had read most of the Bible. The changes made to certain words caused the readings to become inaccurate or unorthodox.

One day the demons confused me by changing numbers. I went to visit my son and when I looked for his apartment number, all of the numbers were different. Instead of Apartment 1306, which was his apartment number, I saw numbers all in the 5900 series. There was no 1306, and I panicked. This was a 12-story locked apartment building, and I had no idea which buzzer to ring. I did not have a cell phone. I can't tell you how hard this was to go through. Finally, another resident who happened to come home let me in the building.

Sometimes I would hear different words spoken by others

than what I believe were being said. For example, I would hear things like *She's very holy,* but I knew this was not actually being said about me. It was a temptation to pride. At other times, I would say, *Jesus is the Risen Lord,* and they would say, *Jesus is the Son of the Risen Lord,* to confuse me.

One Thursday, the demons convinced me it was Sunday and since I hadn't gone to Mass, they convinced me I was in mortal sin. I was so weak by that time, I couldn't think straight and all of my days ran together.

Demons of False Peace

One day Jesus told me in a locution that demons can cause false peace. I received understanding about some things that had been happening to me for years that I had improperly discerned. For example, I would often feel a spirit touching my hair, usually at night. For a long time I thought this was angels, but now I discovered that it was demons. Be careful and never assume anything. I didn't test the spirits when this happened because I had a very peaceful feeling accompany it. Therefore, I was sure it was angels, but I discovered that I was wrong. Always be sure to test the spirits by saying, *Lord Jesus, please rebuke and command any demons of false peace to leave in your Name and cover me with Your Most Precious Blood.* When I began to test the spirits, the evil spirits stopped touching my hair and stopped using that tactic.

I thought a feeling of peace was always from God, but it isn't. Peace from God comes in the heart and soul. With peace from God comes inner joy, a desire to please God, and to be free from sin. True peace is Christ-centered and is a sign of the Holy Spirit acting in the soul.

If you are not obeying the commandments and say you have "peace," the devil may be giving you false peace. Many days when I was in mortal sin, I didn't worry about it. Now I think it was a type of false peace caused by Satan. Satan gets us where he wants us and then makes us complacent. He can send us wealth, power, prestige, immoral relationships, new electronic devices and other distractions so we just bask in worldly things and forget about God. We have false peace. If we prayed and listened to the Holy

Spirit, we would be convicted, but we avoid doing this because we are content and really don't want to change. False peace can become a factor in losing our very souls. Read Psalm 73.

Lying Demons

Demons are liars. Here are some ways they lied to me, and, because of my weakened condition, I believed them. Notice that once again, they used religion against me because I am religious.

- They told me I can save souls. Right Answer: I can *help* save souls.
- They told me that I needed to make atonement (do penance). They constantly would find ways to have me make atonement at all hours of the day and night. One day they had me stand in the bathtub and say *Jesus is the Risen Lord* for four straight hours. I missed a funeral I was going to attend. You see how weak and harassed I was at this time. But doesn't that sound like a legitimate ejaculatory prayer? I later asked a Catholic exorcist about it, and he told me that demons cannot say, *Jesus is My Lord* but they can say "Jesus is the Risen Lord." The demons also said, *Praise God* and *Praise the Risen Lord.* Demons can say things you would think only good spirits can say.
- They told me I was sick and going to die. They convinced me that I had breast cancer. They told me to go the hospital, which I did, but did not stay. On another occasion, they told me to go again to the hospital, but when I was halfway there, they told me to go back home. Then they told me that I was going to have a heart attack and die. They had me going in circles. In my weakened condition, I could not think straight. I was exhausted from lack of sleep and constant harassment. They also told me that I couldn't go to Confession before I died.
- One day when I was in Adoration, I heard *Go to the*

hospital. I was having heart palpitations. Like a dummy, I went. I ended up in the emergency ward for 6-1/2 hours. After doing tests on my heart, everything turned out to be normal. This visit cost me dearly, and I had to make monthly payments for a long time because I didn't have health insurance.

- The demons told me not to look at the Eucharistic Host during the Consecration. We should gaze upon the Lord.
- They told me I could not light blessed candles because it would make me sick. Obviously, this is not true. In fact, for the entire duration of writing this book, I have been lighting a blessed candle daily.

Demons of Accidents

Several times the evil spirits tried to harm me. Once I sprained my ankle. Another time, I fell and bruised my knee. I slipped on the ice twice in early 2006 and almost fell, but my angel helped me. I did fall, however, in my apartment. I stubbed my toe which caused swelling and pain for weeks. I had a dream that demons were causing these accidents, but God was allowing it. Saints rebuked the evil spirits for me. Saints were praying and encouraging me to pray and praise God more.

Demons of Distractions

The demons tried to distract me from going to church or Adoration by causing delays. I misplaced my car keys, I became confused on what the correct time was, and I would do little things that would put me behind schedule such as check the weather on the computer or do a shopping list. I actually missed Mass a few times and didn't get all of my prayers said. They also tormented me so much that I was unable to say the Rosary and the Chaplet of Divine Mercy. When I listened to a CD with the Rosary and Chaplet on it, I would hear their voices on it, too, intermingled with the words of the prayers. However, I persevered and did the best I could.

The demons caused (and still do) the toilet to run to distract me from getting to Mass and as a form of harassment. The toilet runs for about 30 seconds and then stops. It does this during the day and at night. I'm sorry for my poor neighbors who have to listen to this. This is not just a spiritual experience. It actually happens. I had the toilet checked by the maintenance department in the apartment complex where I live and they replaced the parts. However, it continues to happen.

I also have temptations every morning when I am getting ready for Mass. They are usually temptations I have succumbed to in the past. For example, I will think of people who have wronged me in the past. The temptation is to get me to be angry or resentful towards the person all over again.

Satan knows our weaknesses. I don't always handle the temptations well, but reciting a short prayer such as, *Jesus I Trust in You* or calling on Mary for assistance is very effective. Saying the St. Michael prayer always helps, too. I also keep holy water, holy oil and blessed salt around the house and use them frequently. I try not to leave home without using these sacramentals while saying my prayer of rebuke. I also never forget to wear my brown scapular and have blessed medals with me. This is my armor in my battle with the powers of darkness.

The demons often make a loud buzzing noise to distract me. This is mystical but I have learned to cope with it. When they talk in unison, it is similar to a large crowd of people talking in a stadium. This happens daily, often during prayer. But through the years, Jesus has given me the graces I need to tune them out and to lead a normal life, at least on the surface. Playing religious music often stops the din or lessens it immediately, and I have grown to love it. Also, the demons do not like EWTN, so I turn it on to get some peace. In addition, the programming is excellent. The televised Masses are particularly good because demons hate the Mass.

Demons of Infestation

When I go to church, the demons cause loud noises such as raps, knocks and cracking of wood. These are demons of infestation or poltergeist activity, which are discernable by others. When I am at home, the demons slam doors often, usually when they are upset by my praying or doing something efficacious for the Lord, *i.e.* a work of charity. But these sounds are not perceptible to others—doors do not actually physically slam, and I am sure others cannot hear it. (I live in an apartment building which has 25 apartments. I suspect people cannot hear the slamming of doors because it happens often during the wee hours of the morning when people are sleeping. At that hour, if someone was continually slamming doors, it would be reported to the building manager.)

I think the slamming of doors is a spiritual analogy. We open the door for evil spirits and demons to enter when we sin. We let our guard down and leave our door ajar. In order to keep evil spirits out of our lives, we need to pray, attend church (always on Sundays), obey the commandments, do penance and make sacrifices, do works of charity, read the Bible, and resist temptations, among other things. ***Submit yourselves, then, to God. Resist the devil, and he will flee from you.*** (James 4:7 NIV)

The more often we open the door for the evil spirits of the same sin to come in, the more difficult it is to close the door. For example, if one burglar tried to enter your house, you might be able to fend him off. But if several burglars came and forced their way into your home, you would have a more difficult time getting rid of them. They could even seriously harm you.

I learned the hard way that we need to resist all temptations from the very beginning. If we don't, Satan sends in more troops in an attempt to get us to commit a mortal sin. Before we know it, we have an army of demons around us. We live in a perpetual state of spiritual bondage. For someone who has a repetitive sin, it is an endless struggle. But there is always the grace and mercy of Jesus Christ. Never give up. I have conquered many of my temptations and sins, and so can you. ***Though a mighty army surrounds me, my heart will not be afraid. Even if I am attacked, I will remain confident.*** (Psalm 27:3 NIV)

The Demons Request a Book

The demons praised the book on Theosophy, Madame Blavatsky and ascended masters. Then one night they asked me to write a book on Madame Blavatsky. They told me to self-publish it and store the books at the same place I had stored the books on miracles. They said I had enough money to do it. This was their attempt to deliberately get me to write another morally corrupt book on the occult. I recognized the temptation. This was obviously spiritual warfare.

Demons of Obsession

In 2006, Jesus told me that I had demons of obsession with me. I had never heard of this term. From personal experience, this is what I have learned: Demonic obsession is a "preoccupation, fixation, compulsion, fascination, penchant, or strong desire" to do something or to think about something so much that it consumes your time and takes you away from other activities. Obsessions originate as a thought and then we have a choice to act on them or dismiss the thought. What we are thinking about may or may not be sinful, but if we become obsessed with something that is a sin or leads us to sin, it becomes problematic. It gets more difficult each time we give into the temptation.

I realized demons of obsession had been with me all of my life. At this point in my life, the demons with me pretending to be God the Father, Jesus, the Holy Spirit and Mary condemned me for these past sins of obsession. The motive was to make me feel guilty because I had conquered these temptations already.

The demons began to ridicule me for being obsessed with clothes, software and cleaning. They revealed my sins to me, and, of course, they would know them because they tempted me in the first place. They were right. I had been obsessed with these things. Reflecting on my life, I realized I had committed the following sins, and I took steps to correct my faults, although I am still tempted by all of them.

1. Cleaning. For most of my adult life, I was obsessed with

cleaning. I used to clean the house meticulously once a week whether it needed it or not after I was married at age 20. It is the amount of time and detail that went into it that made it time-consuming. If something was not clean, I would clean it right away and could not let it wait or it would really bother me. After company came, I would clean everything meticulously. I learned to temper this obsession. Now I do not clean very often, but do "touch ups" in the meantime. I lost my desire to clean when I began to do more works of charity. I found helping people much more rewarding than cleaning. When I was helping other people, I didn't have time to clean. Now it is only a chore!

However, at times the demons cause me to clean at improper times, *i.e.* getting ready to go to Mass. I control this temptation, although sometimes I will clean something, *i.e.* the toilet, for a few minutes, but still get to Mass on time. I remind myself it is a temptation and try to be prudent and careful, reminding myself of my priorities.

2. Computer Games. I have had demons of obsession with computer games. I played Scrabble online for hours on end and could not seem to let it go. I did this for months before I realized I could make better use of my time, and I was attached to it. I gave it up, but the temptation to do it remained until I had not done it for an extended period of time. The demons gave up, but I can't let my guard down. I know that if I began to play Scrabble again online, I would have difficulty in limiting my time in this activity. Therefore, I abstain.

   I do play a game of Scrabble with family members about three times a year, and I can handle that. I can see how people today become obsessed with the internet, video games, IPods and cell phones and even with television.

3. Shopping. I have had demons of obsession with shopping with me most of my life. I used to buy much more than I needed. In my teenage years, I did not have

much money, so I could not buy many clothes, but after I left home and was married that changed. When my children were little, I would buy so many outfits for them that many went unused. For myself, especially when I worked as a manager in an office, I would spend $1000 at one time on clothes. I had about two dozen pairs of shoes. One day in the early 2000s, I realized my obsession with clothes was demonic and I decided to conquer it. I gave my clothes to the poor.

From that time on, I have spent money in moderation, but I still have the inclination to shop for things I do not need when I go to the stores or to over-buy. I shop mostly at Goodwill now, but they have nice things, too. The solution is to limit going to the stores. Shopping is still a temptation, but I believe I do it in moderation now. I have not been to a shopping mall for years. It helps to give money to the poor, especially when we are poor ourselves. Demons hate this because it is an act of charity. We can give up something we really want and give the money to charity.

Demons of Condemnation

One night the evil spirit pretending to be God the Father said that I was going to Hell because I had not finished the book I was writing, which by this time included parts of my own story, but also a lot of information on Theosophy and Blavatsky. The evil spirits staged a mock trial, which, in my confused state, I believed was really from God.

At my judgment before God, several people came to testify on my behalf. Of course, I realized <u>later</u> that these people were demons masquerading as people I knew. At first, there was good testimony, and they convinced me that I was a saint. I had done a lot of good. I heard testimony from people who said, *She prayed daily for souls in Purgatory. She helped so many people.* It was a really dramatic scene.

The next day I was damned to Hell. New information was given that I had committed the unforgivable sin of blasphemy of the Holy Spirit. I was sentenced to Hell for all eternity. I was shown a vivid vision of what they told me was Hell. In my vision, I saw a large cell and an Iron Gate slamming down full force and with no way out. They told me I was damned, and there was no hope.

I didn't know what the sin of blasphemy of the Holy Spirit was. I discovered that it is despairing of God's mercy, which I had not done. In other words, it means that you believe God will never forgive you for your sins. God always forgives repentant sinners because He is all merciful. However, at the time, the demons tormented me with the thought that I had committed this offense and was going to Hell.

I became convinced that I was damned. The demons told me that I would be going to Hell at 3 a.m. They also told me someone else I knew was going first. I just waited for the time they told me they would be taking me to Hell, resigned to my fate. About 3 a.m. I heard the other person going to Hell, screaming as she descended into a black pit. I actually smelled smoke. But nothing happened to me. By 6 a.m., I realized I was being duped by demons. I was up all night lying on the carpet in the living room, thinking I was going to Hell. When you have strong demons in your life, they become very convincing and cause you to do things you normally would not do. I was in a state of spiritual, mental and physical exhaustion, which made me very vulnerable. So, although this is embarrassing for me to tell you, I am doing it at God's bidding.

Afterwards, I spoke to a priest about everything who reminded me that people are not judged until after they die. Following this incident, I spoke to them because I suspected that they were demons masquerading as God the Father, Jesus, the Holy Spirit and Mary. I shouted, *I wear the brown scapular! What about God's promises? God always keeps His promises! The promises are that whoever dies wearing the Scapular will not suffer eternal fire!* For the first time, there was total silence. They had no answer. When I asked them to identify themselves, there was also silence. Later Jesus counseled me not to communicate with them. Only an exorcist is allowed to speak to them. Since then I have not communicated with them.

The evil spirits complained when I wore the relic of the true Cross, which a good friend had given to me. This was evidence to me that the entities were demons and not who they claimed to be. Near the end of their attempt to convince me they were really God the Father, Jesus, Mary and the Holy Spirit, Mary began to be called "Reverend Mother." This confirmed for me that the female voice I heard was not that of Mary because she is never called by that name. (The devil can't stand the name of the Mother of God, "Mary," because he is so humiliated by a creature who was chosen to bear Jesus and who was created without sin. Mary is the woman who will defeat Satan.)

In the Vatican's document on new age, we read: *A prominent component of Mrs. Blavatsky's writings was the emancipation of women, which involved an attack on the male God of Judaism, of Christianity and of Islam. She urged people to return to the mother-goddess of Hinduism and to the practice of feminine virtues. This continued under the guidance of Annie Besant, who was in the vanguard of the feminist movement. Wicca and women's spirituality carry on this struggle against patriarchal Christianity today.*[89] Madame Blavatsky and her successor, Annie Besant, influenced the feminist movement in the Catholic Church. Some women in the Catholic Church think they should be priests. This is not from God, and the Pope has made it very clear it is not an option. Women do have a role to play in the church, but we should be obedient to papal authority.

When I realized I had brought these demons into my life through reading the book on Blavatsky, I repented and said an act of perfect contrition. This is a sincere act of contrition prior to going to confession when someone is in mortal sin. If someone could not get to confession, for example the person died before he could get there, he would not go to Hell because his sins would have been forgiven. However, the person must go to confession as soon as possible. ***When it arises from a love by which God is loved above all else, contrition is called "perfect" (contrition of charity). Such contrition remits venial sins; it also obtains forgiveness of mortal sins if it includes the firm resolution to***

89 *Jesus Christ the Bearer of the Water of Life, A Christian Reflection on the "New Age"*, www.vatican.va/.../pontifical_councils/interelg/document/rc_pc_interelg_doc_20030203_new-age_en.html - 216k - 2003-02-20, (Section 2.3.2).

have recourse to sacramental confession as soon as possible.[90]

On the evening before Divine Mercy Sunday in 2006, I had a prompting to go to confession by God the Father. Then I had a dream that Jesus was teaching me. When I made an examination of conscience, I had three pages of sins. After my confession on Divine Mercy Sunday, I realized a short while later that I had forgotten to confess an entire page of sins. I went back into the confessional. (They had confessions all afternoon at this parish.) I still was able to attend Mass and receive the Eucharist. I got the plenary indulgence, which takes away all of one's Purgatory up until that point. What a grace and mercy! I had peace in my soul.

These same demons are still with me. I am oppressed by demons of the new age and the occult. My definition of oppression is demonic harassment. I hear a female voice talk constantly who seems to be the leader of the group of evil spirits that are with me. She could be the disembodied damned human soul of Madame Blavatsky. I couldn't have a worse demonic entity with me because *she was one of the most evil and immoral women who ever lived with personal duplicity and profound contempt for humanity.*[91] The demons harass me 24/7. I have learned to tune them out, although not always. It is more difficult when I am tired. They particularly harass me when I go to bed. Jesus taught me to say the St. Michael Prayer over and over until I fall asleep. It works. Most of the time I sleep without a problem now, but if I wake up during the night, they are there. They never leave me. Of course, Jesus is always with me, too, as He is with all of us. But Jesus is not with me like He was in the past when He spoke to me. Now I know He is with me by faith. All of us have God (Father, Son and Holy Spirit), Mary, the saints and angels at our side when we pray for assistance. The Holy Souls in Purgatory also pray for us. One of my tests is to rely on Jesus and trust in Him, realizing that He is in control and will not give me more than I can handle.

My penance is that everywhere I go, the demons go with me.

---

90 *Catechism of the Catholic Church,* Part Two: The Celebration of the Christian Mystery, Section Two: The Seven Sacraments of the Church: Chapter Two: The Sacraments of Healing, Article 4: The Sacrament of Penance and Reconciliation, 1452)

91 Flynn, Ted, *Hope for the Wicked,* MaxKol Communications, Sterling, VA 20166, 2000.

They tempt me and comment on my life or what I am going to do. Sometimes, I can't help but listen to them because it is so distracting. But for me, it's a typical day. However, I couldn't handle it without the grace and mercy of Jesus Christ. Back in 2006, He did come to teach me. The message in the dream came true.

Jesus Comes to Shepherd Me

After I went to confession on Divine Mercy Sunday in 2006, Jesus came to teach me. Jesus helps the repentant sinner. He has always been there when I needed Him, but He will not interfere with our free will. Through locutions, Jesus told me how to cope with the demons and let me know that there are "consequences" for sin. He used that word.

Jesus told me that I had demons of new age and the occult with me, and they were strong. He told me not to speak to them. He said they could read my thoughts so to be careful what I was thinking. This is true. They read my mind, so they know everything I am planning to do. It is my personal cross. Jesus said to eat normally, not to pay attention to them, and that He would help me. Jesus said to rely on the Holy Spirit now, and that He would be with me in Holy Communion and at Adoration. Before He left, I heard His Most Precious Blood falling upon the whole world many, many times. It sounded like a torrential rain.

Shortly after Jesus left, I was led to the passage in the Bible where it says, ***I Myself will shepherd them...*** (Ezekiel 34:15) and to Psalm 25. Jesus did indeed shepherd me after I confessed my sins. He will not abandon us; we abandon Him. We all need to be corrected at times when we begin to go on destructive paths. Jesus' corrections are actually a sign of His infinite mercy.

My Favorite Psalm

Lord, make me know Your ways. Lord, teach me Your paths. Make me walk in Your truth and teach me, for You are God my Savior. The Lord is good and upright. He shows the path to those who stray, He guides the

> ***humble in the right path; He teaches His way to the poor. His ways are faithfulness and love for those who keep His covenant and law. Lord, for the sake of your name forgive my guilt for it is great. If anyone fears the Lord, He will show him the path he should choose.*** (Psalm 25: 4-5; 8-13 NIV)

After Jesus left me, I went through my entire apartment and took 12 diaries detailing my spiritual experiences, my notes, the books I had critiqued on new age, computer files, paper files—almost everything I had accumulated for the previous 13 years in conjunction with my spiritual experiences and study of new age and the occult—and threw them in the garbage. I only saved two diaries as a reminder of how I had brought the demons into my life and how Jesus had helped me. I thought everything in my diaries was from the devil. I did not want anything to come between Jesus and me again. I threw everything out to rid myself of any demonic influences connected with the materials. Reading the demonic experiences in them brought tears to my eyes. I had brought these demons into my life.

However, today I realize that while most of the messages were demonic, many were actually from God. The diaries were my real life struggle between good and evil. This does not mean that Jesus wanted me to bring demons into my life. He allowed it because I had free will. However, God can use everything that happens for good if we repent of our sins.

At the last minute before the garbage men were coming to empty the dumpster, I went out and retrieved one bag of the writings I had accumulated over the previous 13 years. However, all of the diaries I had thrown out were destroyed. I don't know what made me take that one bag out of the garbage, but it was obviously divine intervention because I am using those notes to write this, my book for Jesus.

The fact is that Jesus helped me cope from the very beginning of my involvement in new age and the occult. He counseled me, explained things to me, personally read the Bible to me daily for months, and gave me messages. Because I was so entrenched in demonic warfare, I often did not act on the messages He gave me. I was asked to write several books, but even though I started them, I never finished them. I really am a terrible sinner. He gave me a gift, and I didn't use it. Even demonic experiences can be used as examples for others. Sometimes I was confused, but as I write this He is giving me full knowledge of my faults. I am sorry, and I want this book to be the best gift I can still give Him. It is a synopsis of my life, including some of the spiritual experiences that He allowed me to have.

Jesus showed me that I would have many spiritual tests to test my love for Him, and I do constantly. Once I was shown I would be living the life of Job and then saw the word, **JOB**, on a license plate. I have constant temptations, as many as 100 or more a day.

Until I adjusted (as best as I could) to a life with demons in it 24/7, I got some advice from Fr. John Hampsch, C.M.F., who is an expert on demonology and a prolific writer. The demons were still harassing me continually after Jesus was no longer counseling me, and I didn't know how to discern my experiences. I thought some of them were from God. For example, I heard what I thought was God the Father speaking, but in a rather harsh tone.

Fr. Hampsch called me on the phone after I emailed him. I'll never forget our conversation and what happened. The demons stomped around my living room like a herd of wild elephants. The floor actually shook. The sound was deafening to me. Fr. Hampsch recited a prayer of rebuke and they quieted down. Prayers of rebuke are effective, even from a distance. We can also say them for others.

Fr. Hampsch helped me to discern the voices I heard, especially those harsh ones which claimed to be God the Father, which he confirmed were demons. He was able to identify demons of scrupulosity, infirmity, condemnation, and more. I have often corresponded with him since 2006, and I am grateful for his answers to my questions and words of encouragement.

A few months following Divine Mercy Sunday in 2006, I received Divine Mercy cenacle materials from a total stranger who had called one day to relay a message from a mutual friend. The caller had been going to start a Divine Mercy Cenacle, but something else came up and he couldn't do it. So, he sent the information to me to review.

As I looked over the Divine Mercy materials, my eyes focused on the image of Divine Mercy. It looked familiar. It was then that I remembered a vision I had back in the late 1990s. The vision was of this very image of Jesus that I had in my hands. In my diary I had written: *Tonight I saw an image of Jesus with rays coming from His heart. One was pale and the other was red.* (I had kept notes of this message and some other ones on my computer). I knew then that I was being called by the Holy Spirit to promote the Divine Mercy Devotion.

Subsequently, I began to spread the Divine Mercy devotion in my diocese of Milwaukee. I spoke to small groups in churches (which was difficult for me because I am shy). In conjunction with the short talk, I also showed a short video on Divine Mercy. I started a cenacle, a group which studies the messages of the Divine Mercy devotion given to St. Faustina. As time went on, other parishes started cenacles, too. I began to promote the devotion at religious conferences. I gave Divine Mercy chaplet pamphlets and pamphlets on Divine Mercy Sunday to parishes, charities, prison ministries, schools, and homes for the elderly. I started a Divine Mercy Sunday Mass at a local parish and continued to assist in this project each year. I was successful in setting up a tour for the Marians of the Immaculate Conception to speak in churches in the Milwaukee area. I composed a Divine Mercy Holy Hour for the U.S.A. and it was prayed around the country. A friend and I called other Divine Mercy cenacle leaders in most of the 50 states and many parishes used the program, which I emailed to them or sent by regular mail.

Good fruit came from all of this work. Praise the Lord in all things! God can use anyone, even a repentant sinner to do His work. ***My grace is sufficient for you, for my power is made perfect in weakness.*** (2 Corinthians 12:9) Indeed, I am one of the weakest and most imperfect of God's workers, but I did it all for the love of God and others. My work has culminated with this book, my personal story of Divine Mercy.

Beginning in 2006, I began to rely on the Holy Spirit and prayer, which was quite a change for me after many years of relying on dreams, visions, supplements, demonic messages, coincidences and so on. However, relying on the Holy Spirit and doing reparation has brought me closer to Christ. I thank the Lord for the graces He has given me. Even though I have repented, I still live with the consequences of my sins. But I look forward to eternal life, a life with Jesus in Heaven with no demons. I have hope, and I believe in Jesus' Divine Mercy. ***Therefore, let us offer through Jesus a continual sacrifice of praise to God, proclaiming our allegiance to His name.*** (Hebrews 13:15 NIV).

Chapter Eleven

Hell: The Ultimate Consequence for Sin

Many people do not seem to believe in demons or Hell anymore. I have heard this statement from the pulpit, most recently in Florida. Also, perhaps because of diminishing attendance at Sunday services, there seems to be a tendency, at least in some Catholic parishes, to preach only on subjects that are "neutral." By this I mean that demons and the reality of Hell and sin are not often spoken about because it makes people feel uncomfortable. The evils of contraception, abortion, homosexuality and divorce are not often spoken about either, perhaps because of the fear of losing parishioners. Many people who attend Catholic services believe these heinous sins are morally acceptable and they still call themselves "Catholic."

The existence of Hell, a place of torment and punishment, is documented many times in the Bible. ***Do not be afraid of those who kill the body but cannot kill the soul. Rather, be afraid of the one who can destroy both soul and body in Hell.*** (Matthew 10:28 NIV) One of Satan's best tactics is to get people to believe there is no Hell. If there is no Hell, then there are no consequences for sin.

Unfortunately, we can't brush this subject off so easily. As someone who has been given spiritual experiences both from God and Satan, God has shown me Hell and I have had visits from both evil spirits (demons) and disembodied damned human souls (deceased people who went to Hell). These damned human souls had the features they had on earth, but they had spirit bodies. They emanated negativity, sadness, contempt, hatred, and pure evil.

Hell and demons do exist. Some people don't believe that an all-loving, merciful God would send anyone to Hell. Yet consider the fact that God gives man free will. This means that man has the ability to choose good or evil. If a man chooses evil and does not repent, there is a price to pay. In the Bible, it says that the wages of sin is death. (Romans 6:23)

God, in His infinite mercy, does forgive. We can and should use our free will to ask for forgiveness. It is repentance that is crucial to our day of judgment. Woe to the person who does not repent, for if he is in the state of mortal sin when he dies, he *will* go to Hell.

I saw Hell as a dark, dreary, morbid place full of wretched, miserable deceased people (referred to as disembodied damned human souls) that keep trying to commit the same sins they committed on earth. Each person's condition in Hell is related to the sin(s) they committed on earth. I saw disembodied damned human souls trying to have sexual relations with other disembodied damned human souls, but they had no pleasure in it and only disgust and hatred would permeate their souls. There was no love and no sexual gratification. It was purely an evil act. This was their curse for all eternity.

These reprobate disembodied damned human souls also tempted people on earth with the very sin which caused them to go to Hell. Therefore, disembodied damned human souls have specialties, similar to those in different professions on earth. Reprobate human souls with the same specialties get together to plot how to tempt us with the sin(s) they committed. The devil is clever. Certainly people who committed these sins know the weaknesses of those still living because they are aware of their own folly. Whatever temptations caused them to go to Hell will be their tactics now in tempting us. Most people are in Hell for committing sins of the flesh. What are they? The Bible tells us:

Now the works of the flesh are evident: sexual immorality, impurity, sensuality, idolatry, sorcery, enmity, strife, jealousy, fits of anger, rivalries, dissensions, divisions, envy, drunkenness, orgies, and things like these. I warn you, as I warned you before, that those who do such things will not inherit the kingdom of God. (Galatians 5:19-21 ESV)

In another passage, the Bible says: ***Do not be deceived; neither fornicators, nor idolaters, nor adulterers, nor effeminate, nor homosexuals, nor thieves, nor the covetous, nor drunkards, nor revilers, nor swindlers, will inherit the kingdom of God.*** (1

Corinthians 6:9-10 NASB)

I am going to write about two people, already mentioned in this book, whom God allowed me to know went to Hell when they died. In fact, I had visits from these disembodied damned human souls. This was a difficult chapter to write, but God gave me the strength.

Adultery

Adultery is having sexual relations with someone other than the marriage partner. Adultery can also be committed by a single person with a married person. Adultery is very common today, probably because it is not as frowned upon as it was in the past. Today people seem to accept many sins as normal behavior or are simply indifferent to these choices. Adultery is a sin against the sixth commandment: "Thou shalt not commit adultery." Christ condemned even lust as sinful. ***But I tell you that anyone who looks at a woman lustfully has already committed adultery with her in his heart.*** (Matthew 5:28 NIV).

Marriage should be a commitment between a man and a woman. Sexual relations are a gift from God to propagate the earth within the context of human respect and dignity. Sexual relations should be an act of genuine love for the other person with God at the center of the relationship. Once God is no longer at the center of the relationship, it creates a doorway for Satan to enter. I experienced this on a personal level.

Adultery hurts children in the marriage. It can be embarrassing if their friends find out about it. It can also cause heartache, pain and devastating emotional consequences if the marriage ends in divorce.

If your partner commits adultery, you are called to forgive him/her. This could be a challenge, but for God all things are possible. Once I heard a sermon by a priest who was talking about sacrifices and penance. He mentioned that John the Baptist did penance by wearing a hair shirt. This was a shirt made out of animal hair that people in his day wore on their upper bodies for penance because it was itchy and uncomfortable. The priest commented that, *Your spouse could be your hair shirt!* A lot of people think that divorce is the answer to problems in a marriage, but I can tell you that divorce only brings a new and worse set of problems. ***What therefore God hath joined together, let not man put asunder.*** (Mark 10:9 ASV)

Unfortunately, many people commit adultery. If they do not repent, they can end up in Hell because it is a mortal sin. Although this is probably the hardest story I am going to write about in this book, I am going to tell it to you because I do not want you to make the wrong choices. I had several visits from someone who went to Hell for adultery, and it was my own father. Most of us want to believe that our family members or friends go to Heaven after death, but that is not always the case.

Rude Awakening

One day in September 1994, I got a call from my brother in Madison. He informed me that my father had been admitted to a hospital and diagnosed with a bowel obstruction. Because I had to travel from Milwaukee to Madison for a business seminar just two days later, I decided to schedule a visit with my dad at that time.

When I got to the hospital, my dad was in bad shape. He was vomiting and had lost 20 pounds since he was admitted two days earlier. He weighed only 105 pounds, which for his height of 6′2″, was seriously underweight. There was a tube going down his nose pumping fluids from his stomach. He was being fed intravenously, and was extremely weak. The doctors were debating whether or not to do surgery, which they only wanted to do as a last resort, since they felt he was not strong enough to withstand it.

After the seminar ended, my sister-in-law informed me that my dad had emergency surgery. However, the surgeon said that everything had gone well. They had removed part of the small intestine and pieced the rest back together. I breathed a sigh of relief, and decided to get some rest.

I was staying with my mother, who was now alone. As soon as I arrived at my parents' home, I received a phone call from my brother. The hospital had just called him to say my dad had suffered heart and lung failure and was now on life support. My brother wanted to "pull the plug." I asked him not to do it. Since he had power of attorney, he was in control. My brother agreed to call the doctor and make an appointment for all three of us to meet the following morning in the hospital to review the situation.

When I arrived at the hospital the following morning, my heart sank. My father was in intensive care in a coma on life support equipment. There had been no change from the previous night. He appeared to be dead, as he lay on his back motionless with a number of tubes in his body and machines all around him. Once again, my brother expressed his desire to discontinue life support. He said my dad would not want this. I asked for more time. After some discussion, my brother and the doctor agreed to slowly withdraw the life support measures. If my dad was able to breathe on his own, he would live. If not, he would, of course, die.

I asked the nurse to have the hospital chaplain come to my dad's room and pray, which he did for approximately a half hour. I then went to the chapel to pray. I did not pray for him to be healed, but I left it in God's hands. I knew he was already 81 years old and his death was inevitable eventually. But, I did not believe we should just give up because of his age. I also believe that we should follow the guidelines of the Catholic Church on end of life issues. Many people today end life prematurely and don't pray or try to discern the will of God.

After praying in the chapel, I went back to his room. I had taken some holy water to Madison which I had gotten at the Holy Hill in Conyers, Georgia, an apparition site. I put some on his forehead, praying to the Holy Spirit to help him. As I did so, I saw the first signs of life. His facial expression changed, and he appeared to be concentrating as if something significant was taking place. I have never forgotten his expression. This sacramental was obviously helping him.

I then left the hospital to get some rest. When I arrived at my parents' home, I took a nap. I had a dream. I dreamt that I went back to the hospital to see my dad. In my dream, I took my dad's hand, and he opened his eyes and looked at me. When I awakened, I knew I had to go back to the hospital immediately.

When I arrived, my dad was still motionless and hooked up

to life support equipment. But, as I took his hand, he opened his eyes and looked at me, just as in my dream! I was stunned, but extremely happy; I knew the dream had been God's way of telling me this was going to happen. Looking back, I see that my dad was given more time to repent.

Over the next few days, my father's condition gradually improved. Life support machines were removed one at a time. Within two days, he was off the respirator, breathing on his own. I knew there was a reason why God wanted him to live a little longer.

I left Madison and returned to Milwaukee, uncertain about my dad's future. There was talk that he might have to enter a nursing home for physical therapy. He had had trouble with his left leg, and being bedridden for an extended period of time would not help. A few days later my brother called to tell me that my dad had contracted pneumonia and was not expected to live. Ironically, just a few hours before this call, I sensed my dad was going to get pneumonia. I rushed back to the hospital to be with him.

When I arrived, I barely recognized him. He had lost more weight, and seemed to be in a fetal position. He had an oxygen mask on his face and was again hooked up to machines. I felt so helpless. I said, *Dad, I love you. I'm praying for you.* He responded, *I love you, too.* After visiting for a few hours, I prepared to leave. He threw up his arms and pleaded, *Don't go!* I stayed awhile longer, and finally left close to midnight, tears in my eyes.

That night on the way back to my parents' house, I prayed to the angels to comfort my dad and give him peace. The next day, my father's disposition was completed changed. He seemed actually happy. He was smiling and joking with the nurses and his visitors. Everyone remarked how different he was. My family and I thought he was going to get well. What I wasn't aware of is that some people get a burst of energy shortly before they die. The next evening at 2:15 a.m., my dad passed away.

Exactly one week later to the minute of my dad's death, I was awakened at 2:15 a.m. I felt my dad's presence. I assumed he was in Heaven. However, a few months later I had a dream in which I saw my dad in fire. I thought perhaps he was in Purgatory and began to pray for him.

A short time later, I had a vision in which I saw my dad as a being of light. Then the light was extinguished, and he went below the earth into blackness. I didn't understand this vision—or rather, I did not want to understand it, because going down into blackness to me meant going to Hell.

Over the next four years, I began to have frequent visits from my dad's disembodied spirit. The best way to describe his appearance is that he looked like a ghost. I always felt negative energy, and my dad's disembodied spirit raped me. His disembodied spirit body laid on top of mine. It was very distressing. Often I was paralyzed, and did not have the presence of mind to say a prayer of rebuke right away, but when I did, he left.

One Sunday morning about 5 a.m., I had a dream. I believe this dream was from God. In the dream I saw my dad and his mother (my grandmother) in Hell. Their environment was completely dark and dreary. I felt a sense of foreboding. I woke up screaming because I realized what God had been trying to tell me for almost four years: my dad went to Hell! I called a close friend, who was kind enough to speak with me for about two hours. I just didn't want to believe it. Who would? In fact, I was not going to write about this, but the Lord prompted me to do it. He gave me grace to endure it.

I cried for several days. I then realized that a dream which began in early childhood of my dad having sex with me was prophetic. I had a dream quite frequently that my dad raped me. I had this dream for about 50 years, but I always dismissed it. That is why when I went through therapy sessions with the psychologist after I was diagnosed as a trauma survivor that I suspected that I could have been a victim of incest when he inferred this scenario. I remembered the dream, although I never told anyone, not even my psychologist, about it.

It's not the kind of thing I want to discuss. But I am here, dear readers, because I have been through pain few people are allowed to go through. I am grateful to God for my spiritual experiences, yet they have caused me much sorrow. It has taken me years to come to terms with this situation.

Often my dad's disembodied spirit came to me in dreams—dreams of horrible sexual scenes. Often these dreams took place in the home where I grew up or on that property. Every single experience I have had with my dad since his death has been negative or sinful. I have always felt negative energy when his spirit visits me.

One morning I awoke to see his spirit standing next to my bed. Then he attacked me. I said to him, *Dad, how could you do this to me?* There was no answer. He is a member of Satan's army now and is no longer capable of doing any good.

One night I heard soldiers marching. They were coming closer and closer to me. Then they stopped at my door. I heard male voices. Immediately, I knew it was a group of disembodied damned human souls from Hell, so I began to pray. Then I was attacked with negative energy and paralyzed. "Dad" kept coming to me. I think God was telling me that my dad was among these souls, whose specialty was sins of the flesh. I commanded them to leave in the name of Jesus Christ, and they left.

One night I asked Jesus why my dad went to Hell. In a locution, Jesus told me, *He went to Hell because he had an affair early on in the marriage, and he did not repent of it. Also, he verbally abused your mother, causing her great anguish.* He showed me an example, which I will not repeat. These sins Jesus mentioned were unrepented sins.

Jesus did not mention my dad's other sins, but I know what they were because I witnessed them. My dad took God's name in vain on occasion and did not attend church on Sunday. For many years before his death, he was not charitable. He did not pray. I gave him a Bible a few months before his death, but he barely looked at it. Jesus didn't mention these sins, perhaps because he had repented of them. The bottom line was that he went to Hell for the *unrepented* sins of adultery and verbal abuse of my mother. I realize now I never really knew my dad.

The information I received from Jesus was confirmed. When family members and I cleaned out the family home before we sold it, I found a slip of paper in my dad's handwriting. On this piece of paper was a woman's name and a phone number. On the back of the piece of paper was an address. I knew that she was the woman with whom my dad had the affair. Her name was very familiar to me. I remember hearing my dad talk about her often when I was a young child. *That piece of paper was over 50 years old, and I found it!* If you saw my parent's home, you would know how much of a miracle this was. The home was full of clutter. In fact, my parents built a second story on their garage just for the overflow. Many papers were not filed, and there was an entire closet full of loose papers, old articles and newspapers.

I also found my mother's diaries, which were written over the course of several years. When I read them months later, it confirmed my dad's verbal abuse. I threw them away because I could not stand to read my mother's anguished writings on how much my dad hurt her. Her pain was so enormous, it moved me to tears. Nothing she did pleased him. He tormented her verbally on a daily basis.

My mother went to daily Mass, and he berated her for it. He was upset with her works of charity, especially giving money to the poor. I found cancelled checks she sent to the missions for between $5.00 and $10.00 each. Ironically, when we were cleaning out my dad's room, my siblings and I found $600,000 placed in bank accounts which we had no idea existed. My mother had no idea how much money they had because he handled all of the finances. The small amount of money my mother gave to the missions was a drop in the bucket compared to my dad's wealth.

My father's only concern was taking out the garbage, keeping up the house, and being sure to clip his fingernails. Looking back, I realize how important it is to get our priorities straight. Our relationship with Jesus Christ is much more important than keeping a home immaculate or things that, in the long run, won't help us get to Heaven.

In addition, my mother herself would tell me how my dad caused her such anguish, especially after all of us children left home. She frequently seemed distraught when she talked about it with me on the phone or when I visited her. I think only God prevented her from having a nervous breakdown. My dad was her "hair shirt." She turned to God in prayer for her support.

I have often seen my father in Hell since 1998. Once I saw him lying on a bed. He had bugs crawling on him. He looked so pathetic. My heart grieves for his loss—the loss of Heaven forever. We are only given one opportunity, one life, and if we do not repent and obey God's commandments, we can end up in Hell. It does exist. Sometimes the people we think are in Heaven are not and vice versa.

Some people who think their deceased loved ones are in Heaven, pray to them. Be very careful to whom you pray. We should pray to God the Father, Son and Holy Spirit. We can also prayerfully ask the Blessed Mother, angels, saints and the Holy Souls in Purgatory to pray with us and for us to God as intercessors. We should never pray to anyone except God.

Sometimes my dad's disembodied spirit tried to disrupt my sleep. One night in a dream I was aware that I was sleeping in the bed my dad used to sleep in at our home. I heard my father's voice. It sounded like he was drunk, and he kept making noises in an attempt to wake me up. Finally, the dream did actually wake me up. When I was over at my grandmother's home, I sometimes observed my dad and my grandmother talking in low tones in the kitchen. My dad would open the kitchen cupboard and take out a bottle of liquor, which he took with him. I never saw him drink, and I do know he was not an alcoholic, but I think that he drank at times when no one was around.

Ironically, in 2014 my brother mentioned he had been having bad dreams with my father in them that took place in the basement of the home we grew up in. The dreams would make him violent to the point that he and his wife could no longer sleep together in the same bed. He thought it was a sleep disorder, but actually deceased relatives in Hell are assigned by Satan to other family members to harass and torment them. Their goal is, of course, to cause them to sin because that has become their job as followers of Satan. They work for the kingdom of darkness. Therefore, it is very important to know how demons operate and to say prayers for healing of your family tree. In my opinion, many problems people perceive as having a physical, psychological, or emotional cause are actually being caused or exacerbated by demons.

Memories From The Past Surface in 2014

From a spiritual viewpoint, look at Satan's plan. He tempted my dad sexually early on in the marriage, and he had a brief affair. However, he did not repent of the sin. Therefore, my dad had demons of sexual sins with him all of his life.

When I was writing this book, it brought back memories of the night I was abused. For many years I have thought that the boarder who I flirted with was the perpetrator. In fact, when I wrote the book on miracles, in which I wrote my story, I dismissed important clues that would indicate that my father abused me. I was convinced that the psychic, who told me that the perpetrator was my grandmother's boarder, was correct, and that the information came from God. But psychics work for Satan, and Satan is a liar.

I have come to grips with the matter now. One important clue was that the perpetrator opened the back door with a key. *The sound of the key opening the door is what woke me up*. Then I distinctly remember the sound of footsteps on the linoleum as someone came in. The back door was the one used by family members. The only people who had a key to the back door were my grandmother and my dad. My grandmother was sleeping in the same room as me at the time. *My dad had a key.* I believe that my dad was the perpetrator.

There are other factors that lead me to believe now that my dad was really the perpetrator. If the boarder abused me, why would he go outside around the house to come in the back door? And how did he get in? Would he risk being prosecuted for child molestation knowing my grandmother slept in the same room with me? Despite the fact that I flirted with this man, it does not prove he tried to molest me. I only lived there for a few months.

On the other hand, my dad had motivation. First of all, I suspect that he was being tempted sexually by the devil. My dad was not very religious. He stopped going to church. My grandmother did not go to church either. My dad may not have had sexual relations for a long time. My mother confided to me that she didn't like sex. I think she told me this after the birth of my youngest sister, who was 8 years younger than I. In fact, my parents did not sleep together anymore. My mother slept upstairs, and my dad slept downstairs. My mother was not perfect either. We all sin. Having separate bedrooms on different floors would have made it easy for my dad to leave the house unnoticed.

Although I'm sure that my dad did not want to be discovered molesting me, if my grandmother had witnessed it, she probably would have protected him. They were like glue—it was a *very close* relationship. My father probably saw his mother more than his wife. My grandmother only lived about 7 minutes from my parents' home. My father was a "mama's boy." My father did whatever my grandmother wanted, and my mother had no recourse but to go along with their wishes.

The other factor is that I was not afraid of the boarder during my therapy sessions. Psychologists find that the perpetrator is feared by the victim. I didn't fear my dad either, but I wasn't completely comfortable with him. We did not have a close relationship.

As I write this book today, I am chagrined to think that I was wrong in my conclusion all these years. I didn't want to believe it. Who would want to believe they were abused by their own father?

My dad tried to suffocate me with a pillow because I was screaming, and he wanted to shut me up. After I fell asleep at the play, *Jesus Christ Superstar,* I was screaming when I woke up, which I believe was a duplication of that moment. My grandmother began to wake up when she heard me scream, which is when he ran from the room.

In 1996, I had a dream which I believe was from God. In the dream, my grandmother and I were looking around the house for the intruder (which is actually what we did). While I was alone in the kitchen, my eyes went to a closet. The closet was actually a pantry my grandmother had converted into a closet in which to hang her clothes. It had a horizontal clothes bar the full width of the closet on which hung clothes of all different lengths. It did not have a door on it, but just a curtain that did not go all of the way to the floor. As I glanced towards it, I noticed a pair of men's shoes sticking out at the bottom. I realized someone was in there. Frightened, I returned to bed without saying a word to my grandmother. The dream ended here. This would have been a quick place to hide, and one my father would have been very familiar with. He most likely left quietly after we went back to bed. He may have left through the door on the opposite end of the kitchen, which was right next to this closet.

I do remember my grandmother talking to the boarder I flirted with the very next day. I think she thought the boarder had tried to molest me. I am sure she was aware of my flirtations with him. He probably left because he didn't want to get involved. Of course, if I were her, I would have drawn the same conclusion. She would never have considered that her son would abuse me just as I have had trouble coming to grips with my father's lack of morality for many years. Jesus gave me the spiritual and emotional strength to finally face the truth. I prayed for discernment before writing this chapter.

I lived with my grandmother for only a few months because I missed my family and siblings. I was also very unhappy there. One day, I just walked out and walked home. I never stayed overnight at my grandmother's home again.

In reflecting on the past, I see that I was living the struggle between good and evil just as my friend who was a former psychologist told me. I did block out the memories of the incident. However, I believe that the symptoms were caused by demons; namely, being hit in the center of my forehead instead of the side of the head. I believe that the incident of abuse itself was demonic, a carefully thought out plan by Satan.

I was dreaming about the attack after it had occurred. I was probably struggling with my dad in a recurring dream which duplicated the attack itself when he tried to suffocate me with the pillow.

I do believe that the Blessed Mother helped me. I have been praying for accurate discernment on all of this for many years, and today, after 20 years, I feel I do have the answer. It's been a long time, but prayers sometimes take time to be answered.

After my father's death, he went to Hell because he failed to repent of some of his serious sins. People in Hell commit the same sins they went to Hell for as a consequence for their sins, and they will do this for all eternity. They try to tempt all of us to commit these sins, too. Therefore, my dad tried to tempt me sexually because that was his downfall.

I had many, many diabolical experiences with my father. He attempted to cause me to sin many times by showing me sexual acts in dreams, sometimes with him. I found these dreams repulsive. Most of the time they took place in the home where I grew up. Often these disgusting dreams would occur on a Saturday night to interfere with my sleep. The forces of darkness know that Sunday is the Lord's Day for Christians. Perhaps my dad was doing this so that I would be tempted to miss Mass on Sunday. That happened to be another one of my dad's own sins.

One night I had a dream that my brother and sisters and I were sleeping on cots in my grandmother's home. Then, back in the present moment, I felt someone next to me in bed. As I became cognizant of this fact, I realized that a disembodied damned human soul was really next to me. He tickled me. I didn't completely wake up, so he did it again. It was in my waist area. Then he grabbed me with his hand around my waist. I commanded him to begone in the name of Jesus Christ and he left. It was my dad, who used to tickle me often in the same place when I was a child.

You will note that I also saw my grandmother, my dad's mother, in Hell. This does not surprise me. My grandmother did not go to church on Sunday. I do not know her other sins, but that one alone is enough for someone to go to Hell if she did not repent, which it appears she did not. One of the commandments is to keep holy the Lord's Day, and we do that by attending church to worship and praise the one, true God.

In another dream, my grandmother was stepping on me with her foot. My dad was next to her. They showed me a man who was naked. You can see the recurring temptations to sexual sins which are now their modus operandi.

There are ancestral spirits in families. That means that your ancestry has certain "familiar spirits" which tempt family members in a similar way in every generation. To heal your family tree and stop the progression of these generational sins, say prayers for this intention. You can get a free copy of the

"Healing Your Family Tree Prayer" on the Claretian Teaching Ministry website in English or Spanish, www.catholicbooks.net under "Prayers." Fr. John Hampsch, C.M.F. is an excellent resource on ancestral spirits.

It is too late for the people mentioned in this chapter to repent. But, friends, it is not too late for you and me. Whatever sins you may be committing, repent and confess them. Then try to refrain from committing them again. If you fall back into sin, repent and try again. Satan, demons, and disembodied damned human souls are trying very hard to drag us into Hell with them. Hell does exist, and we may go there. However, we have Jesus, Mary, and the prayers of the Holy Souls in Purgatory and the angels and saints to help us. We also have many efficacious devotions and prayers to aid us.

In my book, *Spiritual Weapons In My Battle With Demons,* I would like to share with you how I have survived my spiritual battle. It's been 20 years now since I have had demons with me. The Holy Spirit led me to several religious practices, prayers and devotions after I repented of my sins. These are the ways I have survived my enormous trials and temptations. I think people who know me will be shocked to read my story. I wish I could say it didn't happen, but it did. I am only alive and close to God today because of Jesus' Divine Mercy and the intercession of the Blessed Mother. I have hidden much pain and sorrow during the past twenty years. I would not have been able to live a seemingly normal life on the surface without the spiritual armor of God. I hope you will purchase this book, too, because I think it will help you survive in these evil times.

Chapter Twelve

Jesus' Unfathomable Divine Mercy

The Man Who Stalked Me

During one of the last conversations I had with Jerry, the man who stalked me, he informed me that he had met a woman he liked, and that he had moved in with her. He confided to me that he was still drinking (to excess), but he said she didn't know it. He drank in the basement when she was not around or late at night. He also told me that he was not attending church services on Sundays even though he had become a Catholic. However, he never practiced the Catholic faith because he did not become a Catholic out of love for God, but out of love for me, a mere creature. He went through the entire RCIA Initiation program in the Catholic Church, but he did it for me, and when I didn't start dating him again, he never attended church services.

I told Jerry that his drinking, neglecting to attend church on Sunday, not practicing the Catholic faith he had professed, and his sins of fornication were going to send him to Hell unless he changed his life. (I had distanced myself emotionally from him because we were going down two different paths. I was trying to change my life and help others.) I will never forget Jerry's response to my comment. He got very angry and said very emphatically, *Well, I feel as if I'm a good person. I pray even though I don't go to church. If God doesn't accept me the way I am, then I'll go to Hell!* He refused to give up his life of drinking, fornication, and not attending church. I have never forgotten that moment because I was horrified!

Jerry's life was totally contrary to Christianity. He didn't read the Bible, he took God's Name in vain, he frequently got angry, he drank to excess daily, he smoked, and he spent most of his time working. His job was his life. He confessed to me that he frequently masturbated. His entire life was a lie. He lied to me many times. Jerry read books from Satan—books that claimed there was no Hell. He refused to go to AA for his drinking problem. He rationalized that he was not hurting anyone, so he was not sinning. This was not true. He was hurting himself spiritually and physically, but most of all, he was offending God.

I once saw a vision in which Jerry was embracing Satan. As I look at Jerry's life, I can see how he aligned himself with Satan and listened to his lies. Jerry was in Satan's grasp, and he didn't care. It was his choice.

God gave him many opportunities to change his life. God kept trying to get his attention. One summer in 1998, he had an auto accident. He described the entire scene to me. His van was forced off the road by another motorist who never saw his vehicle. He plunged down a cliff at 70 mph, narrowly missing the concrete barrier that was on the side of the road, as he headed straight towards a river. On the way down, he had a locution from an angel who said, *You're going to be all right.* The van stopped just short of the river. Jerry had bruises, but was okay. His airbag had inflated and saved him from serious harm; but more importantly, God had intervened and really was the one who saved him. Unfortunately, Jerry did not use that close call to change his life. He shrugged it off. I believe it was a warning. Many times God gives us warnings, but we shrug them off.

After Jerry and I no longer had any contact at all, I decided to pray for him. I wanted to help him save his soul. **When I prayed for him through the years, I asked Jesus to tell me when he was dying so I could pray for him at that critical time.**

In 2012, Jerry's name began to come to me quite strongly over a period of several weeks. I started to pray in earnest for him. In particular, I began to say the Chaplet of Divine Mercy for him. One night a few weeks later, I returned home from Adoration of the Blessed Sacrament. During Adoration I always pray the Chaplet of Divine Mercy for those who are dying and especially those who God places on my heart. As I was walking down the hall in my apartment building to get my mail, Jerry's name came to me and I felt his spirit walking with me. It was peaceful, and I wondered about it.

A couple of days later, I got a call from my son. He had known Jerry because he had worked with him at the same company for awhile. He also knew him because of my relationship with him. My son informed me that Jerry had died. The family had called him, and my son thought I would like to know about his death.

The following day, I got a call from Jerry's daughter. I asked her when Jerry had died and what had happened. I was stunned to discover that he had died *on the very night and at the very time* I had felt his presence while walking down the hall after Adoration. She told me when the funeral was going to be held. I discovered that Jerry had moved to Michigan with his live-in girlfriend, whom he never married, shortly after our last conversation about nine years earlier. The funeral, however, was going to be held in my area because that was where his only daughter lived.

I attended the funeral, but it was so generic. There were pictures of him on a screen and photographs. The people in attendance talked about incidents they remembered in his life. However, what I remember the most about the service was the total absence of prayer.

I hoped that Jerry was saved. I remembered the peaceful presence I had felt on the night of his death as his spirit walked with me down the hall, and so I thought he was saved. I was content and was praying for him.

One day I asked Jesus to confirm for me if Jerry had been saved. That very night, the name "Jerry" came into my mind, and I had a demonic attack. For awhile I thought this was Jerry's disembodied damned human soul. However, the attack wasn't the same as all of the thousands of other demonic attacks I'd had. I had mild negativity, it was very short, and I did not see the spirit body of the attacker, which I did in *all* of the other occurrences.

I began to wonder about it. Shortly after this experience, I went to visit a friend of mine who is a nun. I shared my experience with her and we prayed about it. We rebuked the evil spirits of lies, deceit, confusion, and more with blessed salt and holy water before we prayed. We both had peace that Jerry was saved. My friend got the chills, which she said is usually a sign to her that her discernment is correct. While I do not think we should use this as a single factor in discernment, it may be something God is allowing in her case.

However, a few months later, I decided to contact Jerry's live-in girlfriend, who I did not get an opportunity to speak with alone at the funeral. I wanted to know about his final hours. I asked her if Jerry prayed or went to church or had any signs of repentance prior to his death. She said Jerry did not pray and never went to church. He died at home and had a difficult ending to his life. It was "not peaceful," as she put it. I think demons are with us at the end of our lives when we are destined for Hell, so what she was telling me was not surprising to me. Satan and demons were most likely gathering around him as he died just waiting to add yet another soul to their vast army.

I discovered his live-in girlfriend was a Native American and consulted mediums. Since Jerry's death, she confided to me that she had consulted a medium to speak with him. Mediums work for Satan. I warned her about such practices, but people just don't want to give up their beliefs because Satan has a grip on them. She just defended her beliefs, so all I can do is pray for her.

After speaking with Jerry's girlfriend I began to have doubts about Jerry's salvation. Was he saved? I began to think that he could never have been saved based on his sins and the awfulness of the ending to his life. As a sort of confirmation to this, I had an unusual experience.

One day about eight months after Jerry's death, I was coming out of an assisted living facility after visiting a resident there, and as I approached my car, I saw Jerry get into a van right near me. The distance between us was probably only about six or eight feet. Jerry lit a cigarette in the same manner he always did when he got into his van, something I had witnessed hundreds of times during our relationship. He had a certain manner in which he did things. This was not someone who *looked like* Jerry—this looked **exactly** like the body of Jerry. I got a real good look at him and just stared at him. It really took me aback.

Some saints have seen the devil in human form. Several accounts tell of St. Benedict's struggles with the devil. In one, the devil turned into a beautiful woman to tempt him. To resist giving into sin, St. Benedict threw himself into a thorn bush.[92]

There is also the account of St. Antony of Egypt, Patriarch of Monks (251-356 A.D.) written by St. Athanasius. The devil *harassed him night and day with gross and obscene thoughts. Antony resisted by a strict watchfulness over his senses and imagination, controlling them by austere fasts, acts of humility, and prayer. At last Satan himself appeared in visible form, first as a seductive woman, then as a black and terrifying man. Antony remained unmoved, and the fiend confessed himself vanquished.*[93]

During the time of Saint John Vianney (The Curé of Ars) a girl went to a dance in which worldly music was played. There was a boy who was dancing with every girl except her. She wondered why he didn't dance with her. She later went to confession to the Curé of Ars, and he told her that the boy was the devil in human form and that he avoided her because she was wearing her Brown Scapular.[94] The Brown Scapular is a sacramental given to us through St. Simon Stock by Our Lady of Mount Carmel in the thirteenth century.

The devil can appear as anyone. As I have indicated, the devil has appeared in human form in the lives of some of the saints. So why couldn't the devil take on the body of Jerry who is deceased?

(Conversely, angels working for God can also take human form. For example, in the book of Tobit, the angel Raphael took human form to help Tobit regain his eyesight and assist Sarah in finding a husband. I have seen more than one angel in human form that came to help me and then left suddenly. Whatever God's angels can do is imitated by Satan and demons. Remember that Satan (Lucifer) once was the highest ranking angel in Heaven and still uses his powers, although now he uses them for evil.)

I got a definitive answer to whether or not Jerry was damned or saved one night as I was writing on the Divine Mercy devotion given to St. Faustina Kowalska.

---

92 *Praesidium of Warriors of St. Michael*, http://pwsmri.org/Paranormal%20in%20the%20Church/Saints-Who-Confronted-the-Devil.html.

93 *Lives of Saints*, Published by John J. Crawley & Co., Inc. as an article entitled, *St. Antony of Egypt, Patriarch of Monks 251-356 A.D.*, published by EWTN, http://www.ewtn.com/library/mary/antony.htm.

94 From the booklet *Garment of Grace*, Nihil Obstat: Reverend Lawrence A. Deery, Imprimatur: Most Reverend Timothy J. Harrington, Bishop of Worcester, March 9, 1990.

Jesus appeared to St. Faustina in Poland in 1931. He showed her an image, which he called "The Divine Mercy Image." It depicts Jesus with two rays coming from His heart; one is red and the other is pale, which represent blood and water. The red ray stands for the Blood that is the life of souls. The life of souls is the Sacraments, particularly, Baptism, Reconciliation and the Eucharist. These Sacraments nourish and give life to our souls just like blood gives life to our bodies. The pale ray stands for water, which symbolizes the graces of the Holy Spirit. Underneath the image is written: ***Jesus, I Trust In You.*** St. Faustina was asked to spread devotion to His Divine Mercy.

In 1999, I had a vision of the image of Divine Mercy. At the time I didn't know it was the Divine Mercy Image Jesus had asked St. Faustina to have an artist paint. I had never even read or heard about this devotion. Years later in 2006, the Holy Spirit led me to promote the Divine Mercy Devotion.

An integral part of the Divine Mercy Devotion is recitation of the Divine Mercy Chaplet. Recitation of the prayer is especially efficacious at the 3:00 hour, called the hour of Divine Mercy, because it is the hour that Christ died. Jesus told St. Faustina that He would answer any request made by recitation of the Divine Mercy Chaplet at that hour (if it is in line with His Holy Will). Jesus also asked that the Chaplet of Divine Mercy be recited especially for the sick and the dying. This is encouraged during Adoration. For years now, I have recited this chaplet more than once a day, typically in the morning, at the 3:00 hour in the afternoon, and always during Adoration of the Blessed Sacrament (which I attend daily).

On August 1, 2014, I was writing the book on the spiritual weapons that have helped me during my ordeal with harassment by demons. I was specifically writing about the recitation of the Divine Mercy Chaplet when someone is dying. I was led to a passage in the Diary of St. Faustina, which says: *When I entered the chapel for a moment, the Lord said to me, **"My daughter, help Me to save a certain dying sinner. Say the chaplet that I have taught you for him."** When I began to say the chaplet, I saw the man dying in the midst of terrible torment and struggle. His Guardian Angel was defending him, but he was, as it were, powerless against the enormity* *of the soul's misery. A multitude of devils was waiting for the soul. But while I was saying the chaplet, I saw Jesus just as He is depicted in the image. The rays which issued from Jesus' Heart enveloped the sick man, and the powers of darkness fled in panic. The sick man peacefully breathed his last. When I came to myself, I understood how very important the chaplet was for the dying. It appeases the anger of God.*[95] (Diary 1565)

At this point, an infusion of knowledge came to me. I became very emotional because I realized that despite the awfulness of Jerry's sins, that God, in His infinite Divine Mercy, had given him the grace of repentance at the very last moment of his life! I wept tears of joy. I pondered how the Holy Spirit had prompted me to pray every Chaplet of Divine Mercy for Jerry beginning just a few weeks before his death. Also, what are the chances that I was praying this very chaplet during Adoration ***during the hour of Jerry's death*** that very night not even knowing that he was sick or dying? I am overwhelmed by the awesome mercy of God!

The next morning which was August 2, 2014, the First Saturday of the month, which is a day devoted to making reparation to the Immaculate Heart of Mary, I asked Mary to confirm what I believed was Divine Mercy in Jerry's case. A powerful feeling of peace went in me, around me and through me to the point where I cannot adequately describe it. I have it again right now as I write this story. It's not just a feeling of peace, but peace within my heart and soul. It is so overwhelming now I am moved to tears of joy.

I realized that Satan did not want me to write about the mercy of God. The devil hates the Divine Mercy Devotion because it snatches so many souls from him. I have always been in an intense spiritual battle whenever I try to promote Divine Mercy. But don't let that stop you! Spread the Divine Mercy Devotion.

I hope you, my dear readers, will understand how unfathomable Jesus' Divine Mercy is! He can save even the most wretched sinners from eternal damnation, sinners like Jerry, sinners like me, and sinners like you who may be reading this book. Although we do have up to the last moment of our lives

95 Kowalska, Saint Maria Faustina, *Divine Mercy in My Soul, Diary of Saint Maria Faustina Kowalska,* Marian Press; 3rd edition with revisions (29th printing) 2013.

to repent, I suggest you do it today. Also, those of you who are praying the Chaplet of Divine Mercy now, pray it more often, (especially at Adoration of the Blessed Sacrament) for the sick and the dying. You can help save souls!

Chapter Thirteen

Conclusion

I had a lot of spiritual warfare when I was writing this book. At daily Mass, my pastor always tells us to take one day at a time, and it is good advice.

The demons with me did not want this book written because it demonstrates how they operate. They attempted to put obstacles in my path every day. When I was putting notes together for this chapter, I realized that the demons that came into my life in 2006 and are still with me have been trying to use the same methods they used then successfully to tempt and harass me now. Here is a summary of their methodology while I was writing this book.

Accidents

The demons caused a few accidents. Here are some examples. 1) I tripped and injured my right foot one day and some of my toes and part of my foot were black and blue for several weeks. There was swelling, but my shoe still fit. 2) When I went to the State Fair with my family, a very large sheet of plywood (about 8′wide by 4′ high) that was being used as a barrier fell forward, hitting the right side of my body. It hurt, but I continued on. That night I discovered that most of my right leg was very black and blue and swollen. It took a few weeks to heal. 3) One day I was taking out the garbage and fell quite hard on the cement for no apparent reason. However, my angel must have caught me because, other than a bruise on my little finger on my right hand, I had no other injuries. I think the demons were trying to hurt my fingers because I was getting close to getting the book done and I needed use of my fingers to type. 4) One day I came close to being seriously injured or killed. I was leaving a business and needed to walk around the building to the back parking lot. As I was about to turn the corner to go down the alley that goes to the parking lot, a car came out right in front of me. It missed hitting me by a few seconds!

Some of our accidents are caused by demons, which is why we need our guardian angel. During the last few weeks of writing this book, I felt the presence of my guardian angel almost daily.

Computer Problems

I had many computer problems spanning about 3 months. I didn't learn that Microsoft was going to stop supporting Windows XP until about two weeks before the cutoff date. So I was scrambling to find a new Windows operating system. However, I discovered my computer was too old to support the newer operating system. So I ordered a used computer online. I picked it up at a local store, but when I carried it to my apartment, which is on the second floor of my building, I dropped it on the carpeting. It was in a box so I thought it would be okay. Subsequently, I made arrangements with someone to install the new operating system.

When I got my computer home and started to use it, I discovered the computer made a buzzing noise on and off. I used the computer for a few weeks, but began to be concerned about the noise. I called a local store and took my computer over there to have it checked out. While attempting to carry the computer into the store, I dropped it on the grass. The technician checked out the computer and told me that it was the fan. A different fan was installed. However, the noise did not go away. To make a long story short, it was the hard drive. Although the company I purchased the computer from told me I could return it for a refund even after I honestly told them I had dropped it twice, I could not do this in good conscience. Subsequently, I purchased another used computer. This one had a RAM problem which took weeks to figure out. Apparently, the RAM only works in certain slots and only with similar megabytes. But, finally I got it to work and could begin writing. However, I also purchased another used computer as a backup.

Infirmity (Illness)

Demons of Infirmity caused me to have a lot of gas. On two occasions, they caused severe diarrhea right before I was going to Adoration of the Blessed Sacrament. The first time I didn't go, and I really missed being with Jesus. However, the church where I go to Adoration at night does not have a bathroom that is accessible since it is in a separate chapel. The church does not allow access to the main part of the building. Since the demons were successful in their attempt to cancel my visit to the Blessed Sacrament due to diarrhea, they tried it again a second time a few weeks later. However, I decided to trust in God this time and not let the demons keep me from being with Jesus. So I prayed and I went to Adoration. I was okay!

Harassment

The demons harassed me at night several times, making me physically exhausted the next day. They did this by making noises such as running the toilet, raps, knocks, doors slamming, and constant talking. Jesus did not allow this every night, but it happened periodically, especially during the latter days of writing this book.

They began to chastise me for eating too much. I felt so guilty when I ate, I really cut back on my quantity of food and got very thin. After several months, I realized this was their way of trying to interfere with my energy level so I couldn't write. At times, they convinced me I was in mortal sin from eating too eagerly. However, I did this because I was simply hungry. I do admit, however, that I have an attachment to food, but I was constantly running to Confession to confess this sin even when it was only venial.

Temptations

I had thousands of temptations while writing this book, sometimes as many as 100 or 200 in one day. (I am not exaggerating). Most of them were temptations of pride or attachments to food, bad thoughts, or impatience. It was a constant daily struggle. I did go to Confession at least twice a week (which helped because of the graces) and I attended two Masses daily because the Eucharist is a powerful source of strength. I also went to daily Adoration (with the exception of the one night I had diarrhea).

Materialization

Unfortunately, I made another mistake towards the end of writing the book. I purchased an actual new age book to use as background material. (This obviously was a suggestion placed into my mind by the devil because if you recall I had purchased a book on Theosophy as background material while writing this book in 2006 which brought these demons into my life.) When the book, *The Aquarian Conspiracy,* arrived I was harassed more vehemently. Unfortunately, a second copy arrived that I had cancelled because I had found a cheaper price. I could have returned it, but I decided to throw it out so no one else would read it.

I did not read the books and a few days later I threw them both in the dumpster. They should have been burned, but I have no way to do that because I live in an apartment building. However, demons of materialization began to manifest themselves to me. These are demons of actual faces of people in Hell who manifest themselves to the living. However, it was not a frequent occurrence, probably because I only had the books for a few days.

Mimicry and Condemnation

Towards the end of writing this book, the demons made a final aggressive attempt to stop it from being written. Unfortunately, I fell for their tactics. I began to hear the very loud voice of "God the Father," who chastised me for all of my recent sins. I felt so bad I cried. I was told I was in mortal sin, and the book was being cancelled. He said that it was taking me too long to write it and time was up! He was angry because I was writing too late and not getting enough sleep. He said that I was on the computer too much. I heard the voice of the Blessed Mother (which was actually the voice of a demon) pleading for me for mercy. She talked about all of my good points and tried to persuade God to let me continue to write it. Then I heard Souls in Purgatory pleading to God for mercy for me.

This entire scenario was duplicated nightly for almost a week all night long! It even happened during Adoration, and I couldn't pray. It happened while I tried to pray the Rosary, but I continued on (with pauses to listen to the voices I believed really may be God the Father, Mary, and the Holy Souls in Purgatory). At one point, the voice of Mary said, *You should listen when God the Father is speaking to you,* when I was trying to pray the Rosary and was not listening to the voices. I really didn't know if I was listening to God or demons, so sometimes I listened and sometimes I didn't. But I remember at one point, I was told to tune out all the voices. However, I didn't heed this warning and became confused.

During these episodes, I got very little sleep, was distraught, and in tears much of the time. In the beginning of this farce, the verdict went back and forth. I couldn't write, but then Mary and the Holy Souls would persuade God to let me write. Then the next day, the debate would begin all over.

During Adoration one night, I pleaded with the Holy Spirit to help me. By this time, I was convinced that I had to stop writing the book and that I had failed in my mission. I heard, *There will be an answer. Let it be.* I went home from Adoration and packed up all of my writings, determined to do the will of God and abandon the project despite the fact that I'd spent a year writing this book. However, we are always called to do the will of God.

I was just about to go to bed when Fr. Hampsch (who is a demonologist and an exorcist) called me. He said he had many urgent phone calls to make, but he felt he should call me because I needed help. I told him what had happened and that I had stopped writing the book and packed it away. He told me it was demons who were telling me this. They were demons of mimicry (demons who pretend to be someone else) and demons of condemnation (demons who cause excessive guilt for behavior that is not sinful).

I told him about the message I had received during Adoration a few hours earlier about getting an answer. He said, *Judy, this is your answer. Continue to write. The demons will stop at nothing to prevent this book from being written because it shows how they operate. But God has made it very clear that this book must be written. Your spiritual battle is proof of that.* He said a deliverance prayer for me, and I felt a great sense of peace and happiness in the depths of my soul. When I got off the phone, I resolved to finish the book as quickly as possible.

A Severe Demonic Attack

That night at 3 a.m., Satan attacked me viciously. My heart stopped, and it took a long time to recover. That hour is Satan's hour because it is the opposite of 3 p.m., the hour Christ died. When I did recover, I realized that it was a last ditch effort to stop the book from being written. When I began writing the book again the next day, I accidentally hit a wrong key on the keyboard and guess what came on the screen? The words were: ***The demons will do anything to stop the writing of this book.*** What are the chances of this happening? I do not know how this occurred, but the message was valid. I didn't type it; I just hit one key on the keyboard! It was a message from God.

The harassment orchestrated by Satan was very similar to what happened to me when I tried to write this book back in 2006. Of course, the same evil spirits I had then are still with me, and they obviously figured that if I was duped before in this manner, I might fall for it again. I am chagrined that I was duped so easily again, but Satan can absolutely convince you that you are hearing the voice of God.

Final Comments

My dear readers, I have shared my life and inmost secrets openly and honestly with you in this book for a reason. I do not want any of you to offend God by participating in new age or occult practices. It is my desire that this book of my frank and open testimony will give you all hope. Jesus came to call sinners. Do not despair. If Jesus can help a pitiful sinner such as me, He will help you, too. We have a merciful God who loves us and forgives us no matter what we have done. Obey the commandments, love God and your neighbor. Stay out of new age and the occult.

If you have participated in any new age or occult practice, renounce it by saying prayers of deliverance. Pray, fast and do penance. The closer you become to Christ, the more spiritual warfare you will have. However, trust in Jesus. St. Gemma Galgani (1878-1903) once said, *If I saw the gates of Hell open and I stood on the brink of the abyss, I should not despair, I should not lose hope of mercy, because I should trust in Thee, my God.*[96]

I believe we are living in the End Times. Satan is coming as a demon of light and he is deceiving many people. Learn as much as you can about new age and occult practices by reading the document on the Vatican's website, *Jesus Christ the Bearer of the Water of Life: A Christian Reflection on the New Age,* and other books by reputable Catholic and Christian authors. I learned about new age from reading countless articles, going to Catholic conferences, reading books by select Catholic authors, and from personal experience. Jesus helped me along the way. He has mercy on sinners, of which I am one of the worst. I am grateful to Him for letting me write this book, which I did to help you, my dear readers. I personally do not recommend any of the therapies and practices that are part of the new age and the occult today. They are spiritually dangerous.

In the Bible, we read: ***Woe to those who call evil good and good evil, who put darkness for light and light for darkness, who put bitter for sweet and sweet for bitter.*** (Isaiah 5:20 NIV) This is exactly what is being done today. Satan is presenting evil as good, as light for darkness. Do not fall into his traps. I have seen Hell and it is real. Choose light. Learn the truth. ***The truth will set you free.*** (John 8:32)

There are a lot of new age and occult practices in the world today. Be sure you pray so demons do not bother you. Your prayer life is <u>most important</u>. As I mentioned in this book, the Holy Spirit led me to many prayers and devotions that have been my armor in the spiritual battle. I live with many strong demons 24 hours a day and have for many years. In a separate book, I am including all of the prayers and devotions that I was led to in the

96 *The Voice of the Saints,* Burns & Oates, London. Reprinted by Tan Books and Publishers, Inc., Rockford, IL 61105, 1965.

hope that they will help you, too.

Without my acts of reparation and a strong prayer life, I probably wouldn't be here. Many people despair or turn to a worldly solution, such as drinking, to solve their problems. I have had a huge cross because of my sinfulness. Don't let your guard down and become complacent. Do whatever you can to help others in their spiritual life. ***See to it, brothers and sisters, that none of you has a sinful, unbelieving heart that turns away from the living God. But encourage one another daily, as long as it is called Today, so that none of you may be hardened by sin's deceitfulness.*** (Hebrews 3:12-13)

If you have sinned, repent. Jesus is merciful and His love never ends. Jesus' Divine Mercy is overflowing for all of His children. That includes everyone in the world. That includes you, my dear readers!

This book is the culmination of many years of a spiritual battle raged by demons who did not want this book written. But, here it is, because God is in control. This has been a labor of love for Jesus and truly a work of Divine Mercy!

Give thanks to the Lord for He is good.
His mercy endures forever! (Psalm 118:29 NIV)

There Is Still A Chance That We Will See

By Judy Hankel

One day in 1994
As I was close to Heaven's door
The Blessed Mother came to visit me
And I was healed instantaneously.
She said that I should be prepared
Because my life had been spared
To help bring peace and harmony
To the world which had deliberately
Placed her Son as low priority.
For it is through suffering, prayer, and fasting
That we attain our everlasting
Reward in Heaven with the saints
Who are there to help us with our complaints.
For there is still a chance that we may see
And prevent the terrible catastrophe
That God will send to all mankind
If we don't obey God's laws and find
That we are called to live a life of love
And only worship the God of Heaven above.
Repent and change your life today
Now, get on your knees and pray!

Bibliography

Chapter Five: Dreams, Visions and Locutions

Wise, Russ, Probe Ministries, *Embraced by the Light of Deception,* http://www.leaderu.com/orgs/probe/docs/eadie.html

Chapter Seven: Elemental Spirituality

Christian Apologetics and Research Ministry, *What is Wicca?* http://carm.org/religious-movements/wicca/what-wicca

Wikipedia, the free encyclopedia, *Mediumship,* http://en.wikipedia.org/wiki/Mediumship

Chapter Eight: The Spiritual Dangers of Alternative Therapies

Native American Medicine, *A Cherokee Legend,* Indian Creek Tribe Chickamauga Creek & Cherokee Nation, Inc., Home Remedies and Herb Medicine, http://chickamaugacherokee.org/medicine/

Hoyt, Karen, *The New Age Rage,* The Spiritual Counterfeits Project, published by Fleming H. Revell Company, Old Tappen, NJ 07675, 1987.

Watchman Fellowship, Profiles, *Acupuncture,* http://www.watchman.org/profiles/pdf/acupunctureprofile.pdf

Godwin, Steve, *Project Raphael, Evaluating Acupuncture,* http://www.projectraphael.com/index.php?option=com_content&view=article&id=5:evaluating-acupuncture&catid=7&Itemid=11

Watchman Fellowship, *Index of Cults and Religions*, Chi, Taoism, Yin and Yang, http://www.watchman.org/cat95.htm

Reisser, Paul C., Reisser, Teri I., Weldon, John, *New Age Medicine: A Christian Perspective on Holistic Health*, Arthur F. Whitehead, Jr., Publisher, 1987. Printed at InterVarsity Press.

Chapter Nine:
Catholic Charismatic Prayer Services

Liichow, Rev. Bob, *Slain in the Spirit, non-Christian and unbiblical! Does the Bible Support A Doctrine of Being Slain in the Spirit?* An article and booklet by Rev. Bob Liichow, Discernment Ministries International, 2762 E. Lafayette St. Detroit, Michigan 48207. https://discernmentministriesinternational.wordpress.com